THE WELSH LIFE OF ST DAVID

I
FRANCES
unwaith eto

PREFACE

THIS edition of the Welsh *Life* of St David is meant for students in various parts who study Middle Welsh in the university. Until recently, such students, who came from Wales, were mostly native Welsh speakers, and as was proper, Welsh was the language used in works provided for them. Now, however, provision has to be made for an increasing number of students from Wales and beyond, for whom Welsh is not the first language. In many parts of the world, in Canada and the States, in Japan and Australia, as well as in Europe, languages like German, even Japanese, but more especially English, have to be employed as the medium of instruction and scholarship.

This work is fuller and more detailed than my Welsh edition, which appeared way back in 1959. That edition, however, included some topics omitted here, more especially some references to David subsequent to his *Life*, and subjects relating to text and language. Here, it has been my aim to present a safe and sure guide to the essentials of Middle Welsh prose, and to describe in outline some basic features of the cult of David in earlier times.

It is important that I recognize the debt I owe to some of my colleagues for their interest and consideration. Foremost among them I must mention the Principal of my College, Professor Brian Morris. No head of any college has been more uncompromising and relentless in stressing the importance of research as the hallmark of a centre of learning. Such advocacy of and support for scholarship for its own sake merits acknowledgement and gratitude in times which can hardly be described as propitious for the humanities. I am glad of this opportunity to express my indebtedness to him, and my appreciation of his support and leadership in this matter. To Anne Howells of the University Press Board, and a former student of

St David's University College, I am grateful for help and advice in steering this work through the press; and to Elsie Davies of the Departments of Welsh and English I am much indebted for help, care and consideration in transforming a shaky and doubtful hand into an eminently readable typescript.

The printers deserve acknowledgement and gratitude for their patience and efficiency. And finally, I must place on record my thanks to Mr John Rhys and the University of Wales Press Board for their trust in accepting my work for publication.

D. SIMON EVANS
St David's University College
4 December 1987

CONTENTS

INTRODUCTION

THE HISTORICAL DAVID

OUR knowledge of the historical David, or Dewi, is both meagre and uncertain,[1] but we have a very full and clear picture of the saint fashioned at a later stage by the creative genius of the Welsh. It is possible to trace the growth and progress of his cult, more especially from the twelfth century on, up till the time when he gained general recognition as the patron saint of Wales. The historical David is a much more elusive figure. The difficulty is that there is no reliable contemporary literary evidence. Our knowledge is derived in the main from the findings of archaeologists, historical geographers, and students of language, toponomy, early tradition (as reflected in later literature and quasi historical records), folklore, etc., whose disciplines have produced some valuable information during the last half-century and more.

We can be reasonably certain about some matters. He lived in the sixth century, and may have been born in the early years of that century.[2] For the year of his death we may turn to the Irish annals, where his name occurs, evidence of his renown among the Irish. It is found in Tighernach,[3] and also in the *Chronicum Scotorum*[4]

---

[1] While we are justified in looking to his *Life* for clues, it can in no wise be regarded as providing valid, historical evidence. Welsh *Lives* are notoriously unreliable. Cf. Binchy on Irish *Lives*: 'With the luminous exception of Adamnan no biographer of an Irish saint can be regarded as a genuine historical witness' (*SH* 2 (1962), 57).

[2] See *HW* i. 153, where *c.* 520 is suggested. According to Rhigyfarch, he was 147 years old when he died (*RLSD* 25), in which case the date of his birth would have been around the middle of the fifth century. Cf. *SC* xii/xiii. 41, 43, 44, 48. It is recorded s.a. 458 in *Annales Cambriae* (Mommsen's edition); see *N* 85.

[3] *RC* xvii (1896), 158.

[4] *CS* 62.

s.a. 588. His name, *Dauid Cille Muine*, is not accompanied by the usual *obiit*, but the entry must be interpreted as a record of his death. There can be no question about the entry in the *Annals of Inisfallen*[5] s.a. 589: *Quies Dauid Cille Muine*, clearly a reference to his death.[6] According to Geoffrey of Monmouth,[7] he died during the reign of the kings who followed Arthur in 542, while an early St David's source puts it early in the seventh century.[8]

He belonged to the south-western area of Wales, a part of the country for which there is evidence of Irish settlements at this time.[9] We learn of the migration of the Déisi, an Irish tribe, into these parts.[10] We also find here the concentration of Ogam stones (roughly contemporaneous with the spread of Christianity), most of which are bilingual. In these the Irish form of a name occurs in the Ogam script, while the British form is also given in the Latin alphabet.[11] Such a stone is the one found at Castelldwyran in Carmarthen (*c.* 550),[12] which reads MEMORIA/VOTEPORIGIS/PROTIC-TORIS, and in Ogam the 'Irish' form VOTECORIGAS; *Voteporigis* is genitive of **Uoteporix*, a chieftain who should probably be identified with the *Vortipori* mentioned by Gildas[13] (*c.* 540). A chieftain of the mid-sixth century required a bilingual memorial stone, and this (along with other evidence) must be taken as indicative of a state of bilingualism in at least parts of the south west at this

---

[5] *AI* 78.

[6] Lloyd (*HW* i. 158n) suggested that 589 could be accepted as the year of his death, if he died on a Tuesday (March 1st), as stated in his *Life* (13.27–8). But, as Professor Caerwyn Williams reminds us (*LlC* v. 106), for the second half of the century it could also be 550, 561, 567 or 572. It could also be later, in 606.

[7] *HRB* 502.

[8] In the *Annales Cambriae* s.a. 601 (*N.* 86) we find *Dauid episcopus moni iudeorum*, doubtless intended as a reference to his death, and possibly reflecting the view held at St David's around 955 or later; but likely to have been recorded earlier, as early perhaps as *c.* 795. Cf. *SC* xii/xiii (1977/8), 46, 48. E. W. B. Nicholson (*ZCP* vi (1908), 451) maintains that 547 was the year of his death. Molly Miller thinks that 601 'may be a little too early', *SC* xii/xiii. 41n., also 47. There seems to be no end to the guessing, but cf. M. Miller's serious and authoritative discussion on 'date-guessing' in ibid. 41–60.

[9] See M. Richards, *JRSAI* xc (1960), 133–62. For further sources of information, see *LWS* 22–3. Cf. also *SEBC* 121–3.

[10] Cf. *TC* 1895–6, 55–86; but note also *ZCP* xxvii (1958–9), 14–63.

[11] *LHEB* 151–7.

[12] *ECMW* 107.

[13] *De Excidio Britanniae c.* 31. Cf. Barley and Hanson, *Christianity in Britain 300–700* (Leicester, 1968), 141.

time. It is reasonable to assume that David spoke Irish as well as Welsh (a primitive form of both languages). There must have been close intercourse between this part of Wales and southern Ireland at this time, a state of affairs reflected in the *Lives* of Irish saints, where we are told of visits to St David by saints such as Ailbe, Bairre, Declan, Molua (Mo-Lúa), Aidan, Finnian and Senán.[14]

Two saints, who must have been contemporaries of David, were Teilo and Padarn, the latter possibly a little earlier. The three belonged to the part of the country least affected by Roman culture, and they are to be associated with a movement in the fifth and sixth centuries whereby Christianity entered Wales anew along the western sea routes after the collapse of Roman power, a movement deriving in the main from Gaul.[15] There seems no reason to question the traditional view that the centres of their missionary activity were in western areas, St David's, Llandeilo Fawr and Llanbadarn Fawr (about a mile east of Aberystwyth) respectively. In the more Romanized south east it appears that Christianity had taken root earlier, and may have been at least in part a survival from Roman times. The three more important saints of this area were Dubricius (Dyfrig), Illtud and Cadog, whose names are associated with a tradition of learning (not evidenced in the west), in centres such as Llanilltud (Lantwit) and Llancarfan.

Reference must be made here to the valuable information gained from the researches of scholars such as Professor E. G. Bowen, who has shown the importance of a study of distribution patterns of dedications.[16] In this way we are able to define the area or areas of a saint's cult, but not necessarily the field in which he worked during his lifetime. It is instructive to look at the distribution pattern of *David* churches,[17] although the David may not in every case, especially in eastern parts, be the saint from St David's. He has the largest

[14] Cf. *SC* vii (1972), 31–2, 36–44. It is also worthy of note that some of the early references to David come from Irish sources. Professor Caerwyn Williams suggests that initially he was better known among the Irish than among the Welsh; cf. *LIC* v (1959), 108. In their letter to Honorius II (1124–30) the chapter of St David's maintain that David frequently sent many of his disciples to preach in Ireland; cf. *EAWD* i 250. As for references to him in the *Lives* of Irish saints, cf. *VSH* i. 53, 69 n., ii. 41, 219, 144–8, 153, *LSD* 43–6, *LSBL* 62.
[15] *SCSW* 15–16.
[16] Notably in books such as *The Settlements of the Celtic Saints in Wales*, and *Saints Seaways and Settlements in the Celtic Lands*, and in numerous articles.
[17] See Bowen, *SCSW* 58–65.

number of dedications (more than fifty) of any Celtic saint in Wales, and another feature of some significance is that they are all in south Wales. We find none in the north of Ceredigion, but in the south of Ceredigion they are numerous. We find them also in the old Pembrokeshire and in west Carmarthenshire. Further, we may trace his cult along the south Wales coastal plain in Llangyfelach, in the Gower peninsula and the Bridgend area. Another route will take us along the upper Tywi valley to the vale of Usk, past settlements such as Llywel, y Trallwng, Llan-faes and Llan-ddew. Churches dedicated to David, such as Rhaglan, are to be found in Gwent, and also in northern Brycheiniog and former Radnorshire, and western Herefordshire. His cult seems to have spread eastwards along what remained of the Roman road system in Wales. There is evidence of his cult also in parts of south-west England and in Brittany, but it is doubtful if he himself ever visited those lands.

Quite clearly, the largest concentration of David churches belongs to the south west.[18] To the same area belongs the bulk of Teilo churches which, however, are not so numerous.[19] The two saints must have worked in this part of Wales, and they may well have collaborated in some of their missionary activities.[20] But it appears that David's special field, possibly the area within which he himself actually lived and worked, lay to the west and north of that of Teilo, in west Pembrokeshire and south Ceredigion. Hen Fynyw, a little to the south of Aberaeron on the Cardigan coast, is dedicated to him; so is Llanddewibrefi, some miles to the east in the hinterland; and of course St David's, again on the coast, but much further south. This place may well have been already a focus of influences and activities, and of intercourse with Ireland, with

[18] An area where little, if any, Roman influence can be detected: 'no fact or find has so far been produced to prove that they [the Romans] ever came to the St David's peninsula, or to Ireland, or that the Roman road came any further than Carmarthen'. D. W. James, *St David's and Dewisland*, (Cardiff, 1981), 9–10. One is, furthermore, impressed by the concentration within this area of wells bearing his name, more especially in the St David's area; cf. *DS* 44, 89.

[19] Cf. *SCSW* 56–8.

[20] Teilo also figures in the *Life* of David (4–6). One is here reminded of the words of Professor Bowen, who lays stress on 'the way in which saints linked together in the narratives appear to have dedications close to each other on the ground' (*SCSW* 6). There seems also to have been a tradition that they were educated together; see note on *Paulinus*, p. 35–6.

other Celtic lands, and with western Europe in general, before the
time of David.[21] Concern for and involvement in the Goidelic
element may have been an important factor in his decision ultimately to settle in Mynyw. In any event, if we draw a line from
St David's to Hen Fynyw, to the north, thence to Llanddewibrefi
and back to St David's, we have three important centres in David's
life, which are accorded pride of place by Rhigyfarch, and a tri-
angle, which may give us a fair indication of the area (extending
northwards to the Ystwyth-Wyre line) within which our patron saint
was most active during his lifetime, an area where Dewi churches
are numerous, but where there are no Teilo dedications.

On the nature of the movement with which he was associated,
and the source of its inspiration, there has been considerable specu-
lation. We must take account of the tradition that he was a
dedicated ascetic, a puritan, and also of the view expressed by
scholars that the missionary movement with which he was associated derived from Gaul, and was brought to Wales along the
western sea-routes. 'It was along these routes (which alone in the
fifth and sixth centuries AD were able to maintain contact with what
remained of Roman civilization in Gaul and the Western Mediter-
ranean) that Christianity now entered Wales from the west.'[22]

EARLY REFERENCES TO DAVID

Let us now look at a number of references to the saint, which are to
be found in Welsh, Irish and also English sources, during the five
centuries after he lived, and before the composition of his *Life*
towards the end of the eleventh century.

On a stone in the wall above the chancel door in the church at
Llanddewibrefi, Edward Lhuyd discovered an inscription, which
could have contained an early reference to David. There now survive only two fragments of the stone, built (upside down) in the
external west wall of the church. Questions relating to the inscription have been examined in some detail by Professors R. Geraint

[21] Cf. Bowen, *SC* iv (1969), 56–71.
[22] *SCSW* 19.

Gruffydd and Huw Parri Owen.[23] Our main concern here is whether the inscription in its original form contained a reference to David. According to Lhuyd, his name was on it, and we may with reasonable confidence rely on his final reading, which was: HIC IACET IDNERT FILIVS IACOBI QVI OCCISVS FVIT PROPTER PREDAM SANCTI DAVID. Various interpretations of this inscription are possible, but the following appears to be the most satisfactory: 'Here lies Idnerth, son of Jacob, who was killed because of the despoiling of St David', a memorial to a noble and possibly gallant son, who died defending the church of David against plunder. This may well have happened towards the middle of the seventh century, a date ascribed to the inscription,[24] which would not be long after the saint's death.

David is named in the Catalogue of the Saints of Ireland, the *Catalogus Sanctorum Hiberniae secundum diversa tempora*.[25] The date formerly assigned to this work was the first half of the eighth century (*c.* 730), but Father Paul Grosjean believes that it belongs rather to the ninth or to the tenth.[26] In this obscure document, which seeks to present in outline a history of the church in Ireland from the time of Patrick to the year 665, and which clearly reflects the interests of his church at Armagh, we are told of 'three orders' of Irish saints. The 'second order' belonged to the sixth century (544–98), and consisted mainly of priests, with some bishops. This *ordo* or order received a *missa*, a mode of celebrating mass 'from holy men of Britain', namely David, Gildas and Doccus.[27] Whatever may be the true significance of this document, mention of the British saints in it is indicative of a tradition that Ireland was influenced by them in the sixth century.

In an Irish metrical martyrology, known as *Félire Oengusso Céli Dé* (Martyrology of Oengus the Culdee), the name of David (*Dauid Cille Muni*) is included under March the first.[28] It is thought that this

[23] *B* xvii (1957), 185–93, also xix (1961), 231–2; accompanied by a note on epigraphy and language by Professor Kenneth Jackson, ibid, pp. 232–4.
[24] Cf. Jackson, op. cit. p. 233; also *ECMW* 98.
[25] See *Councils* ii. 292–4, *LSP* 285–7, *SPAI* 88–9.
[26] *AB* lxxiii (1955), 197–213, 289–322.
[27] Ibid. 206–10. But cf. also *CEIS* 72–3.
[28] *MOC* 80. His name occurs also in the notes on the text, which are probably later than the text itself. He is referred to in connection with the Irish saints, Aidan (54) and Molua (182).

was written around the year 800,[29] as was the *Martyrology of Tallaght*, on which it seems to be based. This also records the festival of David.[30] Both were intended for private devotion.

He is mentioned in the *Life* of Saint Paul Aurelian, the *Vita Pauli Aureliani*,[31] a work written in 884 by a monk named Gourmonoc, from the abbey of Landevennec in Brittany. Here *Devius* is named along with Paul himself, Samson and Gildas, as one of the more distinguished pupils of Illtud[32] (at Llanilltud, Lantwit) on the Glamorgan coast. There is clear reference to his asceticism; he lived on bread and water, and was called *aquaticus*.[33] To describe him as a fellow-disciple of Gildas hardly tallies with the evidence of the Vespasian text and Welsh version of the *Life*, where Gildas is obviously thought of as an adult before David was born (2–3), while in the Latin and Welsh *Life*, Paulinus (who is probably the same as Paul) is referred to as David's teacher (3–4 below). The same four are mentioned as disciples of Illtud in the *Life* of Illtud.[34] In the *Life* of Finnian of Clonard, David and Gildas are described as (adult) contemporaries.[35]

Next we have the evidence of a Welshman, namely Asser, author of the *Life* of king Alfred,[36] completed around 893. Sir Ifor Williams maintains that this was intended for the Welsh, in order to win their allegiance to the English king.[37] Be that as it may, the author must have been a Welshman. He says that he was called to Alfred 'from the western and extreme limits of Wales'.[38] He

---

[29] Ibid. vii.

[30] *MT* 20. His name (along with those of the Irish Senán and Moynenn) occurs in the Drummond Calendar of the second half of the eleventh century; cf. *SDL* 9.

[31] Cuissard, *RC* v (1883), 413–60.

[32] Ibid. 421. Also *Doble* i. 13, *LWS* 94–5, 147.

[33] *Sanctumque Devium qui pro eo quod propter artissimam vitae ejus in Christo conversationem et sui a Deo judice laboris firmissimam retributionis spem in pane et aqua vixerit cognomento dicebatur Aquaticus* (*RC* v. 421).

[34] *VSBG* 208. Here Paul's name is given as Paulinus.

[35] *LSBL* 222–3.

[36] *Asser's Life of King Alfred*, ed. W. H. Stevenson (Oxford, 1904), also 1959, rev. Dorothy Whitelock. Further,. cf. I. Williams, *AP* xxvi–xxx; V. H. Galbraith, 'Who wrote Asser's Life of Alfred' in *An Introduction to the Study of History* (London, 1964), pp. 85–128; P. Hunter Blair in *Celt and Saxon: Studies in the Early British Border* (Cambridge, 1963), pp. 94–104, 106; D. Whitelock, *The Genuine Asser* (Reading, 1969); D. P. Kirby, 'Asser and his Life of King Alfred', *SC* vi (1971), 12–35; also *DWB* 16.

[37] *AP* xxvi–xxx.

[38] *de occiduis et ultimis Britanniae finibus* (*ALKA* 63).

answered the call, and was in time made bishop of Sherborne.[39] His death in 909 is recorded in the *Anglo-Saxon Chronicle*.[40]

In this there is a reference to the *monasterium et parochia Sancti Degui*,[41] his monastery and 'parish' or the area of his cult. His kinsman, (*propinquus*) Nobis (d. 873), had been bishop[42] there, as had Asser himself. David was a well-known, powerful saint, who could help those who trusted in him. It is interesting to note that here *Degui* (*Dewi*), and not *Dauid*, is the form of the saint's name, which shows that the author and his readers must have been Welsh.

The cult of David seems to have spread to Wessex. In the ninth century Glastonbury claims to be in possession of his relics. At some time between c. 970, when it was compiled at Glastonbury, and c. 1050, when it was in use at Exeter, his name in the form *Devvi* was inserted in the *Leofric Calendar*. He is commemorated in another calendar from Sherborne, c. 1061. In the litanies (in a tenth-century manuscript of the *Salisbury Psalter*) he is included along with Padarn among the confessor bishops. His cult was probably introduced into these parts through Asser. In another Wessex calendar of about the eleventh century his name appears in the same form as that used by Asser. No doubt, the use of his name in the liturgy would be accompanied by some written material relating to his life.[43] Such material cannot now be traced, whereas some early liturgical sources are probably reflected in certain prayers found in his *Life*.[44]

One ought perhaps to mention here the *Penitential of David*, although problems relating to its date and authenticity remain unresolved.[45] It can no longer be regarded without question as a genuine work dating from the time of David, although it seems to have originated in the Welsh church at an early period.

Finally, we must note the many references to David in the poem *Arymes Prydein Vawr*[46] (c. 930), found in the Book of Taliesin. This

[39] On this, see note ibid. 321–3.
[40] *ASC* 94. Also *Annales Cambriae*; cf. *N* 90.
[41] *ALKA* 65–6; cf. also *EHR* xlvii (1932), 86–8.
[42] archiepiscopum ibid. 66.
[43] See *SDL* 8–11, 69–71; also *SEBC* 133.
[44] See *SDL* 13f.
[45] As for the text and ms., see Hugh Williams, *Gildas* (London, 1899), ii. 286–7; Ludwig Bieler, *The Irish Penitentials* (Dublin, 1963), 70–3, and cf. ibid. 3.
[46] See Ifor Williams, *AP*, and an English edition by Dr Rachel Bromwich in *AP*[1].

is a vaticinatory poem which confidently foretells of victory by the Welsh over their enemies, namely the Saxons who were at the time harassing and oppressing them. There is a reference (somewhat obscure) to reconciliation between the Welsh and the men of Dublin (the Scandinavians), and an alliance between the peoples of the west and north, to be formed no doubt against the oppressor, who has been identified as the Saxon king, Athelstan. He was at that time trying to extend his dominion in the west, and the author of this poem seems to be keen to arouse among his people a spirit of resistance to the oppressive neighbour. He is clearly opposed to Hywel Dda's policy of recognizing the supremacy of the Saxon king, and thus ensuring peace by diplomacy.

It is evident that this poet regards David as championing his cause. This can be inferred from the references to the saint in the poem. The Welsh commend themselves to God and David (1. 51).[47] The foreigners will be put to flight through the intercession of David and the saints of Britain (1. 105).[48] The Welsh will raise the holy standard of David—to lead the Irish (1. 129–30).[49] The foreigners of Dublin—or the Irish—will ask the Saxons why they have destroyed the rights of David (1. 140).[50] And towards the end of the poem the wish is expressed that David be the leader of the warriors (1. 196).[51]

The author was an ecclesiastic who must have belonged to one of the monasteries or churches within the *parochia* of David. This explains the prominence given to the saint in the poem; it does not necessarily indicate any extensive development of his cult at this time. His cult was probably still mainly confined to areas in the south west, and, as Professor Jarman has suggested,[52] the author of the poem must have belonged to that part of the country.

[47] y Dduw a *Dewi* yd ymorchymynynt.
[48] trwy eiryawl *Dewi* a seint Prydeyn.
[49] A lluman glan *Dewi* a drychafant.
y tywyssaw Gwydyl trwy lieingant.
[50] neu reitheu *Dewi* pyr y torrassant.
[51] poet tywyssawc *Dewi* yr kynifwyr.
[52] *LlC* iv (1956), 57. One should mention that there is reference to the grave of 'Dewi' in one of the *Oianau* in the Black Book of Carmarthen: ac a wnant enrydet ar *bet Dewi* 'and they will do honour at the grave of Dewi' *LlDC* 30.39.

His *Life*

We next come to a discussion of the *Life* of Saint David. This, like the *Lives* of other saints, was written many hundreds of years after the time of the saint himself. It is a Latin work, first produced by a cleric named Rhigyfarch. Rhigyfarch died in 1099, at the age of forty-three. We find him commemorated in the *Brut* for his learning, a man acclaimed not only by his own people, but also by the English and the Normans:

> In that year died Rhigyfarch the Wise, son of bishop Sulien, the most learned of the learned men of the Britons, in the forty-third year of his life, the man whose equal had not arisen in the ages before him and whose peer it is not easy to believe or to imagine will arise after him. And he had received instruction from no one save from his own father. After most proper honour by his own people and after most renowned and acknowledged praise by the neighbouring peoples, that is, Saxons and French and other peoples from beyond the sea, moreover with the universal lamentation of all grieving in their hearts, he died.[53]

In order to try and determine why he should have undertaken the composition of a *Life* of St David, we must look at certain events, movements and tendencies in Wales towards the end of the eleventh century. The story of those times has been told and re-told, and although there still remain serious gaps and blurs in our picture, the outlines are reasonably firm and clear, clear enough to enable us to assess the significance of certain events. The Normans had come to England early in the second half of the eleventh century; long before the end of that century their unyielding presence had been felt in Wales also.

The church in Wales up till the Norman period had in large measure preserved its independence, and in comparative isolation had developed a character of its own. The control and authority of Canterbury had not been generally recognized. In the west especially, in centres like Llanbadarn and St David's, it was still probably non-diocesan, 'Celtic' and tribal in organization and outlook.

An important name in the history of the church in this part of Wales during the second half of the eleventh century is that of

---

[53] *BTy RB* 39.

Rhigyfarch's father, Sulien (1011–91).[54] It is our good fortune that
an account of him has been preserved for us in a Latin poem by
another of his gifted sons, Ieuan (d. 1137).[55] Sulien came from a
clerical and learned family, such as were doubtless found in Wales,
as in Ireland,[56] in earlier times. He appears to have received a good
education in Welsh schools, and subsequently at ecclesiastical centres in Scotland and Ireland. From these lands he returned to
Wales, and founded a school at Llanbadarn, to which were attracted pupils from many parts, and among them his four sons, Rhigyfarch, Arthen, Daniel and Ieuan, who perpetuated and fostered the
tradition of learning established by their father. Sulien died in 1191,
probably at Llanbadarn, although we have no details of his final
years. What we do know is that he was bishop of St David's for two
periods, first during the years 1073/4–8, and then for a second term,
1080–5. This is how the Welsh chronicler records his death:

> And then Sulien, bishop of Menevia, the most learned of the Britons
> and eminent for his pious life, after the most praiseworthy instruction
> of his disciples and the keenest teaching of his parishes, died, in the
> eightieth year of his life and the twentieth but one from his consecra-
> tion, on the eve of the Calends of January.[57]

While one has to make some allowance for the chronicler's[58]
devotion and loyalty to the memory of his bishop, one can hardly
question Sulien's renown as a man of piety and learning, although
no written work by him has survived. Along with his family, he must
have played an active and prominent part in the religious and
political life of the time. Together, Sulien and his sons represent an
indigenous tradition of learning, later to be superseded by others
which followed in the wake of the Norman conquest.

[54] For a discussion of the life and work of Sulien and his family, see J. E. Lloyd,
HW ii. 459–61, *The Story of Ceredigion* (Cardiff, 1937), 30–9; *CLlGC* ii (1941), 1–6;
J. C. Davies, *EAWD* ii. 493–506; N. K. Chadwick, *SEBC* 165–73; M. Lapidge,
SC viii/ix (1973/4), 68–106.
[55] *Carmen de uita et familia Sulgeni*, preserved in Corpus Christi College, Cambridge MS 199, ff. 76a–78a (a photographic copy in NLW MS 13213). Printed
(unsatisfactorily) in *Councils* i. 663–7. See now *SC* viii/ix (1973/4), 80–9. The MS
contains a transcript (now incomplete) by Ieuan of St Augustine's *De Trinitate*, a
transcript made at his father's request. Furthermore, the MS displays certain
features in common with Irish MSS of the same period; cf. Lapidge, op. cit. 76.
[56] Cf. *CEIS* 161–4, 210–11.
[57] *BTy RB* 33.
[58] At St David's or Llanbadarn; cf. Lloyd, *The Story of Ceredigion* 31; *BTy Pen
20*[1] xli; *WLC* 21.

We have already referred to his eldest son Rhigyfarch, *Rycymarch sapiens*, as he is described by his brother Ieuan, clearly a man of learning of whose literary activity we have some knowledge. First, there is the manuscript in the library of Trinity College, Dublin, Trinity College MS 50 (A 4.20), which must derive originally from Llanbadarn,[59] but which, like Ieuan's displays features found also in contemporary Irish manuscripts.[60] In this we find Jerome's translation of the Hebrew Psalter and a Martyrology, and more importantly a Latin poem (*de Psalterio*)[61] by Rhigyfarch himself, which may also have been copied by him.[62] However, most of the manuscript was written by one Ithael, while the work of illumination was executed by his brother, Ieuan. Rhigyfarch describes himself as Sulien's (*Sulgen*) son and as Ieuan's brother. Both he and Ieuan could produce Latin verse.[63] Reference has already been made to Ieuan's poem, in which he provides information about his father and the family.[64] The manuscript which contains this poem also has an *inuocatio* and scattered *disticha* in Latin,[65] as well as one solitary stanza in Welsh in praise of *Cyrwen*, Padarn's episcopal staff.[66] The latter may or may not be the work of Ieuan, but whether he composed it or merely copied it, it serves as evidence of at least some involvement with 'Welsh' culture. Rhigyfarch likewise must have known Welsh, and in all probability cherished an intelligent and warm regard for his native culture. But, if he ever wrote anything in Welsh, it has not survived. He has left us only his Latin

---

[59] See H. J. Lawlor, *The Psalter and Martyrology of Ricemarch* (London, 1914). Here (pp. xxi–xxii) it is dated to the year 1079; also Lapidge, *SC* viii/ix (1973/4) 74.

[60] Cf. Lapidge, op. cit. 76–7.

[61] Ibid. 88–9.

[62] Cf. Lawlor, op. cit. xx, 118; and Lapidge, op. cit. 73, 76.

[63] In these works there seems to be evidence of acquaintance with authors such as Vergil, Ovid, Lucan, Juvencus, Prudentius, Martianus Capella, Caelius Sedulius, Boethius, Aldhelm; also possibly Statius, Horace and Juvenal (and the *Hisperica Famina*)—names indicative of acquaintance with a wide range of poetry. Cf. Lapidge, op. cit. 69–70.

[64] Cf. note 55 above.

[65] Lapidge, op. cit. 78, 80. Regarding Ieuan's (uncertain) command of Latin, cf. ibid. 72–3.

[66] See Ifor Williams, *CLIGC* ii (1941), 69–75; also *BWP* 181–9.

works, and among them his 'Lament',[67] a poem of prime importance, concerned with the tragic events of 1093, when the Normans
with their savagery seemed at the time to have subdued all Wales.
Their progress, culminating in the death of Rhys ap Tewdwr of
Deheubarth in 1093, was cause for intense grief and sorrow to
someone like Rhigyfarch, who gives expression to his feelings in this
poem. An effusion of grief certainly, but also strong and fearless
condemnation of his own oppressed and tortured people for their
lack of character and courage. All is lost, and it remains only to seek
heaven and the mercy of the Omnipotent Father.[68]

There is then no lack of evidence of Rhigyfarch's learning, of his
concern for and involvement in the affairs of his day. He was quite
clearly a devoted Welshman, whose regard for his people's traditions and independence, for the old order, made him more than
suspicious of penetration, and consequently of interference and
domination by the Normans. Their savagery caused him anguish,
while the changes which were to follow in their wake must also have
caused him no little concern and worry.

Rhigyfarch died in 1099. His 'Lament' was probably written
about 1094. His de Messe Infelici 'on the Unhappy Harvest' must
have been written at about the same time.[69] The manuscript which
contains the Psalter, Martyrology, and his poem de Psalterio, was
produced probably in 1079.[70] In that year he would be twenty-three
years of age. It is not likely (although not impossible) that he should
have written anything of substance before that time. This means
that the Life of St David, by far his most important work, along
with his other productions, should probably be dated at some time
after, within the period 1079–99, the last twenty years of his life.

Different dates have been suggested for the composition of the
Life. Mrs Chadwick has argued for the year 1081,[71] when it is known
that the bishop (presumably Sulien) gave his blessing to a pact made

---

[67] Preserved in the BL MS. Cotton Faustina C.1, f. 66a (a photographic copy in
NLW MS 12863). See Lawlor, op. cit. 121, etc., SC viii/ix (1973/4), 88–92. The short
poem on 'the Unhappy Harvest' also occurs in this manuscript (ibid. 92), which must
have been copied in the twelfth century, perhaps by a Norman scribe in England, or
in Wales; cf. ibid. 73.

[68] The author in this poem refers to himself by name: Hec ego Ricemarch defleo
mestus.

[69] Cf. note 67 above.

[70] Cf. note 59 above.

[71] SEBC 175–6.

at St David's between Gruffudd ap Cynan of Gwynedd and Rhys ap Tewdwr of Deheubarth.[72] It is recorded also that William the Conqueror visited St David's in that year,[73] and one must not rule out the possibility that he met the Welsh princes there, and came to some sort of understanding with them. Sulien could well have been instrumental in arranging such a meeting, which leads Mrs Chadwick to suggest that the *Life* of St David was written for this occasion, 'both in support of Sulien's policy, and in celebration of the visit of the Conqueror to St David's'; it was 'an appeal by the native Welsh Church to the Conqueror for his protection against encroachment from Canterbury'.[74] In my edition of *Buched Dewi*[75] I was drawn into accepting this view. I still find it attractive, but I am now more inclined than heretofore to question some of the suppositions on which it is based. The Welsh chronicler tells us that William 'came on a pilgrimage to Menevia [St David's] to offer prayers,[76] but one must have reservations about the alleged purpose of such a visit. The king's mission probably had a more practical end, and it appears that we have here the Welshman's version of an expedition made by William through south Wales with the aim of subjugating the Welsh, and also of liberating some imprisoned Normans. He may have gone on to St David's, and there met the two Welsh princes. There are grounds for supposing that some sort of agreement was reached between William and Rhys ap Tewdwr (and possibly between him and Gruffudd ap Cynan also). Be that as it may, contemporary chroniclers from England make no mention of a visit to St David's, but refer instead to William's expedition to Wales. The *Anglo-Saxon Chronicle* (s.a. 1081) says that 'the king led levies into Wales, and there freed many hundreds'.[77] Even if, as is possible, he went on to St David's, and there said his prayers, and even if the bishop took part in negotiations between him and the Welsh princes, it is hard to conceive of the visit as something so elaborately pre-arranged, that the composition of the *Life* of the saint should form part of the preparations.

[72] *HGVK* 14.
[73] *BTy RB* 31.
[74] *SEBC* 176.
[75] *BDe* 24.
[76] *BTy RB* 30, 31.
[77] *ASC* 214. Also other chroniclers; cf. *HGVK* clxi. See *EAWD* i. 103.

A. W. Wade-Evans[78] and Professor W. H. Davies[79] both give
c. 1090 as the date of composition. This, however, must be meant as
an approximation, for we find Wade-Evans a little later in his introduction to the *Life of St David*[80] describing the *Life* as a protest
against interference from Canterbury, more especially by archbishop Anselm, who had suspended Wilfred, bishop of St David's.
This happened in 1095, or a little earlier.[81] J. W. James, who also
favours a date around 1095,[82] suggests that the suspension of
Wilfred in that year may lie behind the account of St David's visit to
the Patriarch of Jerusalem.[83] M. Richter is clearly following James,
when he gives c. 1093–5 as the date, without discussing the
subject.[84] According to Lapidge likewise, it was written probably
about 1093.[85]

   Closely related to the question of date is that of the motive behind
the composition of the *Life*. It should be remembered that 'biogra-
phies' of important figures from the 'Age of the Saints' enjoyed
considerable vogue in the twelfth and thirteenth centuries. What
accounts for the appearance of this 'biography'? The *Life* has been
generally interpreted as the manifesto of the church of St David's,
which seeks to demonstrate that church's claims and privileges,
more especially its authority. This is done by depicting the life and
work of the founder of the church, by appealing to 'history', in a
manner quite common in earlier times. With the great importance
attached to tradition, one can understand why the founder figure
should be regarded as establishing the character of his church. The
tradition and experience of the church are personified in the
account (largely artificial) presented of the founder. In his *Life* of
St David we find Rhigyfarch relentlessly urging the founder's great
gifts and virtues: the miracles he wrought before as well as after his
birth; his great modesty and dedication as a student; his defeat of
the pagan chieftain Boia; the establishing of his own monastery in

---

[78] *LSD* x, *WCO* 148.
[79] *DWB* 838. Likewise J. E. Lloyd, *HW* i 153, and A. H. Williams, *An Introduction to the History of Wales* (Cardiff, 1941), i. 90, and Silas M. Harris, *SDL* 13.
[80] *LSD* xviii.
[81] *EAWD* i. 235.
[82] *RLSD* xi.
[83] Ibid. 19–21, 42–3.
[84] *Journal of Ecclesiastical History* xxii (1971), 183.
[85] op. cit. 73.

Glyn Rhosyn (*Vallis Rosina*), and the code of conduct and quality of life there; his visit to Jerusalem, where he was consecrated archbishop by the Patriarch; his feat at the synod of Brefi, where he was 'constituted archbishop of the entire British race'; the grief universally expressed at the news of his impending death. In all this we see David extolled above all the saints and founders in these islands, a record stuffed with the wondrous and the wonderful, which lays special emphasis on the power of the saint. Little, however, do we learn about the real historical circumstances of his life and times. As we are reminded by Molly Miller, 'Rhigyfarch ... attempts to match the impervious virtue of his ideal founder with a total reticence about historical circumstance'.[86]

Thus did Rhigyfarch seek to bolster up the claims of the church of St David in his own day. But against whom or what? As we have already hinted, there was in the first place an awareness of the danger of interference by the Norman king and by Canterbury, something which required constant vigilance by those concerned with preserving the character and independence of the church in the west. By the seventies of the eleventh century the Normans had established themselves in the border country, with designs of expansion westwards from centres such as Chester, Shrewsbury, and Hereford. In the north, Robert of Rhuddlan, supported by Hugh, earl of Chester, was to gain dominion over Gwynedd, and to be its master until his death in 1088 (or 1093).[87] As early as 1073 and 1074 there were raids into northern Ceredigion. By 1086 Roger of Montgomery, earl of Shrewsbury, was in control on the borders of Ceredigion in the Pumlumon region, ready for the advance into Deheubarth some years later. In the south, especially after the abortive rebellion of the earl of Hereford in 1075, progress seems to have been for a time halted, and it may well have been part of the Conqueror's policy to lend support and encouragement to some native princes, in order to try and prevent his earls on the borders from becoming too powerful. He probably supported Rhys ap Tewdwr in his kingdom in Deheubarth. Later, however, after the Conqueror's death in 1087, the Normans resumed their progress, and advanced deep into Wales on all fronts. They had built a

[86] *SC* xii/xiii (1977/8), 50.
[87] M. Chibnall, *The Ecclesiastical History of Orderic Vitalis* iv (Oxford, 1973), xxiv–xl.

fortress at Pembroke as early as 1091, and from this time forth they were to maintain a firm grip on the south west, which of course included St David's. By 1094 it appeared that all Wales had been subjugated, and the future looked bleak. However, the Welsh were soon to show that their spirit of resistance had not been crushed completely. It is hardly necessary here to record in detail the events of these years.[88] The progress of the Normans was a clear indication of danger, and William's visit to St David's in 1081 must have appeared portentous to men like Rhigyfarch. However, as we shall note later, the danger from the Normans was not the only consideration which occupied the minds of those who were prompted to produce the *Life*.

Over a long period before this time, St David's must have been a centre of some importance. This is evidenced by the references to burning and destruction there, mostly by Saxon and Scandinavian marauders, during the ninth, tenth and eleventh centuries.[89] We also learn of the obits of bishops: Sadyrnfyw in 831,[90] Meurig (Nobis) in 874,[91] Gorchwyl in 908,[92] Nercu in 921,[93] Lwmberth in 943,[94] Eneurys in 945,[95] Morgenau (*Morgynnydd*) in 1025,[96] Joseph in 1063.[97] Furthermore, we find other items of information, such as the reference to the rule (? or consecration) of Meurig (*Nobis*) under 840,[98] and to Lwmberth (*Humbert*) assuming the bishopric in 875.[99] The attention accorded to events at St David's, and the references to its bishops, can doubtless be explained in part by the circumstance that for these years the annals were kept there.[100] All

[88] For a general (and still authoritative) account of these years, see *HW* ii 357–411.
[89] The years 810, 907, 982, 988, 992, 999, 1012, 1022; see *BTy RB* 7, 11, 17, 19, 23. Giraldus makes mention of this; cf. *EAWD* i. 215–16. Also earlier, in 645, according to the *Annales Cambriae*, N 86.
[90] *BTy RB* 7, also *N* 89.
[91] *BTy RB* 9; cf. *BTy Pen 20*[1] 137, and *N* 90.
[92] *BTy RB* 11; but it does not say he was bishop of St David's.
[93] Ibid. 13, referred to only as 'bishop'.
[94] Ibid.
[95] Ibid. 23, referred to only as 'bishop'. As for the name, cf. *BTy Pen 20*[1] 149; cf. also *N* 91.
[96] *BTy RB* 23.
[97] Ibid. 27.
[98] Ibid 7; cf. *BTy Pen 20*[1] 135; and *N* 89.
[99] *BTy RB* 9; cf. *BTy Pen 20*[1] 137.
[100] Cf. *BTy Pen 20*[1] xli; also *WLC* 27; and *WEMA* 201.

this warrants the conclusion that St David's during these times had acquired renown and at least some wealth.

Life for the church and its community can hardly have been peaceful. Onslaught and pillage by marauding bands was an ever-present danger. In some of the entries it is expressly stated, in others it can be inferred, that the death of a bishop was the result of such an attack. It happened in 999, when 'Menevia was pillaged by the Gentiles, and bishop Morgenau was slain by them'.[101] Likewise also in all probability in 1073. In that year 'Menevia and Bangor were ravaged by the Gentiles. And then died Bleiddudd, bishop of Menevia; and Sulien assumed the bishopric'.[102] No doubt, Sulien came there from Llanbadarn, another important ecclesiastical centre in the west (situated at the boundary of commotes Perfedd and Creuddyn), which may well have had an early episcopal tradition, but about which less is known than about St David's. It had apparently proved less attractive to the needy and greedy raider from without, and may well have enjoyed comparative peace over the years.[103] Reference has already been made to the school of learning established there by Sulien. Indeed, a tradition of learning may well have existed already at Llanbadarn, but under Sulien it blossomed anew, and continued to flourish well into the twelfth century. He probably returned to the tranquility of this school at Llanbadarn in 1078, when, as we are told by the Brut, he left his bishopric, and one named Abraham assumed it.[104] The latter, however, did not survive for long, and Sulien had to return, apparently against his will. This happened in 1080. In that year 'Menevia was woefully ravaged by the Gentiles. And Abraham, bishop of Menevia died. And Sulien against his will, assumed the bishopric a second time.'[105] In 1085 Sulien again left, for what reason we are not told:

---

[101] BTy RB 19; cf. BTy Pen 20¹ 147, and GW 163.
[102] BTy RB 29.
[103] Only once does the Brut record pillaging by the Gentiles there—in·988 (see BTy RB 17), when they also ravaged St David's, Llanilltud, Llancarfan and Llandudoch. It was pillaged in 1039—by Gruffudd ap Llywelyn (see ibid. 23). There is no evidence of a Scandinavian settlement in Ceredigion.
[104] Ibid. 31: 'Ac yna yd edewis Sulyen y escobawt ac y kymerth Yvraham'. Two of the latter's sons, Hed and Isac are commemorated in an inscription on a pillar stone, built into the east wall of the south transept of the Cathedral; see ECMW 210–11.
[105] BTy RB 31; cf. BTy Pen 20¹ 155.

'Two years after that, Sulien a second time resigned his bishopric, and Ewilfre assumed it'.[106]

As we have noted, the *Brut* contains a number of references to the deaths of bishops; Sulien is the only one recorded as having relinquished his bishopric during his lifetime. This happened twice, and one is justified in thinking that he left because he preferred the comparative quiet of Llanbadarn to the frustrations and hazards of St David's. It serves to underline his uniqueness as a man, and confirms the impression gained from other sources that on both occasions he was more loath to assume than he was to quit the bishopric.[107] It must have been by a sense of duty, rather than by a desire for power and position that he was drawn away from Llanbadarn, at a ripe age. The church clearly faced trials and tribulations. The danger from Scandinavian marauders was in fact receding, although this may not have been apparent at the time. But it must have become clear to men of judgement and perspicacity, such as Sulien, that a new danger was imminent, coming not over the sea from the west and north, but overland from the east, and that its effects would be more far-reaching than those of the Scandinavian forays, fearful and destructive as they often were. William had shown that St David's was not too remote for him to have an interest in it.

Little or nothing is known of the years 1073–8, but for the second period we have evidence that Sulien played the role of the diplomat and mediator. A brief reference has already been made to this. In the *Life* of Gruffudd ap Cynan[108] we are told that Gruffudd arrived at Porth Clais, near St David's, with troops from Waterford in Ireland. He was met by the bishop (who is not named) and his retinue, and also by Rhys ap Tewdwr, king of Deheubarth, who was in flight before his enemies.[109] An alliance formed between Gruffudd and Rhys is confirmed in the church, and favoured with the

---

[106] *BTy Pen 20*[1] 17. *RB* is in error, when it states that he resigned 'for the *third* time'; cf. *BTy Pen 20*[1] 156.

[107] Such is the impression given by his son, Ieuan; cf. Lapidge, op. cit. 87.

[108] *HGVK* 13.

[109] One can surmise that there had been close and friendly contact between St David's and the princes of south Wales. Here note the words of Giraldus (iii. 154): 'the whole cantref of Pebydiog was conferred on St David's by the pious bounty of the princes of south Wales'. Cf. also *DPGOH* i. 48–9.

blessing of the bishop. From this it can be inferred that Sulien played a not unimportant part in the negotiations between the two princes, who with their joint forces then marched a day's journey to meet their adversaries, Trahaearn ap Caradog, Caradog ap Gruffudd and Meilir ap Rhiwallon, and defeated them at the battle of Mynydd Carn. The *Brut* also (s.a. 1081) refers to this battle,[110] and states that Gruffudd ap Cynan with Irish troops came to the assistance of Rhys ap Tewdwr, but there is no mention of Sulien. We have already referred to the visit to St David's by William, recorded under 1081 in the *Brut*. If he did visit St David's that year, it is reasonable to suppose that he met Sulien, and further that Sulien may have taken part in negotiations between him and the Welsh princes. We learn from *Domesday Book*[111] that 'Riset de Wales' (by which must be meant Rhys ap Tewdwr) paid the king an annual rent of £40. William had probably agreed to Rhys keeping his lands in Deheubarth, in part as a bulwark against further progress by powerful and ambitious Norman leaders. It may well be that he came also to some agreement with Gruffudd ap Cynan about Gwynedd, but the latter was soon to be overthrown by the Norman, Robert of Rhuddlan.[112]

Ieuan describes his father as one 'whom kings, the people, clergy and all land-dwellers venerated unanimously with serene mind'.[113] He may have had behind him a tradition of diplomatic activity, stretching back at least to the days of Asser, some two centuries earlier. We have evidence of his involvement in Welsh politics during his second term at St David's. He may have been instrumental in making secure (at least temporarily) the position and independence of the kingdom of Deheubarth under Rhys ap Tewdwr. He would surely be no less concerned to make secure the position and independence of his church, whose power and influence extended over broadly the same area in the south west.[114] The composition of

---

[110] *BTy RB* 31; cf. note 283.

[111] *Domesday* i. f. 179a.

[112] Cf. Goronwy Edwards, *Proceedings of the British Academy* xlii (1955), 161 n. 1.

[113] Lapidge, op. cit. 87.

[114] It should be remembered that there was no further interference with St David's for some twenty-five years.

the *Life* of St David by his son seems best explained as an indication of this concern.

Everything points to Sulien's second term at St David's as the period during which the *Life* was written, sometime between 1081, when William was there, and 1085, when Sulien finally relinquished the bishopric. As Mrs Chadwick reminds us,[115] Sulien did not hail from Dyfed, and he appears to have been there only for the two terms of his episcopate. Except for those years and the time he spent in Scotland and Ireland earlier in his life, Llanbadarn was his home. He and his sons belonged essentially to that place, and it appears that most of his sons' works were produced there. The manuscript containing the Psalter, Martyrology, and the poem *de Psalterio*, may have been written in 1079.[116] Rhigyfarch would then have been in his early twenties and, as we are reminded by Lapidge,[117] his poem bears the marks of an inexperienced youth, with no adequate mastery of Latin. In this respect it is in marked contrast to the 'Lament', which must belong to a much later period in his life (1094/5), 'after the acquisition of a considerable Latin learning, at a time when the author was in firm command of his poetical powers'. The 'Lament' is 'a remarkable piece', with none of the defects which characterize the earlier work, and also, for that matter, the poetry of Ieuan.[118] Sulien would have been back in Llanbadarn in 1079, when the manuscript containing the Psalter and Martyrology may well have been written. In any event, it appears that St David and his feast-day were not uppermost in the mind of him who wrote the Martyrology, as his name does not appear under March the first. Padarn, however, is entered under April the fifteenth.[119] Sulien was back in Llanbadarn also, when the contents of Ieuan's manuscript (the *de Trinitate* and his poems) were

[115] *SEBC* 166.
[116] See note 59 above.
[117] Op. cit. 74.
[118] Ibid.
[119] H. J. Lawlor, *Psalter and Martyrology of Ricemarch* (London, 1914), xiv, 9, 12. But cf. Silas M. Harris, *St David in the Liturgy* (Cardiff, 1940), 5. There it is suggested as a possible explanation of the omission of David that the MS is a more or less exact copy of the current Continental *Martyrology* of the Pseudo-Jerome. Among the very few Celtic saints commemorated are Patrick (17 March) and Samson (28 July).

written.[120] This work was done between 1085 and 1091, apparently at Sulien's request. St David's is referred to as *ibi* 'there': *bis re-uocatus ibi duodenos egerat annos* 'twice recalled, he spent twelve years *there*'.[121] Here also Padarn figures more prominently than David. The Welsh stanza is clearly concerned with Padarn.[122] One of Ieuan's Latin verses is addressed to him, while he is honourably and piously referred to in the poem on Sulien.[123] David is invoked once, but without much ado, with one possible further mention of him.[124] As for Rhigyfarch's 'Lament' and the 'Unhappy Harvest', they are found in a twelfth century manuscript,[125] and it is not possible to determine the original place of composition.

The works referred to above do not reflect any special interest in St David's or its patron saint. It was apparently against his will that Sulien first got himself involved in the affairs of the bishopric. He left it finally in 1085, and in the poems of Ieuan and Rhigyfarch which were written after this date there is hardly any evidence of further involvement. The 'Lament' of Rhigyfarch has, of course, no reference to St David's, and is so different from the *Life* in its tone and general outlook, that they can hardly have been produced in the same situation.[126] In the *Life* we do not find expressed the anguish of a frustrated patriot, but rather the keen and perceptive mind, also the pride and confidence of an alert observer, who could read the signs of the times. The storm had not yet broken. Large areas in the south and west had hardly been touched by the Normans, in Dyfed, Deheubarth, Brycheiniog, Maelienydd, Elfael, and Ceredigion. But

---

[120] Bradshaw says of this MS, 'written apparently in the monastery of St Paternus in Cardiganshire'. (*Collected Papers* (Cambridge, 1889), 457). One ought perhaps to refer to the view that it seems to have been later at St David's, whence it was sent to archbishop Parker by Richard Davies, bishop of St David's (1561–81); cf. *EAWD* ii, 495. See M. R. James, *Descriptive Catalogue of Corpus Christi College, Cambridge MSS* (1912), i. 481. But there is no firm evidence for this view; cf. further *EAWD* ii. 495, *SEBC* 168.

[121] Lapidge, op. cit. 86.

[122] See above. Furthermore, if we accept Sir Ifor's interpretation of this stanza (*BWP* 185, 189), the author would have us believe that 'Cyrwen is unique, without a peer'.

[123] Lapidge, op. cit. 79, 85.

[124] Ibid. 78: *Antistes Dauid, operi succurre precantis* 'Bishop David, favour the work of one praying (for you) . . .'; *Auxilium Dauidque tuum fer, Sancte Paterne* 'And bring your help to David (?), St Padarn . . .'.

[125] Ibid. 73–4. The MS is BL. Cotton Faustina Cl. Cf. note 67 above.

[126] Cf. Mrs Chadwick, *SEBC* 174–5.

there were ominous signs, and it was not difficult to foresee what would ultimately result from William's visit; the military presence of the Normans in south Wales would be followed by interference in the affairs of the church. Church 'reform' would be imposed, and the old cherished independence lost in the process. St David's and its saint had become the focus of Welsh feeling. The *Life* seems to have been produced in an atmosphere such as must have prevailed after the events of 1081 described above. The position of the Welsh church and state in the west had been rescued, at least for the time being. But the situation still called for vigilance, and had doubtless created a sense of urgency that something be done to promote the honour and dignity of the church of David. This explains the production of the *Life*, which was clearly designed to vindicate the claims of this church. It represents another aspect of Sulien's diplomatic activity at this time, and was probably written at his request, as was Ieuan's manuscript a little later. St David's itself would seem to be the place to produce such a work.[127] The information, be it genuine or spurious, would have been there in abundance,[128] while the environment would certainly be conducive to such an undertaking. To sum up: all the evidence seems to indicate that the *Life* was written, or at least begun, at St David's between the years 1081 and 1085, while Sulien was still there, before he relinquished the episcopate and its problems for the last time.[129]

However, it behoves us to follow developments at St David's for some time after this date. Sulien was succeeded in 1085 by one

[127] Despite *SEBC* 164, 172–3.

[128] Cf. ibid. 153–4. I do not wish to speculate here on the materials (written or oral) available to Rhigyfarch, as our knowledge is so inadequate. But there probably existed documents at St David's and elsewhere, for the saint seems to have been known over a fairly wide area (including Ireland) from as early as the eighth century. There was a flourishing tradition of scholarship at St David's in the time of Asser.

[129] It could, of course, have been completed at Llanbadarn after 1085, and at Sulien's request. But it appears more reasonable to place its completion also within the dates of Sulien's second term as bishop, when he would have been directly and immediately concerned with St David's itself, and when we know from other sources that he was involved in diplomatic activity. Mrs Chadwick would not associate any of the literary works of the family with St David's. They belong to Llanbadarn, the family's literary centre; cf. *SEBC* 172; also J. E. Lloyd, *The Story of Ceredigion* 32, *CLIGC* ii (1941), 5. There are however, strong reasons for supposing that the *Life* is an exception. It would hardly be polite or politic to produce it in Llanbadarn, which after all belonged to Padarn, as we are reminded by Ieuan in his poem. Llanbadarn itself had probably once been the seat of a bishopric. In the *Life* Padarn on the visit to Jerusalem is given a specifically subordinate position; cf. *RLSD* 19–21, 42–3.

named Wilfred,[130] who remained bishop until his death in 1115. Little is known of his background. He must have been a Welshman, and he has rightly been described as the last of the independent Welsh bishops at St David's. Like Sulien, and others before him, he assumed the bishopric without reference to Canterbury. The period of his episcopate was by no means uneventful. We have already seen that St David's was never safe from harassment by pillagers and marauders. In 1089 we learn from the *Brut* that 'the shrine of David was taken by stealth from the church and was completely despoiled near the city'.[131] We are not told who was responsible for such sacrilege, but two years later, in 1091 (the year of Sulien's death), it is recorded that St David's was destroyed by 'the Gentiles of the Isles',[132] probably bands of pirates of mixed Scandinavian and Irish stock operating from the western isles of Scotland.

This is the last reference we have to such raids. Wilfred, unlike some of his predecessors, survived the last onslaught, but it was not long before he encountered hazards from other directions. In 1093 Cadwgan ap Bleddyn attacked Dyfed, and in the same year there were launched fierce and determined onslaughts by the Normans on Dyfed and Ceredigion. Rhys ap Tewdwr, king of Deheubarth, was killed by the Normans of Brycheiniog.[133] But the Welsh did not remain subdued for long. Both north and south we find them in 1094 fighting back successfully in a rebellion which was to continue for some years. The fighting of 1094, we are told in the *Brut*, caused much destruction in Dyfed and Ceredigion.[134]

The Welsh rebellion prompted two expeditions into Wales by the king himself. William Rufus came here in 1095, and again in 1097. These are recorded by the *Brut*,[135] as well as by the English chroniclers.[136] They seem to have been directed in the main against Gwynedd and Powys, but it appears that the king was in south Wales also on at least one of them. Giraldus Cambrensis alludes to

---

[130] *BTy RB* 31. A number of variant forms of his name are attested; cf. *HW* ii, 451 n., *BTy Pen 20*[1] 156.
[131] *BTy RB* 33.
[132] Ibid. 35.
[133] Ibid. 33.
[134] Ibid. 35.
[135] Ibid. 35, 37.
[136] Cf. *HGVK* clxii–clxiv.

his presence in the neighbourhood of St David's on one of his
expeditions, when he indicated his intention of invading Ireland.[137]
It is, of course, possible that Giraldus may be confusing this with
the visit of William the Conqueror in 1081. However, if William
Rufus did visit St David's, it is fair to suggest that he met the bishop
there, although we have no evidence of this. What we do know is
that Wilfred is mentioned again by Giraldus, in connection with the
siege of Pembroke castle. In 1096 the castle was attacked by the
Welsh.[138] Giraldus states that Gerald (de Windsor), who was in
charge of the castle and its defence, hard pressed as he was, signed
a letter with the message that it was not necessary to trouble
Arnulph de Montgomery about coming to their aid for another
four months. It was arranged that the letter should fall into the
hands of Wilfred, who happened to be in the neighbourhood at the
time. When the letter had been read and its contents revealed to
the Welsh, they gave up the siege and returned to their homes.[139] It
is not possible to determine what credence ought to be given to this
story. What we do know is that the Welsh failed to capture Pembroke, a failure which marked a turning point in the revolt in south
Wales. By the end of the century the Welsh were in possession of
Ceredigion and Ystrad Tywi only. But to return to the story, the
main interest in it for us is that it shows Wilfred to be in some way
involved in the struggle on the side of the Welsh. And this seems to
be confirmed by the reference in the *Brut* to an attack on St David's
by Gerald de Windsor in the following year.[140] Furthermore, we
have it on the evidence of Giraldus that on one occasion Wilfred
was captured and held prisoner for forty days by the men of
Arnulph de Montgomery.[141]

The last decade of the eleventh century was doubtless full of
hazards for him. He had to contend with interference from
Canterbury, an eventuality which must have haunted the *clas* at
St David's ever since William's visit in 1081, but which had now
become a reality. Archbishop Anselm suspended him because of
his fault (*culpa*), but shortly afterwards in 1095 at Rockingham he

[137] *GW* 169.
[138] *BTy RB* 37.
[139] *GW* 14–9.
[140] *BTy RB* 37.
[141] *Invect.* ii. 6. Cf. *EAWD* i. 262.

was reinstated.[142] We do not know whether, in order to obtain recognition, Wilfred had surrendered some of his independence, and in some way professed obedience to Canterbury. One must regard with scepticism the evidence for his having been (along with Anselm and others) a witness to the king's confirmation of Arnulph de Montgomery's gift of the church of St Nicholas, Pembroke, and other property to the abbey of St Martin of Séez.[143] In any event, he seems to have won Anselm's support, for we find the latter sometime between the years 1100 and 1102 writing to the Norman leaders with lands in the 'bishopric of Wilfred', expressly and firmly bidding them to recognize him as their bishop,[144] and not least the ecclesiastical right of his church to land, tithes and churches, a clear reference to property which must have been taken by the Norman conqueror. More than once was he obliged without demur to acquiesce in the appropriation of churches and lands by houses in England and on the Continent,[145] and among them, St Peters, Gloucester. In a letter written to the abbot of that house sometime between 1113 and 1115 he mentions a pastoral staff, which they had sent him, and which he was now returning. He confirms grants of churches and lands within his bishopric, allowing them considerable freedom therein, to preach, excommunicate, to shepherd the Flemings (who had been settled in his bishopric), to admit and change their clerks. But he nevertheless makes it clear that in return he expects his episcopal rights and dues to be respected.[146] It must have been necessary for him during the period of his long episcopate at times to assert his rights, for he was constantly being reminded of the power of the Norman.

Wilfred may well have bartered some of his independence in exchange for recognition by Canterbury. Nevertheless, he probably retained too much of it for the liking of king and archbishop, and he left his bishopric essentially unchanged in its organization and character. When he died in 1115 the king showed that he did not want another Welshman at St David's. Already, in the previous year he had been to north Wales on an expedition designed to

---

[142] So Eadmer, *Historia* 72. Cf. *EAWD* i. 235.
[143] Cf. *EAWD* i. 130, 235.
[144] Cf. ibid. i. 130, 236.
[145] Cf. ibid. i. 131, 236–7.
[146] Cf. ibid.

demonstrate his power. In the south, a rebellion led by the young Gruffudd ap Rhys was imminent, and Henry was doubtless already aware of the danger. It is no surprise, therefore, that the *claswyr* of St David's encircled as their church was by Norman lordships, were obliged to accept as their new bishop a Norman, Bernard, chaplain and chancellor to Queen Matilda, who was of course prepared to accept the authority of both king and archbishop.[147] In this way there was achieved ecclesiastical as well as civil conquest of south Wales. Bernard remained in St David's until his death in 1148. During the reign of Henry the First (d. 1135), he seems to have been active as a courtier and English ecclesiastic. He did not, however, neglect the affairs of his church, and set about reorganizing it on a diocesan and Norman model.[148] Sometime between 1124 and 1130 the chapter of St David's addressed to Pope Honorius II a letter claiming metropolitan status.[149] Bernard must have known of this, and supported it. Later, after Henry's death, he became, as is well-known, most resolute in promoting the cause of St David's and his own, and tirelessly endeavoured to obtain recognition from the Pope,[150]—eventually without success, although he seems to have come close to achieving his goal at one stage.[151] Towards the end of the century (1198–1203) Giraldus Cambrensis fought hard to secure metropolitan status but again without ultimate success.[152] These later attempts, and the metropolitan pretensions which continued throughout the century, important as they undoubtedly are, are of little relevance to questions concerning the original composition of the *Life*, though subsequent versions and 'editions' of it, such as the one produced by Giraldus Cambrensis, clearly reflect some of these movements.

[147] Flor. Wigorn. ii. 68; Symeon of Durham, *Hist. Reg.* ii, 249; Eadmer, *Historia*, 235–6; *BTy RB* 83. See *EAWD* i. 133–6. The first Welsh bishop of whom it can be said with certainty that he professed obedience to Canterbury was Urban, bishop of Glamorgan or Llandaff (1107).

[148] Cf. *HW* ii. 453–4, *EAWD* i. 135–45.

[149] Preserved by Giraldus, *De Invectionibus* ii. 10; ed. W. S. Davies, *Cy* xxx (1920), 143–6; see also *EAWD* i. 190–2, 249–50, *SEBC* 207–8, 233.

There is surprisingly no mention of Rhigyfarch in this letter, or in letters sent later (1145–1147) to Eugenius III. There is no reference to him by Giraldus in his *Life* (see p. xl), or in his *Journey through Wales*, where he refers to David's election as archbishop (*GW* 179).

[150] Cf. *HW* ii. 480–2, *EAWD* i. 192–200, 259–65, *SEBC* 216–18.

[151] Cf. *HW* ii. 481, *SEBC* 216–17.

[152] Cf. *HW* ii. 559–60, 623–31, *EAWD* i. 210–32.

In the late eleventh and early twelfth century disputes about primacies were not uncommon, especially in France and England. It was not a phenomenon peculiar to Wales.[153] As we have seen, the composition of the *Life* is related to the claims of St David's and to a movement to promote its interests, to boost its greatness. Rhigyfarch was doubtless aware of similar movements elsewhere, notably in Canterbury itself. We ought also to view the work in the context of the renaissance of historical investigation, for which there is evidence at this time. Another circumstance which ought to be borne in mind is that St David's was in conflict and competition not only with Canterbury, but also with other churches within and without Wales. The conflict between St David's and the newly established diocese of Llandaff, which claimed to be the greatest in Wales, is well-known.[154] In the *Book of Llandaf* there is presented a counterclaim to that of St David's (and of Hereford). It is noteworthy that in his *Life* David is exalted above the saints of other prominent churches. Dubricius and Teilo, who were both claimed by Llandaff, are here shown to be subordinate to David.[155] Likewise Deiniol,[156] the founder of Bangor. David is credited with the founding of important centres in England, such as Glastonbury, and it is furthermore important to note how Rhigyfarch makes him a saint deserving precedence over Patrick.[157] Within Wales, the *Life* reflects conflict among those churches which had already become, or were in the process of becoming, centres of newly formed dioceses.[158] Even within the diocese of St David's itself the author seems to be anxious to establish the precedence of David over other saints, over Padarn and also Teilo. Both of them have to be satisfied with a position subordinate to David before the Patriarch of Jerusalem, a position which may be taken as supporting the case for St David's rather than Llanbadarn as the place of composition. Towards the end of the eleventh century, and at about the same

[153] Cf. *SEBC* 212–13, also *EAWD* i. 200–1. Questions relating to metropolitancy were live issues in Ireland and Wales in the first half of the eleventh century; cf. ibid. 204–7.
[154] Cf. *EAWD* i. 146–90.
[155] See pp. 9.14–16. In *RLSD* 42, Teilo is described as having been at one time a monk in his monastery.
[156] Ibid. 44. Deiniol (Daniel) and Dubricius, 'the holiest and most upright men', were sent from Brefi to try and prevail upon David to come to the synod.
[157] Cf. *RLSD* 29–30, also below pp. 1–2.
[158] Cf. *SEBC* 162.

time as the *Life* of David there was composed at Llancarfan a *Life* of Cadog[159] by Lifris, another son of a bishop, namely Herwald, bishop of Llandaff (1056–1104). Cadog belonged essentially to the south-east.[160] These two *Lives* are the earliest examples of a literary form which became common among the hagiographical productions of Wales in the twelfth century.

THE LATIN TEXTS

We must now turn to examine the *Life* itself, as it has come down to us in various manuscripts. The Revd J. W. James has made a close study of the manuscript sources of the Latin *Life*, which is found in some half a dozen MSS of the middle or second half of the twelfth century.[161] In all some twenty-nine texts (mostly in manuscript) are accounted for, and these may be divided into five groups, representing different recensions. The following are the five listed by James.

The Nero recension. This is found in nine manuscripts, the earliest being BL MS Nero Ei, hence the name. This may well belong to the third quarter of the twelfth century. Other twelfth century manuscripts which contain this recension are the Rouen Municipal Library MSS U. 141 and 19, and a Cardiff Central Library MS. Another which contains it is the thirteenth century Saint-Omer Municipal Library MS 716. Four of the texts, Nero Ei, Rouen 141, the Cardiff MS and Saint-Omer 716, are independent copies of an earlier archetype.

The Digby recension, found in seven manuscripts. The Bodleian Library, Oxford MS Digby 112 was possibly written at Winchester during *c.* 1150–75. Another Bodleian manuscript, Bodley 793, also belongs to the twelfth century, and the *Life* in it is clearly a copy of the text in Digby 112. Another copy is found in the thirteenth-century manuscript Bodley 285, from which some other texts are derived. In fact, all the texts are directly or indirectly derived from

---

[159] *VSBG* 23–141; see also H. D. Emanuel, *CLIGC* vii (1951–2), 217–27; also J. Conway Davies, *EAWD* 506–37. The Vespasian MS contains interpolations from a later *Life* by Caradog of Llancarfan; cf. *SEBC* 235–6.

[160] Cf. *SCSW* 33–48.

[161] See his *Rhigyfarch's Life of St David* (Cardiff, 1967), xi–xliii.

Digby 112. The recension in an abbreviated form was printed in the Bollandists' *Acta Sanctorum*, Antwerp, 1645.

The Giraldus recension, originating with Giraldus Cambrensis (1146–1223). It is based on the Nero recension, and was written probably during the years 1172–76.[162] There are two texts, both apparently deriving from a common exemplar. The one is found in BL MS Royal 13 C1, which belongs to the fifteenth century, and which also contains *Miracula S. Dauidis* (unknown elsewhere) and *Lectiones de Sancta Nonnita* (imperfect). The other occurred in BL MS Vitellius E vii, which was destroyed by fire in 1731. It had, however, been transcribed and printed by Henry Wharton in *Anglia Sacra* (ii. 628–40) in 1691, an edition reprinted by J. S. Brewer in the Rolls Series edition of Giraldus's works in 1862, *Opera* iii. 375–404.

The Vespasian recension. This is fuller than the other four, and is found in the important thirteenth-century manuscript, BL MS Vespasian A xiv,[163] which was written in the early thirteenth century, possibly at Monmouth priory. It must derive from the south-east, and the influence of Gloucester is much in evidence in it, although it has also indubitable links with the west. Another thirteenth-century manuscript which contains this recension, in a drastically abridged form (of about a third in length) from the Vespasian text, is the Lincoln Cathedral Library MS 149. To the first half of the fourteenth century may be assigned the BL MS Tiberius Ei, another abridgement of the Vespasian text. As a result of fire in 1731, less than half is now legible. John of Tynemouth's *Sanctilogium* may well be based on this. Capgrave's rearrangement of Tynemouth's work was printed by Wynkyn de Worde in 1516 in the *Nova Legenda Angliae* (reprinted in 1901 by Carl Horstman). Bodleian Library, Oxford, MS Tanner 15 is a copy of Tiberius Ei, made in 1499.

The Irish recension, found in some four texts, all of Irish provenance. The earliest appears to be Bodleian Library, Oxford, MS

---

[162] *c.* 1200, according to *SDL* 16.

[163] For important discussions of this MS, cf. Kathleen Hughes, *SEBC* 183–200; S. M. Harris, *Journ. of the Hist. Soc. of the Church in Wales* iii (1953), 3–53. The *Lives* in it are printed by Wade-Evans in *VSBG*, that of David in pp. 150–70; also in *Cy* xxiv (1913), 1–74 (trans. in *LSD* 1–33). Variants from it are included at the foot of the page in *RLSD*.

Rawlinson B 485. This was written *c.* 1350, and along with Rawlinson B 505 (*c.* 1400), which is a transcript of it, was connected with the monastery on the Island of the Saints in Lough Ree, Ireland. Rawl. B. 505 seems to have been copied there. The latter was in turn transcribed by Father John Goolde in 1627. This transcript, found in Dublin Franciscan Convent Library MS F2, was printed in John Colgan's *Vitae Sanctorum Hiberniae*, 1636. Finally, there is BL MS Sloane (or Additional) 4788, a manuscript of 1639, which contains a greatly abbreviated version derived from Rawl. B. 505.

The Nero and the Digby recensions can be traced back to the middle of the twelfth century, and seem to derive ultimately from two different copies of an archetype of that date. We are able to reconstruct a mid-twelfth century text of the *Life*, which is the version provided for us, along with copious variant readings, in *Rhigyfarch's Life of St David*. Of the two, the Nero recension[164] seems to come nearer to this text. When one seeks to examine the relationship between the two recensions and the mid-twelfth-century text and the original composition by Rhigyfarch, one can identify some (but not many) features which seem to reflect bishop Bernard's policy and attitude. The need for winning Papal sympathy may account for a possible tendency, only dimly apparent, to play down the significance of the visit to the Patriarch in Jerusalem (*cc.* 44–48), while the wording in *c.* 58, which tells of David being constituted archbishop, may betray acquaintance with forged Canterbury charters produced during the primacy dispute between Canterbury and York.[165]

However, it is reasonable to assume that the two recensions and the earlier lost archetype did not greatly diverge in tenor and content from Rhigyfarch's work. The Giraldus recension is further removed, especially from Digby. According to J. W. James it is based on a text of the Nero recension, and represents more a paraphrase than a copy. It was written about 1176, when the see was vacant, and Giraldus a nominee, his first unsuccessful bid for the bishopric. The Vespasian recension came later. As was stated, it is fuller than the other four, containing material not found in them. Such material accounts for about one-fifth of the Vespasian text. It has more in common with Nero than with Digby, and of the Nero

---

[164] James in *CLlGC* ix. 4: 'it is a very interesting instance of a "Neutral Text".'
[165] Cf. Christopher Brooke, *SEBC* 214, also 242.

manuscripts, it appears that Rouen U 141 represents the text from which Vespasian originated. The accretions and amplifications[166] found in this recension may be divided into two main groups. The first relate to identifications of persons and places of interest in west Wales and in the vicinity of St David's, apparently unknown to Giraldus in 1176, but which were added to a Nero text by someone in St David's about the year 1190, as is suggested. This represents the first stage in the development of this recension. The other group originated, not at St David's, but at the priory where the recension was completed and the manuscript, Vespasian A xiv, written. They were included by the Monmouth scribe, by someone familiar with other *Lives* such as those of Cadog (Lifris), Illtud, Dubricius, and also with other works, such as the *Life* of Gildas and the *Life* of Cadog by Caradog of Llancarfan. These consist of references connected in the main with south-east Wales, and represent the final evolution of the Vespasian recension, completed thus around the year 1200. As we have noted, this recension was found later in the Lincoln Cathedral Library MS 149, and in the version by John of Tynemouth. It is represented also in the Welsh version, which first appeared early in the fourteenth century, and which will be discussed in more detail later.

There is not much that need be said further about the Irish version, save that it is the latest of the five. It is an abridgement, and also in part a paraphrase, based on an early Nero text, possibly Rouen U 141. It can be shown also to have affinities with another Nero manuscript, Bodley 336 of the thirteenth century. It has little affinity with the Digby recension, and none with Giraldus or Vespasian.

THE WELSH VERSION

In order to try and determine the significance of the Welsh version, which was produced more than two centuries later than the original Latin *Life*, we must briefly summarize its contents.

First, we have the rubric, which mentions the subjects to be discussed, namely David's pedigree and part of his life.

Next we are presented with his pedigree on his father's side. It

[166] The additions of the Vespasian MS are given by J. W. James on every page of his edition in *RLSD*.

was important that a saint should have a royal father, and we are here taken back through Ceredig and Cunedda and his immediate forbears, then through a list of some obscure names, ending up with the Virgin's sister.

The *Life* begins with a reference to Ceredig, king of Ceredigion (who gave that land its name) and his reign. He had a son, Sant, who was told by an angel in a dream that he would discover three finds by the river Teifi at Henllan. These are a stag, a salmon and a swarm of bees. He is told (in a sentence which must be corrupt in its present form) that he is to reserve the right of possession of the land for a son not yet born. Two (unidentifiable) places are mentioned, which this son shall possess till the Day of Judgement.

Next, Patrick comes to Glyn Rhosyn, with the intention of settling there, but he is warned by an angel that the place is reserved for a son not yet born, and who will not be born for another thirty years. Patrick expresses disappointment, but is eventually appeased by the angel, who shows him the island of Ireland, where he will be an apostle and will suffer greatly for the love of God. But God will be with him. Before leaving for Ireland, Patrick raises from the dead a man who had been buried for fifteen years, and takes him with him. This man, whose name is Cruchier, later became a bishop.

Then we have a brief account of David's conception and birth, which happened at the end of thirty years. Sant was travelling alone, and met a nun named Nonn. He violated her, she became pregnant, and a son was born to her who was named David. She had been chaste before this encounter, and remained so afterwards.

We are told of a number of wondrous deeds performed by David, both before leaving his mother's womb and shortly afterwards. From the moment she conceived, his mother consumed nothing except bread and water for the rest of her life, and David likewise limited himself to this diet. Gildas failed to preach to a congregation which included David's pregnant mother, and like Patrick is obliged to move on, 'to another island'. The hour David was born there came thunder and lightning, and when Nonn was being delivered, a stone opposite her head split in two, with one half leaping over her head to below her feet. At his baptism a spring appeared, and a blind man (flat-faced from birth) who was holding David was cured and recovered his sight.

David was first educated at a place called *Vetus Rubus* (in Welsh

Yr Hennllwyn), whence he moved on to a master called Paulinus, who instructed him till he became a teacher (*athro*). There is emphasis on David's modesty. Paulinus lost his sight, and after his pupils had failed to cure him, he came at last to David and asked him to look at his eyes. David told him that he had not for the ten years he had been with him looked in his face. The master was amazed at his pupil's modesty, and asked him to put his hands on his face and bless his eyes, which he did. Paulinus recovered his sight and blessed David abundantly.

David then left Paulinus, and undertook an itinerary on which he visited various parts of the country. These consisted of areas in the west of England, the midlands and south Wales, where there were well-known and established centres like Glastonbury and Bath, Crowland and Repton, Colfa and Glascwm, and Leominster. He was also in the old (Welsh) kingdom of Archenfield, where he cured the king, Pebiawc, of his blindness. He founded Rhaglan in Gwent, and Llangyfelach in Gower. In Cydweli two saints, named Boducat and Nailtrwm, joined him as disciples.

He returned to *Vetus Rubus*. His uncle or teacher, Goeslan, was there, and David informed him of what he had been told by the angel, namely that hardly one in a hundred from that place would go to heaven. He showed him another place from which no one went to hell. David, along with his disciples, Aeddan, Eludd and Ismael, then moved to Glyn Rhosyn (or Hoddnant), and we have an account of the conflict between him and the Irish chieftain, Boia, for possession of that area. In the course of this conflict Boia's wife is active in trying to harass David and his disciples. She instructs her handmaidens to display their naked bodies before them. An episode is then related in which she takes her stepdaughter to the valley of the Alun to look for nuts. Her stepdaughter sits on her lap so that she may examine her hair, whereupon she takes a knife and cuts off the maiden's head. A spring appears at the place where the blood fell; this is called Ffynnon Dunawd, because Dunawd was the name of the maiden. The stepmother then flees, and eventually Boia is killed in his sleep in his tower (*twr*) by an enemy. Let all know that God killed Boia and his wife for the sake of David.

Then David built a monastery in Glyn Rhosyn. The place lacked water and David prayed to God, whereupon there appeared a spring, a spring full of wine! After that bishop Gweslan, and a disciple of David named Eludd, both fasted in order to seek from God springs of clear water. Two were obtained, Ffynnon Gweslan and Ffynnon Eludd, in which the cripple, the blind and the sick received a cure.

Next we are told of a conspiracy against David by three members of his community, who had arranged to put poison in bread which he was to eat on the following day. Warning of this was given by the angel to Aeddan, a disciple of David, in his church in Ferns on Easter Eve. A messenger, Scuthyn, was dispatched by Aeddan to St David's in order to warn David. He crossed on the back of a monster, which had suddenly appeared in order to carry him over. He met David and warned him of the evil intention. When they sat down to eat, the deacon who was due to serve David with the bread was forbidden from doing so by Scuthyn, whereupon he sat down greatly surprised. Then David took the poisoned bread. He gave a third of it to a bitch, and a third to a raven, whereupon both of them died instantly. The remaining third he ate himself, with no ill effects, and revealed to the brethren the treachery of his betrayers, who were duly cursed by the whole community.

An account is next given of the synod of Brefi, to which the author quite clearly attaches considerable importance. He has quite a lot to say about it, all redounding to the glory and prestige of David. Labourers and dignitaries from church and state had assembled in large numbers at Llanddewibrefi. It was there agreed that whosoever could preach, so that everyone heard, should be recognized as chief of the saints of the island of Britain. The saints took it in turn to preach, but to no avail. Then Paulinus advised them to go and seek David in Mynyw. He had not come to the synod, and messengers were despatched to bring him there; twice this was done, but he could not be prevailed upon to come. A third time messengers were sent, 'the two chief saints who were there', namely Deinioel and Dubricius. David was eventually persuaded to come with them, and on their way to Brefi, somewhere near the river Teifi, he restored to life the dead son of a widow, who straightway followed him. On arriving at the synod he was greeted by all the saints, who requested him to ascend a high mound where there had been a sermon before. But he declined, and started preaching on the level ground in a clear voice and audible to all, to the farthest as well as to the nearest. And while he was preaching, the ground rose like a high mountain under his feet. This is still clearly visible to all, a high mound with level ground on both sides of it. And that was the miracle and wonder which God wrought for Dewi at Llanddewifrefi.

Then David was unanimously recognized leader of the saints of the island of Britain, because of his being able to preach at that great synod to all the people. And all the saints and all the kings of this island went on their knees to worship him, and made him chief of the saints of the island of Britain.

Next there is reference to David's right of protection or sanctuary, in St David's and also within an area between Dyfi (corr. Tywi) and Teifi. It is declared that there is right of protection wherever there is land consecrated to David who, it is maintained, received right of protection before everyone, since God and men set him up as head of the whole island. Anyone who would violate David's protection, the saints excommunicated with the concurrence of the kings.

As David was listening to his scholars at a service on the last Tuesday of February, he heard an angel converse with him, informing him of his impending death. When the brethren heard this, there was great grief and lamentation. This is all described in a very vivid and dramatic manner, the sorrow and sense of loss expressed as the angel carried the news throughout this island (Britain) and Ireland.

David's last message is recorded, followed by a description of the general grief.

We are given an impressive account of David's death on the first day of March, when Jesus Christ took away his soul with great victory and joy and honour. And the angels brought it to the place where there is light without end, rest without labour, and joy without sadness, the celestial abode in which dwell people of renown such as Abel, Enoc, Noe, etc., the angels and archangels and the King of kings for ever.

Finally there is an epilogue, which asks for the help and intercession of the saint for those/him who recorded his life and deeds on this earth, that they/he may obtain mercy in time to come.

The Welsh *Life* contains some five thousand words, the Nero E1 and Digby 112 manuscripts some six thousand three hundred, and

the Vespasian text seven thousand nine hundred.[167] It has already
been noted that the Vespasian recension is fuller than those of
Nero and Digby. The Welsh *Life* is shorter than all three, and a
cursory comparison with them will readily show where material
has been omitted by the Welsh redactor.

Let us briefly note the parts he has left out. The introductory
chapter of the Latin is missing,[168] as are the sentences explaining
the significance of the three gifts.[169] There is no reference to the
two stones which appeared at the time of Nonn's conception, one
at her head and the other at her feet.[170] There is a reference to
the thunder and lightning which accompanied the birth of David,
but no mention of the tyrant who had intended to kill Nonn;
neither is there mention of the church built at the spot where he
was born.[171] His ordination is not referred to.[172] The sections
dealing with the manner of life and code of conduct in David's
monastery,[173] which occur immediately after the reference to the
building of it,[174] are entirely missing in the Welsh *Life*. No
mention is made of Constantine, king of Cornwall, joining the
community.[175] He was one of the kings and princes attracted to
the monastery; later he departed for another land and built a
monastery there. Omitted also is the section describing how
David at the request of a man, named Terdi, draws water from
the ground with the point of his staff.[176] The Welsh *Life* speaks of
Aeddan as David's disciple, but he is already at Ferns in Ireland.
In the Latin *Life* we find him at St David's. At the bidding of the
prior he left an open book he was reading out of doors, and with
two oxen went to carry timber from the valley. The oxen and the
waggon fell down a precipice, but were miraculously saved by the
sign of the Cross made over them. After completing his journey,
Aeddan returned to the open book, which had remained dry

---

[167] See James, *CLlGC* ix. 4.
[168] c.1. The references here are to the chapters as found in *RLSD*, and in *VSBG*
and *LSD*.
[169] c.2.
[170] c.4.
[171] c.6.
[172] c.9.
[173] cc.21–31.
[174] c.20.
[175] c.32.
[176] c.34.

despite a downpour of rain.[177] When his education had been completed, Aeddan left for Ireland, where he built a monastery at
Ferns.[178] The Welsh *Life* has not included the story of the Irish
abbot, Bairre, who on his return from the shrines of Peter and Paul,
called at St David's and was given David's horse to cross the sea, as
his ship had been delayed by lack of wind.[179] On his way he met
St Brendan. Later, after it died, a statue was made of the horse
to commemorate the miracle, a statue still to be found and renowned for its miracles.[180] There is in the Welsh version no mention
of Midunnauc, who was attacked by a workman, and saved by David
who saw the incident from afar.[181] After many years Midunnauc
departed for Ireland. All the bees followed him, and after he had
three times returned to bring them back, David eventually gave him
permission to take them with him. He blessed them, and as a result
they increased in Ireland, a land which was thus 'enriched in an
overwhelming abundance of honey'.[182] We are next given the
account of the visit to Jerusalem by David, Teilo and Padarn.[183] On
their journey they come to Gaul, where 'they heard foreign languages spoken by different peoples'. But David had the gift of
tongues, so that they had no need of an interpreter, and could
'confirm the faith of others with the Word of Truth'. The Patriarch
in Jerusalem had three thrones made ready for them, and 'advanced
David to the archbishopric'. They are urged to preach to the Jews.
This they do, and many are converted, others confirmed in the
Faith. The Patriarch gave David four wondrous gifts possessing
miraculous powers, an altar, a bell, a staff and a tunic woven with
gold.

[177] c.35. A similar incident is recorded in the *Life* of Cadog; *VSBG* 52–4.

[178] c.36.

[179] c.39.

[180] c.40.

[181] c.41. c.42. Is found only in the Vespasian text. There it is stated that about a
third or a quarter of Ireland is subject to David. His disciple Aeddan, when sailing to
Ireland, had forgotten the little bell, Cruedin, given him by David. A messenger was
sent for it, but the bell was carried across the sea by an angel, who reached Aeddan
before the messenger had returned.

[182] c.43.

[183] cc.44–48. Mentioned also in the *Life* of Padarn, *VSBG* 258, and of Teilo, *LL*
103. It is related of other saints in *Lives* composed in the eleventh and twelfth
centuries that they visited Jerusalem; cf. *Doble* iii. 9, and see *VSBG* 56, 80, 87, 94
(Cadog), 234 (Cybi). Such accounts may well have been inspired by the Crusades,
which occurred during this period.

While the Welsh *Life* attaches great importance to the synod of Brefi, it is not as in the Latin *Life* associated with the question of heresy. After the synod we are told of the expulsion of heresy, and the confirmation of catholic decrees, decrees enjoined by David, which 'in very old documents of the father are in part extant'.[184] After some years, another synod, called the synod of Victory, is held. In this decisions are reaffirmed and new provisions added. All the churches of the land take their standard and rule by Roman authority from these two synods, and David himself is credited with having committed the decrees to writing with his own hands.[185] In the next section there is reference to the building of monasteries, to churches, to charitable offerings, and above all to David as 'the supreme overseer, the supreme protector, the supreme preacher'.[186]

In further sections there are references to his age, 147 years,[187] and to his burial in the grounds of his monastery.[188] Next, the author emphasizes that he has been able to commit to writing only a few of David's deeds and virtues 'out of the very many that are scattered in the oldest manuscripts of our country, and chiefly of his own monastery'.[189] Finally, Rhigyfarch names himself, and asks for the prayers of those who read his work. He aspires to a place 'within the portals of the celestial gates, there endlessly to behold God, who is blessed above all things, for ever and ever, Amen'.[190]

But the Welsh *Life* contains words and sentences not found in the known Latin texts. There are also cases where the Welsh differs from the Latin. For the most part, these consist of mere stylistic additions and variations, and are of no consequence. Some will be referred to in the notes, but it will be convenient here to bring together the more important divergences, since in this way, along with the differences mentioned above, they could help to assess the significance and character of the Welsh version.

The Welsh version is alone in inserting 'Wyry, vam Iessu Grist'

[184] c.54.
[185] c.55.
[186] c.56.
[187] c.58.
[188] c.65.
[189] c.66.
[190] c.67.

(1.6) after 'Veir' (*Mariae*). It alone has the reference to Ceredig ruling in Ceredigion, and to his having given that land its name[191] (1.7–8). The Latin *Life* does not contain the sentence, 'ef bieiuyd deu le hyt Dyd Brawt, y rei a dywetpwyt vchot, Lin Henllan a Liton Mancan' (1.13–14). Neither does it contain the following: 'ehun' '*alone*' (2.18), 'a dauid a rodet yn enw arnaw' (2.20–1), 'Kynntaf gwyrth a wnaeth Dewi' (2.23), 'Eil gwyrth a wnnaeth Dewi' (2.26), 'a yrreis i ... Heb y' (3.3–4), 'Gwyrth arall a wnaeth Dewi' (3.11), 'Gwyrth arall a oruc Dewi' (3.15), 'val y dylyynt' (3.21), 'yng Kymraec yw yr Henllwynn' (3.22–3), 'yn y gylch' (3.25). In Latin Paulinus is described as disciple of Germanus (Germani discipulum ND, discipulum Sancti Germani episcopi V) but in Welsh as 'disgybyl ... y escob sant a oed yn Rufein' (3.26–7). The Welsh seems to be alone in including the following: 'A hwnnw a elwir yr Enneint Twymynn' (4.13), 'Dyoer' (5.6), 'Yn bugelyd ni a dywedassant ymi' (5.18–19), 'ny allwnn ni diodef hynn, nac edrych ar' (5.33–4), 'Tidi vorwyn,' heb hi, 'kyuot ac' (5.37–8), 'yn y gyfeir' (6.5), 'Ac eissyoes, sef y damweinawd y bore trannoeth' (6.12), 'Satrapa' (6.16). Missing also are the details relating to Gweslan and Eludd (Teilo), and the springs named after them (6.27). Aeddan is addressed as 'Tidi, wrda gwynuydedic' (7.1–2) in the Welsh version only. In that version only is there a specific reference to betrayal by the three members of St David's monastery (7.4–5), and to a request that he be warned not to eat the poisoned bread (7.7). There only do we find the words, 'ual y galler y chaffel' (7.10), and there only do we learn that Scuthyn was at St David's by noon on Easter Sunday (7.16). More details are given in Welsh of the meeting between Scuthyn and David (7.18–25); they met at a place called *Bed Yscolan* (7.19). In addition to the categories of people attending the synod of Brefi named in the Latin texts, the Welsh *Life* mentions 'athrawon ... a'r ieirll, a'r barwneit, a'r goreugwyr a'r ysgwiereit' (8.13–14). Paulinus is described as '*hen* escob' (8.27). Only in the Welsh version does he specifically name David as the one who should be brought to the synod (9.5–7). Only here does he refer to his having become an '*athro*' (9.2). A place had been reserved for him in the

---

[191] But cf. the *Life* of Carammog: Keredic autem tenuit Kerediciaun, et ab illo nuncupata est (*VSBG* 148).

kingdom of *Demetica* (Dyfed), namely 'Mynyw yn y deheu' (9.4–5). It is said of him that he loves God greatly and preaches Christ (9.6–7). Messengers are sent to dinas Rubi, where David is engaged in praying and teaching (9.9). 'o'e garyat' (9.12) is found in the Welsh version only. Likewise the following words and sentences, 'a dygwch yma dyfuwr gloyw o'r ffynnawn' (9.18–19), 'a'r dwfyr a aeth yn win ar hynt' (9.23), 'Vrth hynny ... at y ketymeithonn hynny' (9.27–30) 'a chwitheu, gwediwch y Tat pennaf, ... a rodet yni o'r nef' (9.31–4), 'kyuodi yn hollyach a oruc y mab' (10.14), 'a syrthyaw ar dal y glinyeu' (10.23), 'gann dyrchauel ohonaw y benn brynn vchel, y lle y buassei bregeth kyn no hynny' (10.23–4), 'Eissoes ef a gymerth venndith y kyffredin' (10.28), 'pann vei hanner dyd' (10.33–4), 'A phann oed Dewi ar warthaf y llawr gwastat a dywedwyt vchot' (10.35), 'A'r gwyrth a'r ryuedawt hwnnw a oruc Duw yr Dewi yn Llanndewiv-reui' (11.3–4), 'gann dywedut ... yn Ynys Prydein' (11.6–13), 'am bregethu ohonaw ... namyn ef' (11.15–17), 'Ac ef a'e haedawd' (11.19), 'Honn yw nodua Dewi ... a vo moe' (11.21–4), 'Sef a oruc ynteu yna, dyrchauel y wyneb y vynyd' (12.5–6), '.ac na at vi y drigyaw a vo hwy yn y drygeu hynn' (12.12–13), 'a decuet y daear ... a hynny a daw y gyt a thi' (12.16–19), 'a gwediaw' (12.27), 'A'e gyuryw kynn noc ef nys clywysbwyt, a gwedy ef byth ny chlywir' (13.7–8), 'y bregeth ac' (13.9–10), 'a chwioryd' (13.12), 'bychein' (13.13), 'a phoet grymus ywch vot ar y dayar' (13.15–16), 'a digrifwch' (13.24), 'megys y gadawssei yn y vawrhydri, a'r heul yn eglur yn egluraw y'r holl luoed' (13.26–7), 'y gyt a mawr uudugolyaeth ... a'e vedwl am y byt' (13.28). The long, rhetorical, closing section, 'ac y dugant y'r lle y mae goleuni heb diwed ... yn yr oes oesoed. Amen' (13.32–14.17) does not occur in the Latin texts, but a passage resembling it is found at the end of Cybi's *Life*.[192]

As we have noted, the Welsh *Life* is shorter than the Latin texts. The differences between it and them are often not easy to explain, but there are some which can help us to understand the more

---

[192] *VSBG* 248, 250.

essential features of the Welsh version. The latter seems to concen-
trate upon the diocese of St David's, upon the monastery and its
immediate environs. It has certain delicate (but deliberate)
touches, apparently calculated to create a more familiar, intimate,
and less formal atmosphere, the kind of atmosphere suited to the
circumstances and aspirations of a Welsh audience. Note the reference to Ceredig, and the explanation of the name Ceredigion, the
mention of the two place-names, Lin Henllan and Liton Mancan,
the Welsh for *Vetus Rubus*, the two springs named after Gweslan
and Eludd, the place called *Bed Yscolan* where Scuthyn and David
met. The reference to 'earls' and 'barons' and 'squires' at the
synod of Brefi is delightfully anachronistic, but would cause no
offence to a Welsh audience, and would be 'understood'. Demetica
is explained as 'Mynyw yn y deheu' (*Mynyw in the south*). Further,
there is the reference to David's great love of God and his preaching
of Christ. The messengers who came to St David's find him praying
and teaching, and he beseeches them to depart in the peace of God
and his *love*. It is for the love of God that he finally decides to go to
the synod, and urges that His help be sought in prayer. The
members of the synod fall on their knees when he arrives, and his
feat there is explained as a miracle and wonder wrought by God for
David. It is expressly stated that it was for this that he was acclaimed
chief and leader of the saints of Ynys Prydain. The area of
David's right of sanctuary is defined. Finally, we may note certain
small additions, such as those of 'chwioryd' in 13.12, and of
'bychein' in 13.13, which serve to confirm the impression that
the Welsh *Life* was intended for a 'public' different from that of
Rhigyfarch and the others, less sophisticated, and certainly less
concerned with the weighty 'political' issues and circumstances
which originally produced the Latin *Vita*. Apart from certain specific additions which would be meaningful to a Welsh listener or
reader, there is in the Welsh *Life* generally emphasis on David's
simple goodness and godliness, on his humility and devotion, on his
miracles, to the exclusion of other aspects. The authority derived
from the Patriarch of Jerusalem is not mentioned, neither is the
pilgrimage to that place by the three saints.[193] More prominence is

---

[193] Cf. *EAWD* i 249–50, 262–3. Here the Welsh *Life* seems to be more in agreement with the letters of the chapter of St David's than generally with Rhigyfarch; cf.
note 85 above.

accorded to Rome. One may note the references to Paulinus as having been taught by a bishop in Rome, and (as in L) David is described as having been consecrated archbishop there. More Roman then, apparently, than Rhigyfarch. Also, less Irish. By comparison, the Welsh *Life* gives scant attention to David's Irish disciples, and to the links with Ireland, although there is no lack of emphasis on his influence and authority in that country (4.32–5.2, 12.28–9, 31–3). The question of doctrine and orthodoxy is given little prominence; and we observed that there is no account of the life of the community at St David's. The Welsh author does not seem disposed to stress David's extreme asceticism; he is throughout content to demonstrate in a general way the chastity and integrity of the saint, his powers and gifts; as the elect of God his pre-eminence and authority have been ordained from the beginning.

Notwithstanding the divergences, the Welsh *Life* is clearly based on a Latin text or texts, either a direct translation or, as seems more likely, an adaptation. J. W. James has shown that it is an abridgement of the Vespasian version,[194] which means, of course, that it must be dated post 1200. We can note readings, sentences and passages, where it agrees specifically with the texts of the Vespasian manuscripts.[195] There are marked correspondences with the

[194] *CLlGC* ix (1955/6), 5–6.

[195] Such as 1.2–6 (the genealogy, which in V , however, occurs at the end; cf. *RLSD* 28, *LSD* 32–3), 1.10–11 (ger lan auon Teiui), 2.18, (lleian), 2.19 (ymauael a hi) 2.26–7 (y warandaw pregeth), 2.31 (y rwg y dor a'r paret), 3.13–14 (ac a neidyawd … ynn escor), 3.23–4 (seilym yr holl vlwydyn a'e llithion a'r offerennev), 3.24–5 (a gyluin eur idi), 3.25 (yn gware), 3.27–8 (A hwnnw … athro), 3.28–30 (Ac yna … ol yn ol), 3.33–4 (edrych … dy lygeit), 3.35–6 (a ryuedu kewilyd y mab), 3.36 (Kannys velle y mae), 4.1–2 (A phann … holl yach), 4.3–4 (Ac yna … yn y newyd), 4.18–19 (yg Gwyr), 4.20–1 (Deu sant … idaw), 4.22 (hyt y lle … *Vetus Rubus*), 4.30 (hyt y … hwnnw), 5.3 (Yscot), 5.13–17 (Ac yna … yn eu kyueir), 5.19–20 (yn holl … an deueit), 5.22–4 (Ac yna … hynn), 5.25–6 (Ac yna … y Dewi), 5.26–8 (A phann … yn yach), 5.30 (hyt yr auon), 5.31–3 (Holl … ymeith), 5.37–9 (Ac yna … trannoeth), 5.40–6.4 (Trannoeth … kyllell), 6.7–8 (A hyt … Ffynnawn Dunawt—*Martirium* Dunaut), 6.9–11 (Yna … lawenhassant), 6.11 (Yna … Dauyd), 6.15–16 (Gwybydet … Dewi), 6.21–2 (val … hwnnw), 10.7 (yn emyl … Teiui), 10.8 (syrthyaw … corff), 10.9–13 (a gwediaw … dayar), 10.17–18 (drwy … vlwynnyded), 10.18–19 (A phawb … Duw), 10.29 (A gwrthot … brenn), 10.30–2 (A dechreu … eglur), 11.17–18 (holl … Dewi), 11.24–5 (aet … sant), 12.24 (vn vedwl), 12.24–5 (a pha … mwy), 12.26–7 (y bawp), 12.28 (yn oet vn dyd), 12.31 (at y Arglwyd), 12.33–13.6 in V¹ only (O! … tat), 13.17–21 (Yna … angheu).

Lincoln text (L).[196] Whether that text was used by the author of the Welsh recension, it is impossible to determine. Nothing is known of its early history. We know that it found its way to France, where it was acquired during the Commonwealth years by Dr Honeyman. He became dean of Lincoln after the Restoration, and presented the manuscript to the Cathedral library. In any event, there is evidence that the author of the Welsh *Life* consulted a text or texts other than L.[197] It may well have been based on a text different from V and L, but one which contained features found in both.

I tried to show in my Welsh edition that the language of the text seems to point to the fourteenth century as the period of composition, probably sometime in the first half of that century. We are reminded by Professor Glanmor Williams that 'the circumstances of the latter half of the fourteenth century ... were distinctly less propitious for clerical learning than those of the first half of the century'.[198] It is not possible to determine precisely the circumstances which produced this version or the place where it was written, St David's itself, or more likely Llandddewibrefi? But, wherever or whenever it was written, it may be taken as reflecting spiritual and

[196] Such as 1.16–17 (Adaw ... etwo), 2.26–7 (a'e vam ... pregethu), 2.29–31 (Ac elchwyl ... paret), 3.13 (yn ... deu hanner), 3.30–1 (ac nyt ... idaw), 4.6 (vynet odyma), 4.7 (y petheu ... wnneuthur), 4.10 (dwfyr ... wenwyn), 4.29 (a llawer y gyt ac wynt), 5.7 (trist ... llidyawc), 5.11–12 (a llad ... gannyat), 5.20–1 (ac eu bot ... agoret), 5.29 (Ac yna ... llawuorynyon), 5.30 (a diosglwch awch dillat), 5.34 (Ac yna ... y ni), 7.3 (dy athro di), 7.5 (dodi ... bara), 7.12–16 (Sef ... arall), 7.28–9 (y wassanaethu ... gantaw), 7.32 (mynet y eisted), 8.15 (a ymgynnullassant ... Vreui), 8.16–21 (Ac amot ... bregeth), 8.21–2 (Yna ... gilyd), 8.24–9 (nat oes ... idaw), 9.7 (a myui ... gras), 9.8 (y seint), 9.9–18 (A phan ... mor), 9.20–1 (A'r kennadeu ... kinyaw), 9.22–3 (a'r dwfyr ... win), 9.23–7 (A Dauyd ... aros di), 9.30–1 (yr hwnn ... gallaf), 9.32 (yny ... y ni), 9.36–10.1 (A chynn ... mab), 10.2–5 (A phann ... varw), 10.8 (a dodi ... mab), 10.14 (A phann ... Dewi), 10.18 (y gyt a ... Duw), 10.20–3 (Odyna ... bregethu), 10.25–7 (Ac escussaw ... idaw), 10.28 (ac a vfydha awd vdunt), 10.33–4 (ac yn gynn gyffredinet ... bawp), 10.35 (A hynny ... bawb), 11.17–19 (A'r dyd hwnnw ... Ynys Prydein), 12.4–5 (y peth ... mynnych), 12.11 (Sef ... vchel), 12.15 (a naw rad nef), 12.20–4 (A'r brodyr ... vedwl).

[197] The words 'Yn ol hynny ... y dwy ffynnawn hynny' (6.23–9) appear to be an elaboration of the last sentence of 6.17–22, which does not occur in L. The Welsh seems occasionally to favour N and Di, but this is rare. Cf. nyt a neb y vffern (4.26) = inferni penas luet (NDi) = misericordiam consequetur (V) = misericordiam dei consequuntur (L); see *CLlGC* ix (1955/6), 10, *RLSD* 9. The section dealing with rights of sanctuary is found only in V¹ (c.57 in *RLSD*); likewise the passage describing the general grief at the news of David's impending death (12.33–13.6), which however, occurs later in V¹, before the account of his burial (c.64 in *RLSD*, pp. 26–7).

[198] *WCCR* 176.

cultural vitality and vigour in Wales, for which there is evidence from other sources. It was an age of bishops, renowned for scholarship as well as administration, men like Thoresby, Fastalf, Houghton and Gilbert in St David's;[199] and at a somewhat lower level we witness in the fourteenth century increased activity in the production of Welsh texts and manuscripts, containing both secular and religious material. We may mention works such as the White Book of Rhydderch, the Book of the Anchorite of Llanddewibrefi, and a little later the Red Book of Hergest, the Red Book of Talgarth (Llanstephan 27) and others, the work of nameless writers and copyists, probably all clerics. Welsh prose now had centuries of tradition and cultivation behind it. The Welsh version of the *Life* of St David is only one of many translations and adaptations of works of a religious content produced during this period,[200] more especially during the thirteenth and early fourteenth centuries. Not only prose, but poetry also, for we witness in the fourteenth century a resurgence of poetry in the compositions of Dafydd ap Gwilym and other poets, who initiated a new development in Welsh verse.

The Welsh Texts

There are extant some fourteen manuscripts which contain the Welsh *Life*. We shall look briefly at five of the earliest among them:[201]

[199] Ibid. 129.

[200] See *WCCR* 88–104. One must, of course, take account of developments at an earlier period, in the thirteenth century, when we know that translations and adaptations were produced, copies of some of which are to be found in the *Book of the Anchorite*. We are reminded by Sir Idris Foster of the appointment of that important figure, Thomas Wallensis, to the see of St David's in 1247; cf. Foster, op. cit. p. 216; also J. Conway Davies, *EAWD* ii. 558–61.

In 1287, another bishop of St David's, Thomas Bek, founded a collegiate church at Llanddewibrefi, where the Welsh *Life* may have been composed.

[201] The following are the other MSS in which the *Life* occurs: Pen. 15, fifteenth century, a copy of A (*RMWL* i. 334–6); Pen. 27, 1475–1500, a paraphrase in the hand of Gutun Owain (ibid. i. 355–8); Pen. 225, 1594–1610, in the hand of Sir Thomas Wiliems (ibid. i. 1049–53); Llan. 34, end of the sixteenth century, in the hand of Roger Morys of Coedytalwrn (ibid. ii. 474–7); Hav. 10, *c.* 1620 (ibid. ii. 312–13); Pen. 120, end of seventeenth century, in the hand of Edward Lhuyd, a copy of A (ibid. i. 730–40); Card. 36, beginning of the eighteenth century, in part a copy of C, and in part of Llan. 34 (ibid. ii. 231); Llan. 104; beginning of the eighteenth century, probably a copy of Llan. 34 (ibid. ii. 564–5); Pen. 319 (ibid. i. 1123), a copy of A.

Pen. 225, Llan. 34, Hav. 10, and Llan. 104 probably belong to the same group. The Pen(iarth) and Llan(stephan) MSS are to be found in the National Library of Wales, Aberystwyth, the Hav(od) MSS in the Cardiff Central Library.

On the relationship between the above texts cf. J. W. James, *CLIGC* ix (1955/6), 1–3; also Caerwyn Williams, *LIC* v (1959), 112–17.

A. *Jesus College MS 119*, or *Llyvyr Agkyr Llandewivrevi*
93a–103b. (See *RMWL* ii. 30–1; also Thomas Jones, 'The Book of
the Anchorite of Llanddewi Brefi' (Llyvyr Agkyr Llandewivrevi)'
TCAS xii. 63–82; and Idris Foster, *The Book of the Anchorite*, The
John Rhŷs Memorial Lecture, British Academy, 1949). It was
edited and published by J. Morris-Jones and John Rhŷs in the
volume *The Elucidarium and other tracts in Welsh from Llyvyr
Agkyr Llandewivrevi*, AD 1346 (*LlA*).

In a note which occurs after the preface to the first text in the
manuscript, namely *Hystoria Lucidar* or the *Elucidarium*, we find
the following words:

> Gruffud ap ll(ywelyn) ap phylip ap trahayarnn . o kant(r)ef mawr
> aberis yscriuennv yllyuyr hwnn . o law ketymdeith idaw. nyt
> amgen.gwr ryoed agkyr yr amsser hwnnw yn llandewyureui . yrei y
> meddyanho duw y heneideu yny drugared. Amen.
> anno d(omi)ni mCCC. Quadrages(im)e Sexto.
>
> (Gruffudd ap Llywelyn ap Phylip of Trahaearn of Cantref Mawr
> caused this book to be written by the hand of a friend, namely a man
> who was an anchorite at that time at Llanddewifrefi: whose souls may
> God hold in His mercy. Amen.)

This manuscript then was compiled for Gruffudd ap Llywelyn ap
Phylip ap Trahaearn, a nobleman who dwelt in Rhydodyn, near
Llansawel, in the Cantref Mawr, which comprised the northern
uplands of Carmarthenshire. Gruffudd hailed from a family renowned for its protection and patronage of Welsh culture, and this
work for which he had asked, consists of a collection of religious
texts, translated or adapted from Latin.[202] It may be described as
one of the manuals of religious instruction, which were produced in
medieval times for the benefit of the educated layman of noble
stock.[203]

It is fortunate for us that the anchorite noted the year, namely
1346, the kind of information which is very seldom provided, but we
should like to know to what precisely he refers. As Professor Caerwyn Williams says,[204] he is not necessarily referring to the year when

---

[202] Cf. Foster, op. cit. p. 218.
[203] This kind of literary activity, whereby noblemen employed the services of
learned clerks to produce translations and adaptations, is attested also in
Morgannwg and Gwent in the same period, as was noted by Professor G. J.
Williams, *TLlM* 146–9.
[204] *B* xi (1944), 156.

all the texts in the manuscript were copied. It may be that he is thinking only of the *Hystoria Lucidar*, and that the other texts were copied later, or even earlier, although that is less likely.

B.   *Llanstephan 27* or *The Red Book of Talgarth* 62b–71b (see *RMWL* ii. 455–62). In this also we find a collection of religious texts, probably compiled for the nobleman, Hopcyn ap Tomas ab Einion of Ynystawe (north of Swansea), as was the more famous Red Book of Hergest,[205] large parts of which display the same hand as that of Llanstephan 27. The latter thus belongs to the end of the fourteenth century.[206]

C.   *Llanstephan 4*, the fourth volume of *Y Didrefn Gasgliad*.[207] Here the text is defective; only three sections are extant, 522a–523b, 524a–525b, 528a–531b (see *RMWL* ii. 424–7, *ChO* xxxiv–xlii, *CLlGC* ix (1955/6), 1–2). It is dated *c*. 1400 by Gwenogvryn Evans and Ifor Williams,[208] and is, therefore, of about the same age as B.

D.   *BL Cotton MS Titus D xxii* 138a–155b (see Sir Idris Bell, *VSBG* xiii–xvi). The text of the *Life* in it was published, full of errors, by W. J. Rees in *Lives of the Cambro-British Saints* 102–16 (*LCBS*).

This manuscript also consists in the main of religious texts, and among them the *Lives* of Gwynllyw and Cadog (in Latin), and of Margaret, Catherine and David (in Welsh). Its contents differ markedly from those of A and B, the *Life* of David and Ebostol y Sul being the only texts common to all three. Considerably more than half of D is in Latin.

Sir Idris Bell came to the conclusion that it is all the work of one hand, and he is of the opinion that it was written in the first part of the fifteenth century, not long after 1429.

E.   NLW MS 5267 B (*Dingestow 7*). *Y Casgliad Brith*, a defective text with only two sections extant, 85a and b, 86a and b (see *Handlist of Manuscripts in the National Library of Wales*, Series 11, Number 8, p. 81; also *CLlGC* ix (1955/6), 2 and *B* ix (1938), 221–2). This manuscript contains a miscellaneous collection of prose texts,

---

[205] Cf. *TLlM* 13–14, 147.
[206] 1400 is the date given by Gwenogvryn Evans in *RMWL* ii. 455.
[207] See Ed. Lhuyd, *ABr* 254a.
[208] *ChO* xl, xlii.

and it probably belongs to the fifteenth century,[209] to the middle of that century as seems likely.

In my Welsh edition I gave some details of the relationship between these earlier texts,[210] which need not be repeated in full here. It appears that B and D (and C and E) derive originally from the same archetype, which is now lost, but which was different from A. That text and A must have come either directly or indirectly from the same text, which, however, could hardly have been the original copy. All the extant copies have inherited errors made by an early copyist in an earlier text from which they all derive. This earlier text must have been itself a copy, made not long after the original composition of the work in the first half of the fourteenth century. It should be noted here that there are few serious textual divergences among the extant manuscripts. There may, however, be some slight evidence of a Welsh version other than the one represented in the extant manuscripts. This whole question requires further detailed investigation of sources, comprising missals, breviaries, etc., which relate to the saints' cultus over the centuries.[211]

In my Welsh edition I published a composite text, based in the main on B, with readings from other manuscripts sometimes included. Textual variations were given at the foot of every page. Here I have decided to publish the text from A, as I thought it would be useful to have available two early texts (probably the earliest) for the purposes of comparison. Variant readings are not given, but textual matters are mentioned in the notes at the end.

The text has been edited in the manner to which we have now long been accustomed. It has been divided into paragraphs and sections, for which headings are provided. I have followed the manuscript in every detail, except for punctuation, and also for the representation of w [u]. In those places in the manuscript where 6 and w are used (indifferently) for it, I have throughout used w, as it

---

[209] 'xvii cent.' in the *Handlist* must be an error for 'xv cent'.

[210] It is interesting to note that the *Life* of Beuno immediately follows that of David in A and B (and originally in C also; see *RMWL* ii. 426–7). Beuno does not occur in D or in E, but it does occur in some other manuscripts which contain the *Life* of David: Pen. 15 (*RMWL* i. 335), Pen. 225 (ibid. i. 1052), Llan. 34 (ibid. ii. 476), Hav. 10 (ibid. ii. 312), Pen. 120 (ibid. i. 731), Card. 36 (ibid. ii. 231).

[211] *SDL* 54.

appeared that no useful purpose would be served by employing the two characters, which in some cases might cause confusion. Forms abbreviated in the manuscript are indicated by italics, and letters added by the editor are given within square brackets.

HYSTORIA O UUCHED DEWI

[Jesus College MS 119, 93a–103b]

Yma y treithir o ach Dewi, ac o dalym o'e uuched.

[DAVID'S GENEALOGY]

Dauyd vab Sant, vab Keredic, vab Kuneda, vab Edern, vab Padarnn Peisrud, vab Deil, vab Gordeil, vab Dwuyn, vab Gordwuyn,
vab Amguoel, vab Amweryt, vab Onut, vab Perim, vab Dubim, vab
Ongen, vab Auallach, vab Eugen, vab Eudoleu, vab chwaer Veir
Wyry, vam Iessu *Grist*.

[SANT AND THE TREASURE TROVE]

Keredic vrenhin a wledychawd lawer o vlwynyded, ac o'e enw ef y
kauas Keredigyawn y henw. A mab a uu idaw, ac enw y mab oed
Sant. Ac y hwnnw yr ymdangosses angel yn y hvn, a dywedut
wrthaw: 'Auory,' heb ef, 'ti a ey y hely, a thi a geffy tri dyuot ger lan
auon Teiui, nyt amgen, karw a gleissat, a heit wenyn y mywn prenn
vch benn yr auon, yn y lle a elwir yr awr honn Henllan. Dyro dylyet
y tir y gadw y vab ny anet etwo; ef bieiuyd deu le hyt Dyd Brawt, y
rei a dywetpwyt vchot, Lin Henllan a Liton Mancan.

[PATRICK]

Odyna y doeth Pad*ric* hyt y Glyn Rosin, ac y medylyawd dwyn
yno y uuched. Ac angel a doeth at Padric, ac a dywat vrthaw: 'Adaw
ti,' heb ef, 'y lle hwnn y vab ny anet etwo.' Sef a oruc Padric, llidiaw
a dy[w]edut, 'Paham y tremygawd yr Arglwyd y was, a uu yr yn vab

yn gwassanaethu idaw drwy ouyn a charyat, ethol ohonaw ynteu yr awr honn mab ny anet, ac ny [93b] enir hyt ympenn dec mlyned ar hugeint?'

Ac ymparatoi a oruc Padric yndaw, ac ydaw y lle hwnnw y'r Arglwyd *Grist*. A'r Arglwyd, eissoes, a garei Padric yn vawr, ac a anuones angel attaw y duhudaw. A'r angel a dywat vrthaw, 'Padric, byd lawen. Yr Arglwyd a'm hanuones i attat ti y dangos yt Ynys Iwerdon o'r eistedua ysyd yn Glyn Rosin (ac a elwir yr awr honn Eistedua Padric). Kannys ti a uydy ebostol yn yr ynys a wely di, a thi a diodeuy lawer yno o garyat Duw; a Duw a vyd y gyt a thi, beth bynnac a wnelych.

Ac yna y llonydwyt medwl Padric, ac y gedewis Padric y Dewi y lle hwnnw. A pharatoi llong yn y porthloed idaw, a chyuodi o varw gwr a gladyssit yno ar y morua yr ys pymthec mlyned; Kruchier oed y enw. A mynet a oruc Padric y Iwerdon, a'r gwr hwnnw y gyt ac ef; a hwnnw gwedy hynny a uu escob.

[CONCEPTION AND BIRTH OF DAVID]

Ac ym penn y deg mlyned ar hugein wedy hynny, val yr oed y brenhin a elwit Sant yn kerdet ehun, nacha lleian yn kyfuaruot ac ef. Sef a oruc ynteu, ymauael a hi a dwyn treis arnei. A'r lleian a gauas beichogi (enw y lleian oed Nonn); a mab a anet idi, a Dauid a rodet yn enw arnaw. A gwr ny bu idi na chynt na gwedy; diweir oed hi o vedwl a gweithret.

[SOME OF HIS MIRACLES]

Kynntaf gwyrth a wnaeth Dewi : o'r pann gauas hi veichogi, ny mynnawd hi vwyt [94a] namyn bara a dwfuyr yn y hoes. Ac ny lewas Dewi vwyt namyn bara a dwfuyr.

Eil gwyrth a wnnaeth Dewi, a'e vam yn mynet y'r eglwys y waranndaw pregeth y gan Gildas sant. Gildas a dechreuawd pregethu, ac nys gallei. Ac yna y dywat Gildas: 'Ewch oll o'r eglwys allann,' heb ef. Ac elchwyl proui pregethu a oruc, ac nys gallei. Ac yna y gouynnawd Gildas a oed neb yn yr eglwys onnyt euo ehun. 'Yd wyf i yma,' hep y lleian y rwg y dor a'r paret. 'Dos ti,' heb y sant, 'ydieithyr yr eglwys, ac arch y'r plwyf dyuot y mywn.' A phob vn a doeth y le y eisted, val y buassei. Ac yna pregethu a oruc y sant yn eglur ac yn

vchel. Yna y gouynnawd y plwyf idaw, 'Paham na elleisti pregethu y
ni gy*nn*hev, a ninhev yn llawen yn damunaw dy warandaw di?'
'Gelwch,' heb y sant, 'y lleian y mywn, a yrreis i gynnev o'r eglwys.'
Heb y Nonn, 'Llyma vivi.' Heb y Gildas yna, 'Y mab ysy yg kroth y
lleian honn ysyd voe y vedyant a'e rat a'e vrdas no mivi, kannys idaw
ef ehun y rodes Duw breint a phennaduryaeth holl seint Kymry yn
dragywydawl kynn Dyd Brawt a guedy. Ac am hy*n*ny nyt oes,' hep
ef, 'fford y mi y drigyaw yma hwy o achos mab y lleian raco, y rodes
Duw idaw pennaduryaeth ar bawp o'r ynys honn. A reit yw y mi,'
heb ef, 'vynet [y] ynys arall, a gadaw y'r mab hwnn yr ynys honn.'

Gwyrth arall a wnaeth Dewi. Yn yr awr y ganet [94b] ef, ef a
doeth taraneu a mellt. A charrec a oed gyfuerbynn a phenn Nonn a
holltes yny uu yn deu hanner, ac a neidyawd y neill hanner idi dros
benn y lleian hyt is y thraet, pann yttoed hi ynn escor.

Gwyrth arall a oruc Dewi. Pann vedydywyt, ef a ymdangosses
ffynnyawn o'r dayar, lle ny buassei ffynnyaon eiroet. A dall a oed yn
daly Dewi vrth vedyd a gauas yna y olwc. Ac yna y dall a wybu vot y
mab yr oed yn y daly vrth vedyd yn gyfulawn o rat. A chymryt y
dwfuyr bedyd, a golchi y wyneb a'r dwfuyr. Ac o'r awr y ganet, dall
wynebclawr oed. Ac yna y olwc a gauas, a chwbl o'r a berthynei
arnnei. Sef a wnaeth pawb yna, moli Duw val y dylyynt.

[HIS EDUCATION]

Y lle y dysgwyt Dewi yndaw a elwit Vetus Rubus, yng Kymraec
yw yr Henllwynn. Yno y dysgwyt idaw ef seilym yr holl vlwydynn a'e
llithion a'r offerennev. Yno y gwelas y gytdisgyblon ef colomen a
gyluin eur idi yn dysgu Dewi, ac yn gware yn y gylch.

Odyna yr aeth Dewi hyt at athro a elwit Paulinus, a disgybyl oed
hwnnw y escob sant a oed yn Rufein. A hwnnw a dyscawd Dewi
hyny vu athro. Ac yna y damweinawd colli o athro Dewi y lygeit, o
dra gormod dolur yn y lygeit. A galw a oruc yr athro attaw y holl
disgyblon ol yn ol, y geissaw y gantunt ganhorthwy am y lygeit, ac
nyt yttoed yr vn yn y allel idaw. Ac yn diwethaf oll galw Dew[i] a
oruc. [95a] 'Dauyd,' heb yr athro, 'edrych vy llygeit, y maent y'm
poeni.' 'Arglwyd athro,' heb y Dauyd, 'nac arch y mi edrych dy
lygeit. Yr ys deg mlyned y deuthum i atat ti y dyscu, nyt edrycheis i
ettwo y'th wyneb di.' Sef a oruc yr athro yna, medylyaw a ryuedu
kewilyd y mab, a dywedut: 'Kannys velle y mae,' heb ef vrth y mab,

'dyro di de law ar vy wyneb i, a bendicka vy llygeit; a mi a vydaf holl yach.' A phann rodes Dauyd y law ar y lygeit ef, y buant holl yach. Ac yna y bendigawd Paulinus Dauyd o bop bendith a geffit ynn ysgriuennedic yn y dedyf hen, ac yn y newyd.

[THE FOUNDING OF CHURCHES]

Yna y doeth angel at Paulinus, a dywedut vrthaw val hynn: 'Amser,' heb yr angel, 'yw [y] Dauyd sant vynet odyma, y wneuthur y petheu ysyd dyghetuen y gan Duw idaw y wnneuthur.

Odyna y deuth Dewi hyt yn Glastynburi, ac yno yr adeilawd ef eglwys.

Dewi a deuth y'r lle yr oed dwfyr llawn o wenwyn, ac a'e bendigawd, ac a wnaeth y dwfuyr hwnnw yn dwymynn hyt Dyd Brawt. A hwnnw a elwir yr Enneint Twymynn.

Odyna y deuth Dewi hyt yg Krowlan, a hyt yn Repecwn.

Odyna y deuth y Gollan a Glasgwm.

Odyna yr adeilawd Lannllieni y glann Hafuren.

Odyna y rodes waret y Pebiawc, vrenhin Ergyng, a oed yn dall.

Odyna yr adeilawd eglwys yg Gwent, yn y lle a elwir Raclan. [95b]

Odyna yr adeilawd eglwys yn y lle a elwir Llanngyfuelach yg Gwyr.

Deu sant a oed yg Kedweli, a elwit Boducat a Nailtrum, a ym-rodassant yn disgyblon idaw.

[THE DEFEAT OF BOIA]

Odyna yr ymhoelawd Dewi hyt y lle a elwit Uetus Rubus. Ac yno yr oed escob a elwit Goeslan, a hwnnw a oed vrawt ffyd y Dewi. A Dewi a dywot vrthaw, 'Angel yr Arglwyd a dywot y mi y mae o vreid yd a vn o gant o'r lle hwnn y teyrnas nef. A dangosses y mi le arall, ac o'r lle hwnnw nyt a neb y vffern o'r a vo ffyd da a chret gantaw. Ac a gladher y mynnwent y lle hwnnw heuyt, nyt a y vffernn.

A dydgweith y deuth Dauid a'e disgyblon, nyt amgen, Aedan ac Eliud ac Ysmael, a llawer y gyt ac wynt, hyt y lle a vanagassei Duw vdunt, nyt amgen, hyt y Glyn Rosin: Hodnant y gelwir y lle hwnnw. Kyntaf lle dan yr awyr y kynneuassant wy tan uu yno. A phann gyneuassant tan yno y bore glas, y kyuodes mwc ac y kylchynawd y

mwc hwnnw yr ynys honn oll, a llawer o Iwerdon; a hynny o'r bore
glas hyt bryt gosper.

Ac yna yd argannuv tywyssawc a elwit Boya (ac Yscot oed) y mwc
hwnnw. Ac o lit eisted a oruc y mywn creic vchel o'r bore hyt pryt
gosper, heb uwyt, heb diawt. A'e wreic a vedrawd arnaw yno, ac a
ovynnawd idaw paham na mynhei na bwyt na diawt. 'Dyoer,' heb
ef, 'trist wyf a llidyawc.' 'Mwc a weleis hediw', [96a] heb ef, 'yn
kyuodi o Hodnant, ac yn kylchynu llawer o dinassoed. Y gwr,' heb
ef, 'a gynneuawd y tan hwnnw, y veddyant ef a gerdha fford y
kerdawd y mwc.' Heb y wreic, 'Yr wyt yn ynvyt. Kyuot y vynyd,'
heb hi, 'a chymer dy weisson y gyt a thi, a llad y neb a gynneuawd y
tan hwnnw ar dy dir heb dy gannyat.'

Ac yna y doeth Boya, a'e ysgiwereit y gyt ac ef, ar vedwl llad Dewi
a'e disgyblon. A phann doethant tu a'r lle yd oed Dewi, y dygwydassant yn y kryt, hyt na ellynt wy wneuthur dim drwc yn y byt y
Dewi nac y disgyblon, onyt eu gwattwar, a dywedut geireu
tremygedic yn y kyueir, ac ymhoelut adref. Ac val y bydynt velle,
nachaf wreic Boya yn kyuaruot ac wynt, ac yn dywedut, 'Yn bugelyd ny a dywe[da]ssant y mi ry varw yn holl ysgrybyl ni, nyt amgen,
an gwarthec, an ychen, an greoed, an deueit, ac eu bot oll yn veirw
ac eu llygeit yn agoret.

Ac yna kwynnvan ac vdaw a griduan a oruc Boya a'e wreic a'e
dylwyth, a dywedut, 'Y sant hoyw y buam ni yn y wattwar a wnaeth
hynn.' Sef y cawssant hwy yn y kyngor, gwediaw y sant, a cheissaw y
vod ef a'e dylwyth. Ac yna y rodes Boya yn dragywydawl Hodnant y
Dewi, ac ymhoelut adref a oruc Boya a'e dylwyth y gyt ac ef. A
phann deuthant adref, wynt a gawssant y hanyueileit yn vyw ac yn
yach.

Ac yna y dywat gwreic Boya vrth y llaw[96b]uorynyon: 'Ewch,'
heb hi, 'hyt yr auon ysyd ger llaw y sant, a diosglwch awch dillat, ac
yn noeth dywedwch vrthunt geireu aniweir kywilydus.' Holl disgyblon Dewi a uu anawd gantunt diodef y kywilyd hwnnw, ac a
dywedassant vrth Dewi: 'Fown odyma ymeith,' heb wy, 'ny allwnn
ni diodef hynn, nac edrych ar y gwraged drwc.' Ac yna y dywaut y
sant, 'Ponyt gwell y ni peri vdunt wy adaw y lle hwnn y ni?' Ac yna
Dewi a'e disgyblon a dyrwestassant y nos honno hyt trannoeth.

Trannoeth y dywat gwreic Boya vrth y llysuerch: 'Tidi vorwyn,'
heb hi, 'kyuot, ac awnn yn dwy y Lyn Alun y geissaw kneu.' Heb y
vorwyn vrth y llysuam: 'Parawt wyf i,' heb hi, 'y vynet.' A cherdet a

wnaethant hyt y gwaelawt y glyn. A phan doethant yno eiste a oruc y
llysuam, a dywedut vrth y llysuerch, 'Dyro dy benn y'm harffet; mi a
dihaedaf di benn.' Sef a oruc y vorwyn da, diweir, war, gymenn,
rodi y phenn yn arffet y llysuam. Sef a oruc y llysuam, tynnv kyllell a
llad penn y vorwyn santes. Ac yn y gyfeir y dygwydawd y gwaet y'r
llawr, yd ymdangosses ffynnyawn. A llawer o dynyon a gauas yechyt
a gwaret yno. A hyt hediw y gelwir y ffynnawn honno Fynnnawn
Dunawt, kanys Dunawt oed enw y vorwyn.

Yna y ffoes y llysuam drwc, ac ny wybu neb o'r byt hwnn pa
anghev a'e duc. [97a] A Boya a dechreuawd drycaruaethu, a Dewi
a'e disgyblon a lawenhassant. Yna y medylyawd Boya lad Dauyd
a'e disgyblon. Ac eissoes, sef y damweinawd y bore trannoeth dyuot
y elyn hyt y twr yd oed Boya yndaw yn kysgu, gwedy caffel y pyrth
yn agoret, a llad penn Boya yn y wely. Ac yn diannot y doeth tan o'r
nef, a llosci yr holl adeiladeu hyt y llawr. Gwybydet bawp ry lad o'r
Arglwyd Duw o achaws Dewi Boya a Sat*ra*pa y wreic.

[FOUNDING OF ST DAVID'S]

Odyna yr adeilawd Dewi y Glynn Hodnant.

[THE APPEARANCE OF SPRINGS]

Ac nyt oed yno dim dwfyr, onnyt chydic o dwfyr redegawc. Ac
yna y gwediawd Dewi ar yr Arglwyd, ac yn diannot y kyuodes
ffynnawn eglur. Ac yn oes Dewi y bu y ffynnawn honno yn llawn o
win, val na bu arnaw yn y oes ef eisseu gwin da. Llyna rod teilwng y
gan Duw y'[r] ryw wr hwnnw.

Yn ol hynny, Gweslan escob, brawt ffyd y Dewi, a disgybyl y
Dewi a elwit Eliud, ell deu a dyrwestassant y geissaw y gan Duw
ffynnhonnev o dwfyr croew; kanyt oed dim yn y dinas o dwfyr, a rac
sychet yr amsser. Ac yna y cawssant y gan Duw dwy ffynnawn, ac a
elwir hyt hediw Ffynnawn Gwestlan a Ffynnawn Eliud. A'r
crupleit, a'r deillonn, a'r cleiuon a geffynt waret yn y dwy ffynnawn
hynny.

[THE PLOT AGAINST DAVID]

Ac ymysc hynny, yr oed Aydan sant yn y eglwys ehun yn dinas
Gwernin yn gwediaw, nyt amgen, nos Pasc, nachaf angel yr

Arglwyd yn dy[97b]vot attaw, ac yn dywedut vrthaw: 'Tidi, wrda
gwynuydedic, pony wdosti,' heb ef, 'yr hynn yd ys yn y darparv y
Dauid sant, dy athro di, y Glyn Rosin?' 'Na wn, dyoer,' heb yr
Aedan. Heb yr angel, 'Neur deryw y tri o'e dylywyth o'r vanachol
gwnneuthur y vrat, nyt amgen, dodi gwenwyn y mywn bara, a'r bara
hwnnw a rodir idaw ef avory o'e vwytta. Vrth hynny, anuon gennat
hyt at dy athro, ac arch idaw ymoglyt y bara a'r gwennwyn yndaw.'
Sef a oruc y sant, tristav ac wylaw. 'Arglwyd,' heb ef, 'pa delw yr
anuonaf i gennat yno? Mor vyrr yr oet ac y mae. Nyt oes long yn
barawt, val y galler y chaffel.' 'Anuon,' heb yr angel, 'dy gyt-
disgybyl, nyt amgen, Scuthyn, hyt y traeth, a mi a baraf idaw vynet
druod.' Sef a oruc Scuthyn yn llawen, gwneuthur yr oedit yn y erchi
idaw, a dyuot y tu a'r traeth, a cherdet yn y dvfuyr racdaw, yny
deuth y dwfuyr idaw hyt y linyeu. Ac yn deissyuyt, llyma anghenuil
o'r mor yn y gymryt ar y geuyn, ac yn mynet ac ef drvod, yny vv ar y
tir arall. Ac erbyn hanner dyd dyw Pasc yr oed ef y gyt a'e athro.

Ac val yr oed Dewi yn dyuot o'r eglwys gwedy offerennev, a
gwedy pregethu y'r holl vrodyr, nachaf y guelei ef y gennat yn
kyuaruot ac ef yn y lle a elwir Bed Yscolan. Sef a oruc Dewi yna, bot
yn llawen vrthaw a mynet dwylaw mynwgyl [98a] idaw, ac amouyn
ac ef am anssawd Maydawc sant, y disgybyl; a mawr y carei Dewi y
disgybyl. A gwedy daruot y'r gennat menegi idaw ef o gwbyl anssawd
Maydawc y disgybyl, galw a oruc Scuthyn Dewi attaw ar neilltu, a
datkanu idaw y gennadwri, a megys a'r mod y dywedassei yr angel
vrth Vaydawc sant. Sef a oruc Dewi yna, kynnhewi a medylyaw, a
dywedut diolwch mawr y Duw, a dyuot racd[a]u y'r vanachloc.

A gwedy eiste pawb yn y mod y dylyynt, gwedy daruot y gras,
kyuodi a oruc y diagon, yr hwn a wassannaethei ar Dauid, y wassan-
naethu a'r bara gwennwynic gantaw. Sef a oruc Scuthyn, kyfuodi y
vynyd a dywedut: 'Tidi,' heb ef, 'ny wassanaethy di hediw. Miui,'
heb yr Scuthyn, 'a uyd gwassanaethwr hediw.' Sef a oruc hwnnw,
mynet y eisted a synnyaw arnaw yn vawr; ef a wydyat kared a oed yn
y vedwl.

Ac yna y kymerth Dewi y bara gwennwynic a'e rannv yn teir rann,
a rodi vn y ast a oed yn seuyll allann odieithyr y drws. A'r awr y
llewas yr ast y bara, y bu allmarw, ac y syrthyawd y blew oll yn enkyt
y trawyt yr amrant ar y llall, a thorri y croen y amdanei, a syrthaw y
holl perued y'r llawr. Sef a oruc yr holl vrodyr pann welsant hynny,
synnyaw yn vawr arnunt. Ac yna yd anuones Dewi yr eil rann o'r

bara y vran a oed yn gorwed ar y nyth y mywn onnen [y rwng] y
ffreutur [98b] ac auon a oed y tu a'r deheu. Yr awr y kymerth hi y
bara yn y gyluin, hi a syrthawd o'r prenn yn varw y'r llawr. Y tryded
rann o'r bara a gymerth Dewi, ac a'e bendigawd, ac a'e bwytaawd.
Sef a wnnaeth yr holl vrodyr, edrych arnaw a ryuedu yn vawr, ac
ofuynhav yn ormod am Dewi.

Ac yna y menegys Dewi y damwein y'r holl vrodyr, mal y mynnassei y twyllwr y wenwynaw. Ac yna y rodes yr holl vrodyr eu
hemelltith ar y gwyr hynny, ac y gyt a hynny rodi ar y tat o'r nef hyt
na cheffynt hwy yn dragywydawl gyurann o teyrnnas nef.

[THE SYNOD OF BREFI]

A gwedy kadarnnhav ffyd a chret yn yr ynys honn, holl lauurwyr
yr hynys hon a deuthant y gyt hyt yn dor sened Vreui. A'r escyb, a'r
athrawon, a'r offeireit, a'r brenhined, a'r tywyssogyonn, a'r ieirll,
a'r barwneit, a'r goreugwyr, a'r ysgwiereit, a'r kreuydwyr yn llwyr,
a phawb heb allu rif arnadunt a ymgynnullassant y sened Vreui.

Ac amot a wnaethpwyt yn y gynnulleidua honno: pwy bynnac o'r
sened o'r seint a pregethei val y clywei y niuer hwnnw yn gyffredin,
gadv ohonunt yn bennadur ar seint Yny[s] Prydein. Ac yna y dechreuawd y seint bregethu bop eilwers. Ac yna y dywat vn dros y
kyffredin: 'Y kannvet dyn o'r gynnulleidua honn', heb ef, 'ny chlyw
dim o'r bregeth; yr ywch yn llauuryaw yn ouer o gwbyl.' Yna y
dywat [99a] pob vn o'r seint vrth y gilyd, 'Nyt oes neb ohonom a allo
pregethu y'r niuer hwnn, a ni a'e prouassam pob eilwers; a ni a
welwnn nat oes gras y neb ohonam ni y bregethu y'r niuer hwnn.
Edrychwch a medylywch a wddawch chwi a oes neb mor deilwng ac
y gallo pregethu y'r hwnn yniuer yma.

[DAVID INVITED TO THE SYNOD]

Yna yd attebawd Paulinus sant, a hen escob oed ef: 'Myuy,' heb
ef, 'a wnn was ieuangk, tec, adwyn, ac angel yn wastat yn getym-
deith idaw. A mi a'e hadwen,' heb ef, 'y vot ef yn gymenn ac ynn
diweir, ac yn caru Duw yn vawr, ac a wnn y car Duw ynteu, a'e vot
yn gyurannawc ar yr holl voesseu da. Miui,' heb ef, 'a wn y mae
mwyhaf dyn [a] rat Duw arnaw yn yr ynys honn yw hwnnw, a Dauid
sant y gelwir. Yn gyntaf, ef a dyscawd llen a berthynei idaw y dyscu

ar y dechreu. A gwedy hynny, ef a dyscawd y gennyf ynhev yr Yscrythur Lan, ac a uu athro, ac yn Rufein a vrddwyt yn archescob. A mi,' heb ef, 'a weleis angel yn dyuot attaw, ac yn galw arnaw, ac yn erchi idaw vynet y wlat y gyuanhedu y lle a barchassei Duw idaw yn teyrnnas Demetica, sef yw honno, Mynyw yn y deheu. Ewch a gelwch attawch hwnnw, ef yssyd yn caru Duw [yn] vawr, ac yn pregethu y Grist; a miui a wn y mae idaw ef y rodes Duw y gras.'

Ac yna yr anuones y seint gennadeu hyt yn dinas Rubi, y lle yr oed Dauid sant, gwas y Duw, yn gwediaw ac yn dyscu. A phann gigleu [99b] ef neges y kennadeu, llyma yr atteb a rodes ef, nyt amgen: 'Nyt af vi,' heb ef, 'yno; ys gwell gennyf wediaw Duw yman. Ewchwi,' heb ef, 'yn tagneued Duw o'e garyat.' A'r eilweith y seint a w[a]hawdassant Dewi sant, ac ynteu a rodes yr vn atteb a rodes gynt. Tryded weith, o gyduundeb yr holl seint, yr anuonet at Dewi yn gennadeu y deu sant bennaf a oed yno, nyt amgen, Deynioel a Dubricius. A'r nos kynn dyuot y kennadeu at Dewi, Dewi a dywat vrth y disgyblon, 'Vy meibon i, gwybydwch chwi y daw kennadeu yma avore. Ewch y byscotta y'r mor, a dygwch yma,' heb ef, 'dyfuwr gloyw o'r ffynnawn.'

A'r kennadeu a deuthant y dyd y dywat Dewi vrthv[nt], ac ynteu a baratoes vdunt hwy eu kinyaw. Disgyblon Dauid a rodassant ar y bwrd ger bronn y seint piscawt digoned a dwfyr o'r ffynnawn, a'r dwfyr [a] aeth yn win ar hynt. A Dauyd a dywat vrthunt, 'Bwytt-ewch, vrodyr, yn llawen.' Ac yna y dywat y deu sant vrthaw, 'Ny chemerwn ni na bwyt na diawt,' heb wy, 'onnyt edewy ditheu dyuot y gyt a nynhev y'r sened vawr anryued, y lle y mae llu ny ellir y rifuaw y'th aros di.' 'Vrth hynny,' heb yr hwynt, 'dabre y gyt a ni yr Duw, ac yr bendith hynny o seint, onny mynny haedu y hemelltith.' Heb Dewi yna: 'Mi a af,' heb ef, 'yr caryat Duw at y [100a] ket-ymeithonn hynny. Eissoes,' heb ef, 'yr hwnn a erchwch y mi, nys gallaf i. Miui,' heb ef, 'a gerdaf y gyt a chwi hyt y sened, a chwitheu, gwediwch y Tat pennaf, yny rodho ef gannhorthwy y ni druein, a mynhev a'ch gwediaf chwitheu, vrodyr, yny gymeroch chwitheu bwyt a diawt o'r alussen a'r gardawt a rodet y ni o'r nef.'

[RESUSCITATING THE WIDOW'S SON]

A gwedy hynny, kyuot a oruc Dewi y gyt a'r kennadeu y sened Vreui. A chynn y dyuot y'r gynnulleittua honno, nachaf y gwelynt

yn dyfot yn y herbyn gwreic wedw gwedy marw y hun mab, a'r wreic
yn gweidi ac yn disgyryaw. A phann welas Dewi y wreic yn y
dry[g]yruerth hwnnw, kysseuyll a oruc, a gollwng y kennadeu o'r
blaen. Sef a oruc y wreic druan, a glywssei glot Dewi, syrthaw ar dal
y deulin, a menegi idaw bot y hun mab yn varw. Sef a wnaeth Dewi
yna, trugarhav wrthi, a throssi y gyt a hi y'r lle yr oed y mab yn varw
yn emyl auon a elwit Teiui, a dyuot y'r ty, y lle yr oed gorff y mab. A
syrthyaw a oruc Dewi ar y corff, a dodi y eneu vrth eneu y mab, a
gwediaw yr Arglwyd a dywedut, 'Vy Arglwyd Duw i, ti a disgynneist o arffet y Tat o nef y'r byt hwnn o'n hachaws ni bechaduryeit, y
an prynu ni o sauan yr hen elyn, trugarhaa, Arglwyd, vrth y wreic
wedw honn yman, a dyro yn y hun mab y eneit dracheuen, val y
mawrhaer dy enw di yn yr [100b] holl dayar.'

A phann daruu y Dewi y wedi, kyuodi yn hollyach a oruc y mab,
mal bei atuei yn kyuodi o gyscu, a Dewi erbyn y law deheu yn y
gyuodi a'e rodi yn hollyach y vam. Sef a oruc y mab o'r lle y kyuodet
ef o veirw, kannhlyn Dewi o vedwl a gweithret. Ac ef a uu drwy
lawer o vlwynnyded y gyt a Dewi yn gwassannaethu Duw. A phawb
o'r a welsant hynny a volyassant Duw.

[DAVID AT THE SYNOD]

Odyna y kerddawd Dauid y gyt a chennadeu y seint hyt y sened yr
oedit yn y aros. A phann deuth Dauid yno, y kyuodes yr holl seint yn
y erbyn pann welsant ef yn dyuot. A chyuarch gwell idaw, a
syrthyaw ar dal y glinyeu, ac erchi idaw pregethu gann dyrchauel
ohonaw y benn brynn vchel, y lle y buassei bregeth kyn no hynny.
Ac escussaw a oruc ef ar dalym o enkyt vrthunt, a dywedut na
be[i]dei ef ac na allei wnneuthur y peth yd oedynt wy yn y erchi
idaw.

Eissoes ef a gymerth venndith y kyffredin, ac a vfydhaawd vdunt.
A gwrthot a oruc ef ysgynnv y benn y brenn, a dywedut na mynnei ef
le y seuyll onnyt ar y llawr gwastat. A dechreu pregethu odyno a
oruc Dewi o gyureith Grist a'r Euegyl, a hynny megys llef kornn
eglur, a[c] yn amlwc hynny y bop dyn, y'r pellaf yn gynn egluret ac
y'r nessaf, ac yn gynn gyffredinet ac y bydei yr heul y bawp pann vei
hanner dyd. A hynny a uu [101a] ryued gann bawp.

A phann oed Dewi ar warthaf y llawr gwastat a dywedwyt vchot
yn pregethu, y kyuodes y llawr hwnnw megys mynyd vchel dan y

draet, a phawb o'r gynnulleitua honno yn edrych ar hynny, yr hwnn yssyd etwo yn vrynn vchel yn amlwc gann bawp, ac yn wastatir o bop parth idaw. A'r gwyrth a'r ryuedawt hwnnw a oruc Duw er Dewi yn Llanndewivreui.

[DECLARED CHIEF OF THE SAINTS OF BRITAIN]

Ac yna yn gytuun y rycgtunt ehunein moli Dewi sant a orugant, ac adef yn duhun y vot ef yn tywyssawc ar seint Ynys Prydein, gann dywedut mal hynn: 'Megys y rodes Duw pennadur yn y mor ar bop kenedyl o'r pyscawt, a megys y rodes Duw pennadur yn y dayar ar yr adar, velle y rodes ef Dewi yn pennadur ar y dynyon yn y byt hwnn. Ac yn y mod y rodes Duw Matheu yn Iudea, a Lucas yn Alexandria, a Christ yg Kaerussalem, a Pheder yn Rufein, a Martin yn Ffreinc, a Sampson yn Llydaw, y rodes y Dauid sant vot yn Ynys Prydein.

Ac vrth hynny y gwnaethpwyt Dewi sant yn tywyssawc ac yn pennadur ar seint Ynys Prydein, am pregethu ohonaw yn y sened vawr honno y'r holl bobyl, yn yr honn ny allawd neb bregethu namyn ef. A'r dyd hwnnw holl seint yr ynys honn a'r brenhined oll a ostynghassant ar eu glinnyeu y adoli y Dewi, ac a roddassant idaw vot yn bennaf ar seint Ynys Prydein. Ac ef a'e haedawd.

[RIGHT OF SANCTUARY]

A'r dyd hwnnw y rodet y Dewi y nodua[101b]eu, ac amdiffynn y bop kyuryw dyn o'r a wnnelei drwc o'r a ffoei y nawdir Dewi. Honn yw nodua Dewi y bawp o'r a vo yn dinas Rubi, yn nawd Dewi ac a dan y amdiffynn: o byd reit idaw, kennat yw idaw vynet o Dyfi hyt ar Deiui, ac or byd reit idaw vynet a vo moe, aet yn ragor rac pob sant a brenhin a dyn yn yr ynys honn. Nodua Dewi yw pa le bynnac y bo tir kyssegredic y Dewi sant, ac na lauasso na brenhin na tywyssawc nac escob na sant rodi nawd idaw ymblaen Dewi, kanys ef a gauas nawd ymlaen pawb, ac nys cauas neb yn y vlaen ef, kanys ef a ossodes Duw a dynyon yn bennaf o'r holl ynys.

Ac yna yr ysgymunawd hynny o seint o duundeb y brenhined y neb a dorrei nodua Dewi sant.

[THE ANGEL'S WARNING]

Ac odyna, val yd oed Dewi duw Mawrth diwethaf o vis Chwefrawr yn gwaranndaw ar yr yscolheigyon yn gwassanaethu Duw,
nachaf y clywei angel yn ymdidan ac ef, ac yn dywedut vrthaw val
hynn: 'Dauid,' heb yr angel, 'y peth a geisseisti yr ys talym y gann dy
Arglwyd Duw, y mae yn barawt yt pann y mynnych.' Sef a oruc
ynteu yna, dyrchauel y wyneb y vynyd, a llawenhau, a dywedut val
hynn, 'Yr awr honn, Arglwyd, kymer dy was di ythagneued.' Sef a
oruc yr ysgolheigonn a oed yn gwarandaw y deu ymadrawd hynn,
synnyaw arnunt yn vawr, a syrthyaw megys dyny[102a]on meirw.
 Ac yn yng ar hynny, nachaf y clywynt llef didan ac arogleu teccaf
yn llewni y dinas. Sef a oruc Dauid yr eilweith, dywedut yn vchel:
'Arglwyd Iessu Grist,' heb ef, 'kymer vy eneit, ac na at vi y drigyaw
a uo hwy yn y drygeu hynn.' Ac yn ol hynny, wynt a glywynt eilweith
yr angel yn dywedut vrth Dewi, Dauyd sant ymparattoa, y dyd
kynntaf o Vawrth ef a daw dy Arglwyd di, Iessu Grist, a naw rad nef
y gyt ac ef, a decuet y dayar, y'th erbyn, ac a eilw y gyt a thi o'r rei a
vynnych ti, o yscolheic a lleyc, gwiryon a phechadur, ieuang a hen,
mab a merch, gwr a gwreic, croessan a phutein, Idew a Sarascin, a
hynny a daw y gyt a thi.'
 A'r brodyr, kymein hun, pann glywyssant hynny, drwy wylyaw a
chwynaw, ac vdaw ac vcheneidyaw, a dyrchauassant eu llef ac a
dywedassant, 'Arglwyd Dewi sant, canhorthwya yn tristit.' Ac yna y
dywat Dewi vrthunt hwy, gann eu didanu a'e llawenhav, 'Vy
mrodyr, bydwch wastat ac vnvedwl, a pha beth bynnac a welsawch
ac a glywyssawch gennyf i, kedwch ef a gorffennwch beth mwy.' O'r
dyd hwnnw hyt yr wythuet nyt aeth Dewi o'r eglwys o bregethu y
bawp a gwediaw.
 Y chwedyl, eissoes, yn oet vn dyd a aeth drwy yr holl ynys honn ac
Iwerdon gann yr angel. Sef val y dywedei yr angel, 'Gwybydwchwi
pann yw yn yr wythnos nessaf yssyd yn dyuot yd a Dewi sant, ych
argluyd chwi, o'r byt hwnn yma at [102b] y Arglwyd.' Yna y gwelut
ti gyfuredec gann seint yr ynys honn a seint Iwerdonn, o bop parth
yn dyvot y ymwelet a Dewi sant. O! bwy yna a allei diodef wylouein
y seint, neu vcheneideu y meudwyot, neu'r offeireit, a'r disgyblonn
yn dywedut, 'Pwy a'n dysc ni?' Kwyn y personnyeit yn dywedut,
'Pwy a'n kanhorthwya ni?' Annobeith y brenhined yn dywedut,
'Pwy a'n hurda ni, pwy a vyd tat kynn drugarocket a Dewi, pwy a

wedia drossom ni ar yn Harglwyd?' Kwynvan y tlodyon a'r cleiuon yn vdaw. Y myneich a'r gwerydon a['r] rei priawt a'r penydwyr, y gweisson ieueing a'r morynyonn, y meibon a'r merchet, a['r] rei newyd eni ar eu bronnev yn gollwng eu dagreu. Beth a draethaf vi, onnyt vn kwyn gann bawp: y brenhined yn cwynaw eu brawt, yr hyneif yn cwynaw eu mab, y meibon yn cwynaw y tat.

[HIS LAST MESSAGE]

Dyw Sul y canawd Dewi offerenn, ac y pregethawd y'r bopyl.' A'e gyuryw kynn noc ef nys clywysbwyt, a gwedy ef byth ny chlywir. Nys gwelas llygat eiroet y sawl dynyon yn vn lle. A guedy daruot y bregeth a'r offerenn, y rodes Dewi yn gyffredin y vendith y bawp o'r a oed yna. A gwedy daruot idaw rodi y venndith y bawp, y dywat yr ymadrawd hwnn, 'Arglwydi, vrodyr a chwioryd, bydwch lawen a chedwch ych ffyd a'ch [c]ret, a gwnewch y petheu bychein a glywys-sawch ac a welsawch gennyf i. A mynheu a gerdaf y fford yd aeth an tadeu idi, ac ynn [103a] yach ywch,' heb y Dewi. 'A phoet grymus ywch vot ar y dayar, a byth bellach nyt ymwelwn ni.

Yna y clywit gawr gyffredin yn kyuodi gann gwynnvan ac wylouein a dagreu, ac yn dywedut, 'Och, na lwnck y dayar ni! Och, na daw tan y an llosci ni! Och, na daw y mor dros y tir! Och, na syrth y mynyded ar an gwastat ni! A phawb hayach a oed yna yn mynet y angheu. O dyw Sul hyt dyw Merchyr, gwedy marw Dewi, ny lawssant na bwyt na diawt, namyn gwediaw drwy dristit.

[HIS DEATH]

A nos Vawrth ynkylch canu y keilawc, nachaf lu o engylyon yn llewni y dinas, a phob ryw gerdeu a digrifwch ym pob lle yn y dinas yn llawn. Ac yn yr awr vore, nachaf yr Arglwyd Iessu Grist yn dyfot, a chyt ac ef naw rad nef, megys y gadawssei yn y vawrhydri, a'r heul yn eglur yn egluraw y'r holl luoed. A hynny dyw Mawrth, y dyd kynntaf o galan Mawrth, y kymerth Iessu Grist eneit Dewi sant y gyt a mawr uudugolyaeth a llewenyd ac anryded. Gwedy y newyn a'e sychet, a'e anwyt, a'e lauur, a'e dyrwest, a'e gardodeu, a'e vlinder, a'e drallawt, a'e brouedigaetheu, a'e vedwl am y byt, y kymerth yr engylyon y eneit, ac y dugant y'r lle y mae goleuni heb diwed, a gorffwys heb lauur, a llewenyd heb tristit, ac amled o bop ryw da, a

budugolyaeth, a chlaerder, a thegwch, y lle y mae molyant ryswyr
Crist, y lle yr ysgaelussir y kyuoethogyon drwc, y lle y mae yechyt
heb dolur, [103b] a ieuengtit heb heneint, a thagneued heb anuundeb, a gogonyant heb orwagrwyd, a cherdeu heb vlinder, a
gobrwyeu heb diwed, y lle y mae Abel y gyt a'r merthyri, lle y mae
Enoc y gyt a['r] rei byw, lle y mae Noe y gyt a'r llongwyr, lle y mae
Abraham y gyt a'r pedrieirch, lle y mae Melchisedech gyt a'r offeireit, lle y mae Iob y gyt a['r] rei da eu diodef, lle y mae Moysen y
gyt a'r tywyssogyonn, lle y mae Aaron gyt a'r escyb, lle y mae Dauid
y gyt a'r brenhined, lle y mae Ysaias gyt a'r proffwydi, lle y mae
Meir gyt a'r gwerydon, lle y mae Pedyr y gyt a'r ebestyl, lle y mae
Pawl y gyt a gwyr Groec, lle y mae Thomas y gyt a gwyr yr Yndia, lle
y mae Ieuan y gyt a gwyr yr Asia, lle y mae Matheu y gyt a gwyr
Judea, y lle y mae Lucas y gyt a gwyr Achaia, lle y mae Marcus y gyt
a gwyr Alexandria, lle y mae Andreas y gyt a gwyr Sithya, lle y mae
yr engylyon a'r archengylyon, a cherubin a seraphin, a Brenhin y
brenhined yn yr oes oesoed. Amen.

[EPILOGUE]

Ac val y coffayssam ni Dewi yn y vuched ehun, a'e weithredoed
yn y dayar yma, velle y bo canhorthwywr yntev, ac y grymoccao y
eirawl y nynheu geir bronn y gwir Greawdyr ar gaffel trugared rac
llaw.

NOTES

   treithir o, 'is discussed, related'. In MW *o* 'of' is used with verbs meaning 'to speak, relate', etc., where *am* is later found.

     talym, now *talm o amser* 'a period of time, a while'. Formerly its meaning was more general, and it meant sum, piece, part, as in *talm* o alaw 'a piece of lily' *GDG* 143.3, aur *dalym* 'a piece of gold' *GO* 177.17, *talym* o uara gwynn 'a piece of white bread' *WM* 394.15, a *thalym* o'r paladyr trwy[d]aw 'and a length of the shaft through him' 421.32–3, *talym* o'r llyfyr 'a part of the book' *SGr* 75.31. Cf. Ir. *tamall*; see *Celtica* i. 339. Note the epenthetic vowel between *l* and *m*, represented as is usual in MW by *y*. This reflects the tendency of sonants to become syllabic after a consonant; see *GMW* 12.

     Dewi, the form most commonly found in the Welsh *Life*, also *Dewi sant*; *Dauyd* and *Dauyd sant* also occur. In the Latin versions the form is *Dauid*, but it is added that the ordinary people call him *Dewi* (*uulgus autem Dewi clamat RLSD* 1).

     Dauid (in an Irish garb) is found in the Irish *Lives*, and in other *Lives* where there are references to the saint. But *Dewi* occurs twice in the *Life* of Illtud (*VSBG* 208, 222), *Devvi* in the *Life* of Gildas by Caradog of Llancarfan (*Gildas* ii. 400), *Devium* in the *Life* of Saint Paulinus (*RCv.* 421), *Dewi* in the *Life* of Kentigern by Jocelyn (*c.* 1180); cf. *SEBC* 313–14. We find *De(u)gui* in Asser (*ALKA* 65, 66)—a work with an unmistakable Welsh orientation, and *de(g)ui* in *LL* 275. Forms resembling these are found also in some Wessex calendars, as well as in Cornwall and Brittany; cf. *SDL* 73–4. Generally speaking, it can be said that the use of *Dewi* is indicative of a vernacular as opposed to a learned and Latin source. It is found in *Armes Prydein* (*c.* 930), and among the Gogynfeirdd and later poets; for examples cf. *G* 320.

     Both are borrowings, at different stages, from the Latin. *Dewi* is the earlier, and comes from *Dauīd*. *Dafydd* is later, and seems to be from a form *Dauidus*.

     On this use of dual nomenclature, found also in the *Life* of Cadog, cf. Emanuel, *B* xxi (1965), 133–5.

vab, note the soft mutation, common in a noun in apposition after a personal name; cf. *GMW* 15.

Sant, 'Saint', but here a personal name. According to the Genealogies, his mother was *Meleri*, daughter of Brychan Brycheiniog; cf. *EWGT* 15, 18, 43, 82 (*Eleri*). In some of the texts of *Bonedd y Saint* Sant is made a son of 'Kedic, son of Keredic'; see *EWGT* 54, and cf. *SC* xii/xiii (1977/8), 43.

He is not included in the royal pedigree of Ceredigion in Harleian 3859, (*EWGT* 12), and in the Breton *Buez Santes Nonn* 'The Life of Saint Nonn' Ceredig is named as the father of Dewi (*RC* viii 236, 258–68).

Keredic, cf. now M. Miller's view that 'Ceredig's name represents a settlement from eastern Severnside in or immediately after 577' (*SC* xii/xiii (1977/8), 59). The claim to descent from Cunedda was made later: 'it seems possible to say that the obit date and pedigree of St David were established by about 800, and the affiliation of Ceredig to Cunedda shortly afterwards, apparently by 829' (ibid. 59–60), some three centuries, therefore, before the time of Rhigyfarch.

Kuneda, also frequently referred to as *Kuneda Wledic*. His name is often found in the genealogies of the saints, most of whom are descended from him through his son *Keredic*; cf. *EWGT* 54–5. His name is first linked with Manaw Gododdin, a kingdom around Stirling and the northern shore of the Forth in the south of Scotland, whence according to the *Historia Brittonum* (c. 62) he emigrated with his eight sons to Wales. This happened towards the end of the fourth century, or during the early part of the fifth; cf. *LWS* 35n. He drove out the Irish, and is clearly thought of as having occupied a large area of the country. We are told (in Harleian 3859, see *EWGT* 13) that the territory of his sons extended from the Dee to the Teifi (Gwaun, according to the *Life* of Carannog, *VSBG* 148), and the names of some of them (e.g. Ceredig—*Ceredigion*) occur as eponyms of later Welsh kingdoms. He was a name of importance in early Welsh tradition, and in his character and movements appears to reflect a state of Romanization among the native aristocracy. It has been noted that his immediate forbears appear to have Roman names: Edern (Eternus), Padarn (Paternus), also Tagit (Tacitus), not found here; but cf. *HGVK* 1. Furthermore, the names Donatus and Marianus, attributed to two of his sons, indicate that he was a Christian.

It will be noticed that David's genealogy, like that of most other Welsh (and Irish) saints, is aristocratic. His affiliation to the pedigree of Cunedda may well have been a late development. Cf. under *Keredic* above, also *SG* 112.

2–3   **Padarnn Peisrud,** 'Padarn of the red tunic', possibly indicative of service in the Roman administration—an officer of high rank

p.   *l.*

1   (Rhys, *Celtic Britain*, 1884, 118, and Lloyd, *HW* i. 116–20, although another explanation is possible; cf. *EC* x (1962–3), 470.

In the MS, *srud* in *Peisrud* is largely obliterated. The genealogy here omits a number of names found elsewhere; Harleian MS 3859: Tacit map Cein map Guorcein (*EWGT* 9). *Life* of Cadog: Guorceng genuit Ceint. Ceint genuit Tacit (ibid. 25). *Life* of Carannog: Tacit m. Cein m. Guorchein (ibid. 26). History of Gruffudd ap Cynan: Tagit, m. Yago, m. Guidauc, m. Kein, m. Gorgein (*HGVK* 1). Pedigrees from Jesus College MS 20: Tegyth m. Iago m. Genedawc m. Cein m. Gorein (*EWGT* 44). Cf. further *HGVK* ccx.

3   **Deil,** but elsewhere *Doli*; cf. *EWGT* 9, 25, 26, 36, 44, 109.

Gordeil, elsewhere *Guordoli* (*EWGT* 9, 25); *Gurdoli* (ibid. 26, 36), *Gwrdoli* (ibid. 44), *Gwrddoli* (ibid. 109).

4   **Amguoel,** elsewhere *Amguoloyt, Amguoloid* (*EWGT* 9, 26), *Amgoloit* (ibid. 25), *Afloyd* (ibid. 109). The Latin *Life* has *Amguoil* (ibid. 27).

Amweryt, *Amguerit* in the Latin *Life* (*EWGT* 27), and in the *Life* of Carannog (ibid. 26). Forms with *-n-* are also attested: *Anguerit* (*EWGT* 9, 25), *Anwerit* (ibid. 36), *Anuueret* (ibid. 44), *Anweryd* (ibid. 109).

Onut, note forms in other texts: *Oumun* Harleian 3859 (*EWGT* 9), *Oimiud* The *Life* of Cadog (ibid. 25), *Omnid* The *Life* of Carannog (ibid. 26), *Onnet* History of Gruffudd ap Cynan (*HGVK* 1), *Eimet* Jes. Coll., MS 20 (*EWGT* 44), *Onwedd* Achau Brenhinoedd a Thywysogion Cymru (ibid. 95), *Onwet* (ibid. 109).

Perim, *Perum* in the Latin *Life*. Not attested in other genealogies; but *Peryf* in 'Gwehelyth *Dogveiling*' (*EWGT* 109).

Dubim, note the variant forms in other texts: *Dubun* (*EWGT* 9), *Dubunn* (ibid. 25, 26), *Dobun* Latin *Life* (ibid. 27), *Diuwng* (ibid. 36), *Dibun* (ibid. 44), *Diwng* (ibid. 109); and cf. further *HGVK* 42.

In other versions of this genealogy, there follows here the name *Brithguein* (*EWGT* 9, 25), *Britguenni* (ibid. 26), *Brychwein* (*HGVK* 1, *EWGT* 95), *Prydein* (*EWGT* 44), *Brochwein* (ibid. 109).

5   **Ongen,** *Iouguen* in the Latin *Life*. Elsewhere *Eugein* Harleian 3859 (*EWGT* 9), *Euguein* Life of Cadog (ibid. 25), *Eugen* Life of Carannog (ibid. 26), *Ewein* History of Gruffudd ap Cynan, Pedigrees from Jesus College MS 20, 'Gwehelyth *Dogveiling*' (ibid. 36, 44, 109).

Auallach, *Abalach* Latin *Life*, *Aballac* Harleian 3859 (*EWGT* 9), *Aballach* (preceded by *Baallad*) *Life* of Cadog (ibid. 25), *Aballach* Life of Carannog (ibid. 26), *Auallach*

History of Gruffudd ap Cynan (*HGVK* 1), Pedigrees from Jesus

1   College MS 20 (ibid. 36, 44).

Eugen, vab Eudoleu, in the Latin *Life Eugen* is the son of *Eudolen*, son of *Eugen*, who is described as the son of the sister of Mary. In other versions of this pedigree the list of names ends with *Beli* (*Fawr*) and his mother Anna, who is described as cousin/kinswoman (*consobrina*) of Mary; cf. *EWGT* 9, 25, 26, 44 (Anna is not mentioned in the History of Gruffudd ap Cynan, *HGVK* 1, or in 'Gwehelyth *Dogveiling*', *EWGT* 109). In Harleian 3859 (*EWGT* 9), Beli is father of *Amalech*, father of *Aballac*. In the *Life* of Cadog he is father of *Aballach* (ibid. 25), in the *Life* of Carannog, father of *Canalech*, father of *Aballach* (ibid. 26). In the History of Gruffudd ap Cynan he is father of *Aflech*, father of *Auallach* (*HGVK* 1), while in the Pedigrees from Jesus College MS 20 his son is *Amalech*, father of *Auallach* (*EWGT* 44). In 'Gwehelyth *Dogveiling*' *Beli mawr* is father of *Affllath*, father of *Afallach* (ibid. 109).

5–6   **Veir Wyry,** 'the Virgin Mary'. Note the soft mutation in *Veir* (*Meir*), a genitive after a feminine singular noun, *chwaer* 'sister'; cf. *GMW* 14.

Wyry: from *gwyryf* 'virgin', with soft mutation of a noun in apposition. This is common after a personal name, both feminine and masculine; cf. *v*ab above, *v*am here in line 6, and Keredic *v*renhin in line 7; cf. *GMW* 15.

It is noteworthy that the references to the Virgin are few in the *Life*; not once is she addressed.

7   **Keredic vrenhin a wledychawd,** 'King Keredic ruled'. Note the order *Subject + a + Verb*, one of the types of Abnormal Sentence commonly found in Middle Welsh; cf. *GMW* 179–80. Examples abound in this text.

gwledychawd, 3 sing. pret. of *gwledychu* 'to rule', a denominative verb formed from *gwlat* 'country'. The stem is formed by the addition of *-ych-* to the noun; cf. *chwenychu* (*chwant*) 'to desire', *pesychu* (*pas*) 'to cough'. See *WG* 381, 383.

blwynyded, pl. of *blwydyn* 'year', by metathesis from an earlier *blwydyned HGVK* 6.8. See *GMW* 33.

7–8   **o'e enw ef y kauas Keredigyawn y henw,** 'from his name Ceredigion got its name', another type of Abnormal Sentence commonly found in Middle Welsh, with the order *Adverb/Adverbial expression + y(d)/yr + Verb*; see *GMW* 179–80. Examples abound in this text.

8   **kauas,** 3 sing. pret. of *cael* 'get, receive', the only verb in MW where *-as* is invariably used as the ending of the 3 sing. pret.; see *GMW* 122.

Keredigyawn, a kingdom in west Wales, co-extensive with former Cardiganshire. It consisted of four cantrefs, and ten commotes. The cantref of Penweddig in the north (with Ystwyth

1   forming its southern boundary) consisted of the three commotes
of Genau'r Glyn, Creuddyn and Perfedd. Further down there
were the three commotes of Mefenydd, Anhuniog and Penardd,
which with Penweddig formed Uwch Aeron. To the south we
have Is Aeron, consisting of four commotes, Caerwedros,
Mabwnion, Iscoed and Gwinionydd.

9   **Sant,** see 1.2. *Sant* above. In the Latin *Life* it is said that he
later laid aside his royal power, 'to procure for himself a
heavenly kingdom' (*RLSD* 29).

ymdangosses, 3 sing. pret. of *ymdangos* 'appear', a verb consisting of the reflexive prefix *ym-* + *dangos* 'show'. Verbs containing *-o-/-oe-* in their stems regularly take the ending *-es* in the
3 sing. pret. in MW; see *GMW* 122.

dywedut, 'say, speak': a verbal noun used instead of a finite verb,
a very common construction in narrative MW prose. Usually, but
not invariably, a finite verb precedes. Note also 2.1, 13, 3.18,
4.5, 6.15, 7.3, 4, 8, 9, 8.9; and see further *GMW* 161.

10   **ey, keffy,** the ending of the 2 sing. pres. indic. in MW is *-y*; cf.
GMW 115–16.

hely, 'hunt'. *-y* is non-syllabic, and derives from an earlier *g*
(**selg*). Mod. W. *hel(a)*. See *L & P* 33, *GMW* 10.

dyuot, 'a find, prize, treasure-trove', something found by acci-
dent, also *dyouot, douot*; see *G* 425, *PKM* 153–4, *GPC* 1072.
Lat. *tria ... munera* 'three gifts' *RLSD* 1.

The three finds are a stag, a salmon and swarm of bees, and, as
Wade-Evans (*LSD* 60–1) reminds us, they are to be associated
in some way with possession and claim to unoccupied land. Note
how the angel, after referring to the three finds, declares that the
right to the land is to be reserved for a son not yet born.

In the *Life* of Cadog (*VSBG* 64) it is said that Cadog on the
banks of the Neath saw a wild boar, bees in a hollow tree, and
the nest of a hawk at the top of a tree. He then sent these as gifts
to king Arthfael, who granted him the land to inhabit and possess. According to Lhuyd, St Baglan built his church at a place
where he 'found a tree with a litter of pigs at the root, a hive of
bees in the body, and a crow's nest in the top'. Cf. *LBS* i. 193.

In the *De Situ Brecheniauc* the following episode is related of
Drichan and his *alumnus* Brachan:

> Drichan autem in fine etatis sue cecus factus est. Et dum
> idem uigilans iacuisset, quidam aper venit de silua, stetit-
> que iuxta ripam fluminis Ischir, ceruusque retrorsum erat in
> flumine necnon sub uentre cerui piscis erat, que tria por-
> tendebant Brachan opulentie copia felicem futurum.
> Adhuc etiam fagus secus fluminis predicti litus stabat, in
> qua mellificabant apes. Dixitque Drichan alumpno suo bra-
> chan, 'Ecce hanc arborem de apibus et melle, auro quoque

et argento plenam, do tibi, et gratia Dei eiusque dilectio
tecum maneat semper hic, et in futuro.' (*VSBG* 313).

Here we have mentioned a boar, a stag and a fish, all three
portending that Brachan would be blessed with wealth. Further,
there is the beech tree, where bees were making honey, and
Drichan tells Brachan, 'Behold this tree full of bees and honey,
also of gold and silver, I give to you, and may the grace of God
and his love abide with you always, now and in the future'. Thus
the fish, stag and the bees are associated with possession and
right for Brychan, as they are for David. Note the account of
Kentigern fixing his abode near the river Elwy; cf. *LBS* ii. 236;
also of Cyngar fixing the site of his monastery, ibid. 249, and
Dyfrig, ibid. 366.

In the *Life* of Saint Paul Aurelian (*RC* v 417–58) it is related
that the saint, having reached the place which was to be the
centre of his work and mission (namely, Saint Pol-de-Leon),
found within the *castellum* (ibid. 443) a wild sow with a litter of
pigs, whose progeny for many years maintained the king's herd
of swine. In a hollow tree a swarm of bees and a plentiful supply
of honey was discovered. A bear, which had been ravaging the
countryside, fled and fell into a deep pit called *pars Brochana*.
The saint also drove out a wild ox.

Loth suggests (in *Chrestomathie Bretonne*) that *pars Brochana* is indicative of a link with the legend of Brychan (here cf.
Doble i, 22, 34–5). Be that as it may, it appears that in the case of
David, Cadog, Brychan, and St Paul Aurelian, where circumstances relating to the founding of a centre are mentioned, we
are given some insight into practices concerned with rights of
possession of uncultivated and unoccupied land. Ownership of
such land was signified by claiming right to the honey, fish and
wild animals on it. These only would represent the value of such
land. Here we may refer to the Laws: Maer a chyghellawr bieu
cadw diffeith brenhin hyny wnel y vod ohonaw, ac wynt o gy-
freith a gaffant y mel a'r pyscawt a'r bwystuileit bychein gwyllt.
'The *maer* and *canghellor* are to keep the king's wasteland until
he do his pleasure herewith, and they by law are to have the
honey, fish, and the smaller wild animals' (*LlB* 48–9). Cf. also
WEMA 34.

In the third branch of the Mabinogi, after the feast and the
provisions were ended, and the enchantment had fallen upon
Dyfed, making the land without life and habitation, it is said of
Manawydan and his company, 'dechreu a wnaethant ymborth ar
kic hela, a physcawt, a bydaueu' (*PKM* 52. 14–15).

The explanation in the Latin *Life* is quite different; see *RLSD*
1–2, 29. There it is said that the three gifts foreshadow his life:
'For the honeycomb declares his wisdom . . . The fish proclaims

p.   *l.*

1   his abstinence ... The stag signifies his power over the ancient serpent'.

ger lan, this would mean 'by the bank (of)', with *lan* a mutated form of *glan* 'bank'. However, the soft mutation is not normal after *ger* 'by'. Other MSS (e.g. B. Llanstephan 27) have *llaw* 'hand', which seems the better reading, *ger llaw* meaning 'beside, near to'.

11   **auon Teiui,** 'the river Teifi'. This river, with its source in the Pumlumon mountains, forms the southern boundary of Ceredigion, and enters the sea at Aberteifi, Cardigan.

karw, in the Latin *Life* it is said that Sant 'will kill a stag near the river' (*RLSD* 29).

12   **Henllan,** on the banks of the Teifi, not far from its estuary in Cardigan (Aberteifi). In the earlier versions of the Latin *Life* the location is not mentioned, but in the Vespasian text we find *in loco qui uocatur Linhenlanú* 'at a place which is called Linhenlanú (for Linhenlann)' (*RLSD* 1). These words, like the Welsh *yn y lle a elwir yr awr honn Henllan*, seem to form part of the angel's message, however inappropriate. The whole clause is best explained originally as a gloss. The author of the Welsh *Life*, having observed *Linhenlanu* in the Latin version, substituted *Henllan* for it, the form of the name known to him, and added *yr awr honn* 'at this time'. However, the Latin may originally have had some form such as *nunc/nūc*, which could explain the *-u* at the end of the Latin form of the name (*Linhenlanu*). Another possible explanation of *yr awr honn* is that it is wrongly placed from the Latin: ad Maucanni monasterium; quod *nunc* usque Depositi monasterium uocatur (*RLSD* 1).

dylyet, 'right', cognate with Irish *dliged* 'law'; see *L&P* 30. In the Welsh form we have an example of an epenthetic vowel (*y*), having developed between two consonants (*d* and *l*) at the beginning of a word, whereas it is usually found at the end; see *GMW* 13.

13   **bieiuyd,** 'will own', from *pieivyd*, which consists of *pieu* (*pi* + *eu*) and *byd*, 3 sing. fut. of the verb 'to be'; see *GMW* 80–1.

deu le, the whole sentence is hard to explain as it stands, and there is nothing corresponding to it in the Latin *Life*. There has been no previous reference to 'two places', *deu le*. It appears that the reference to 'two places' is the result of bungling by some editor or copyist. It may be that the original reading was *dylyet* (see above): ef bieivyd *dylyet* hyt Dyd Brawt 'he will own the right till Domesday'. y rei a dywetpwyt uchot 'those mentioned above' could well have been originally a marginal note on *dylyet*, referring to the three finds and their significance. *linhenllan* and *litonmancan* may also have been glosses originally, written by a scribe after consulting a Vespasian version with its *Linhenlanú* and *Maucanni monasterium* (*VSBG* 150.15, 17–18).

Subsequently, these notes could have been incorporated in the text, and *dylyet* altered to *deu le*, in order to try and get some meaning out of the jumble.

14   **Liton Mancan,** MS *litoninancan*. In the Latin *Life* it is said that the honeycomb, and a portion of the fish and of the stag are to be set aside, and sent to Maucannus's monastery, 'there to be preserved for a son who will be born of you' (*RLSD* 29). It is further stated that this monastery 'to this day is called the Monastery of the Deposit'—*depositi Monasterium* (ibid. 2). The Welsh for deposit is *adneu*, which reminds us of the Llann *adneu* mentioned by Gwynfardd Brycheiniog (twelfth century) as one of the churches of David; see *HGCr* 46, 190. *Litonmancan* is doubtless a reference to this monastery. It is difficult to decide as between *Mancan/Maucan*. The latter would correspond to Mawgan, also Meugan; see *LHEB* 440–1. On this saint and his connections, see *LBS* iii. 478–81, *LSD* 58–9, *SCSW* 87–91, *HWW* 209, *Doble* ii. 34–44. There is evidence of his cult in Cornwall and in Brittany, as well as in various parts of Wales, especially in north Pembroke, e.g. Llanfeugan in Cemais, the main centre of his cult with which, according to Wade-Evans (*LSD* 60), *Liton Mancan* is to be identified. There is some (late) evidence that Patrick embarked for Ireland at *Port Maugan*, and that there was a town by the sea called *Portus Maugan*; cf. *LSD* 58, also 2.15 *mynet a oruc Padric y Iwerdon* below, where mention is made of *Porth Melgan* nearby. There is a farm in the vicinity of St David's called *Trefeugan*. We may further mention *Pistyll Meugan, Cwm Meugan, Dyffryn Meugan*, close to the river Teifi. Also *Ffair Feugan* 'Meugan's Fair', held on the Monday after Martinmas, 11 November.

Slover (p. 91) suggests that we have here the Irish saint, *Mancan*, and that the Irish *Liath Manchan* lies behind the form in our text.

The first element also presents difficulties, which may in part be due to an early scribal error. The third letter could be *c*; even if it were, it would not help. The word ought to denote some meaning, such as *monasterium*, and could be *litu* (or ? *litou*), later *llydw*, meaning 'a host, household, community'. In *LL* 120 we have *lytu* yr ecluys and *lytu* teliau, for *populus* (ibid. 118). On *litu*, see Ifor Williams, *B* v (1929), 6. J. Lloyd-Jones (*Llenor* ii. 195–6) suggested that we should take *liton* as the form here, with the meaning 'servant, captive, community', and finally 'monastery'. Cf. Carn *Llidi*; see under 2.9 *Eistedua Padric* below, and cf. *LBS* ii. 293.

15   **Padric,** the patron saint of Ireland, who lived in the fifth century and probably hailed from some area of western Britain. Here, as elsewhere in the *Life*, we seem to have an echo of the conflict between Brython and Goidel in this part of Wales.

1   The 'orthodox' view of Patrick's mission was that he was sent
        to Ireland in 432 by Pope Celestine, as successor to Palladius,
        who had died that year and who had been sent there in 431. He
        spent the rest of his life in Ireland, where he laboured, more
        especially in the north and west of the country. His mission was
        most successful, and when he died in 461 almost the entire
        country had been converted to the Christian Faith. This is the
        view of Patrick expounded by J. B. Bury in his *Life of St Patrick*.
        It was later questioned, and by some, notably T. F. O'Rahilly,
        rejected. The latter sought to interpret the early evidence for the
        existence of two famous missionaries in Ireland in the fifth
        century. The first, he maintained, was Palladius who went to
        Ireland in 431, and remained there till his death in 461. Another
        name for him was Patricius. He was followed, probably in 462,
        by Patricius the Briton, who died in 492. See *The Two Patricks*
        (Dublin, 1942). The Patrician question has continued to attract
        attention. One may refer to the studies of L. Bieler, e.g. *The
        Life and Legend of St Patrick* (Dublin, 1948) and *St Patrick and
        the Coming of Christianity* (Dublin, 1967). He in general sub-
        scribes to the 'orthodox' view, as do scholars like Ryan, Shaw
        and Aubrey Gwynn (cf. *Studies*, 1961), also the distinguished
        Bollandist P. Grosjean (cf. *SH* ii. 25–6). Not so, however,
        James Carney, who believes that Patrick came to Ireland in 456
        and died in 493; see *SILH* 324–73, and later *The Problem of
        St Patrick* (Dublin, 1961). For yet another view we may refer to
        Mario Esposito (*IHS* × (1956), 131–55), who proposes that
        Patrick preceded Palladius and died about 430, after a fairly
        successful mission. For a useful and concise presentation of the
        more important theories, see *Saint Patrick* (Thomas Davis
        Lectures, Dublin, 1958). These were critically examined by
        D. A. Binchy in a lengthy study in *Studia Hibernica* ii. (1962),
        7–173. Finally, mention should be made of a work by R. P. C.
        Hanson, *Saint Patrick His Origins and Career* (Oxford, 1968).
        He believes that there was only one Patrick, and that he be-
        longed to the first half of the fifth century. He was a product of
        the British Church, was made bishop in Britain and sent from
        there to Ireland. Here we may perhaps note the reference in the
        letter sent by the chapter of St David's to the Pope (1124–30) to
        the 'histories', which state that it was from their see that Patrick
        was sent to Ireland; see *EAWD* i. 250. P. A. Wilson (*SC* xiv/xv
        (1979/80), 344–79) thinks that he was of British background, but
        that his mission was of Gallo-Roman origin. *c*. 440–*c*. 470 were
        the years of his missionary activity in Ireland.
            It is probable that large areas of the east and south of Ireland
        had been Christianized before the coming of Patrick.
            Two Latin works are attributed to him, his *Confession* and
        Epistle to Coroticus (probably the earlier of the two). They are

p.   *l.*
1   translated (with commentary) by L. Bieler in *The Works of St Patrick* (London, 1953). His earliest biographers were Muir-chú and Tirechán, both of whom wrote towards the end of the seventh century.

Here, as in other parts of the *Life*, Rhigyfarch is anxious to underline David's superiority over some other notable saints of the period.

Glynn Rosin, Latin *Vallis Rosina*, the name used by Rhigy-farch for Mynyw or St David's. Of the cathedral Giraldus Cambrensis writes, 'The place where it stands is called *Vallis Rosina*. A better name for it would be the Valley of the Marble, for it is in no sense rosy or remarkable for roses, whereas there are plenty of rocks all over the place' (*GW*166). However, the *ros* in *rosin/rosina* is hardly the word for 'rose'. As Wade-Evans reminds us (*LSD* 67), the name *Rhoson* occurs in the area as the name of a farm; also *Carn Roson, Carreg Rhoson, Maen Rhoson*. *Rhoson* may well be for *Rhosan*, a form attested in the *Liber Communis* of the Cathedral Church, *HASD*, 375, 378, etc., where it is spelt *Rossan*; also in Owen's *Pembrokeshire* i. 113. Carreg *y rossan*. Ross on Wye is *Rosan ar wy* in *RMWL* i. 920, and there is a brook called Rhosan in Cil-y-cwm, near Llandovery, Dyfed. These forms seem to contain a diminutive of *rhos* 'moor', cognate with Irish *ross* 'wood, promontory' (*rosan* 'small wood'), Breton *ros* 'hill', cf. Sanskrit *prastha-s* 'plateau', see *L&P* 21, and cf. further *SSSCL* 216–19, also *Y Genhinen* x (1959–60), 242–3.

According to the Latin *Life* (*RLSD* 2), Patrick first came to Ceredigion, where he remained for a short while before entering Dyfed.

16   **dywat,** 'said, spoke': 3 sing. pret. of *dywedyt*; see *GMW* 124. Also *dywot*.

17   **Sef a oruc Padric, llidiaw,** 'What Patrick did was to become angry', or rather 'Patrick became angry'. A common construc-tion in MW prose is this use of *sef* (*ys* 'is' + *ef* 'it') + *a* (rel. pron.) + (*g*)*oruc* 'did', followed by a verbal noun; see *GMW* 52n. The construction is frequently found in this text: 2.19, 3.35, 6.3, 4, 7.8, 12, 19.25, 29, 31, 38, 10.4, 5, 16, 12.5, 7, etc. It is a variant of the construction *verbal noun* + *a* + *goruc*; cf. 2.4 below.

2   1   **ouyn,** 'fear'. Here we have an example of the epenthetic vowel, which is commonly found in the form *y* in MW in certain groups of consonants, usually at the end of a word; see *GMW* 12–13.

         ethol ohonaw, 'he chose': the verbal noun here used instead of a finite verb; see under 1.9. *dywedut* above. The subject of the verbal noun is denoted by being placed after it, governed by the prep. *o*, a common construction in MW; see *GMW* 161.

p.   l.

2   2-3   **ny enir hyt ympenn dec mlyned ar hugeint,** 'who will not be
born till the end of thirty years'. Geoffrey of Monmouth tells us
how Patrick had foretold that Mynyw had been reserved for
David. Cf. *BD* 186: Canys Padric a daroganassei idav ef y lle
honno kyn no'e eni. Furthermore, we have the entry in the
Annales Cambriae (MS B) relating to the birth of David: *anno
tricessimo post discessum Patricii de Menevia* 'in the thirteenth
year after Patrick's departure from Menevia'; see *N* 85. Also the
Life of Carannog, where it is stated that that saint followed
Patrick to Ireland thirty years before the birth of David: *xxx.
annis ante natiuitatem sancti Dauid filii Sant, bene Carantocus
susceptus est in Hibernia* (*VSBG* 142); see *SEBC* 157-8, and
Doble iv. 38.

In the *Life* of the Irish saint Ciaran, Patrick tells him (in Italy)
that he will follow him to a fountain (*Fuaran*) in the middle of
Ireland, *after thirty years*; cf. *Doble* iv. 8. In the *Life* of St Moling
it is said that Brénainn had intended building his monastery near
the river Barrow in Leinster, but he is told by an angel, 'Do not
make an abode here now, for in prophecy it is not for thee to
make an abode here; but the boy *who will be born at the end of
thirty years from today*, he it is, Moling of Linn mór, that will
make a dwelling there' (*BLSM* 19). But Moling is already there,
having leapt over the thirty years: he also was a child of sin!
(ibid.).

4   **ymparatoi a oruc Padric,** 'Patrick prepared', a common construction in MW, where we have the order *verbal noun + a +
goruc/gwnaeth* 'did', usually equivalent in meaning to a simple
form of the verb: 'prepare he did' = 'he prepared'; see *GMW*
160. For a variant of this construction, see under *Sef a oruc
Padric, llidiaw* above.

yndaw 'in him'. This clearly requires emendation. The
meaning requires a verb such as *ymadaw* 'depart'. Cf. the earlier
versions of the Latin *Life: uadam* 'I will depart' (*RLSD* 2); in the
Vespasian text we have *Parauitque fugere* 'And he prepared to
flee' (ibid.).

4-5   **ac ydaw y lle hwnnw y'r Arglwyd Grist,** 'and leave that place
to the Lord Christ'. In the Vespasian text of the Latin *Life* we
find *et dominum suum Iesum Christum deserere* 'and to abandon
his Lord, Jesus Christ' (*RLSD* 2). It is fair to suggest that the
Welsh version originally read 'ac adaw yr Arglwyd Grist', but
the reading was emended in order not to attribute an unworthy
thought to Patrick, and the words *y lle hwnnw* were added. This
would be in keeping with other references in the text to a place
being left to someone else: *adaw* ti ... y lle hwnn y vab 1.16,
ac y *gedewis* Padric *y* Dewi y lle hwnnw 2.12, a *gadaw y*'r
mab hwnn yr ynys honn 3.10, peri vdunt wy *adaw* y lle hwnn y
ni 5.35.

2   6   **y duhudaw,** 'to pacify him'. In the form *y* the prep *y* 'to' and
the infixed genitive pron. 3 sing. *y* have coalesced; see *GMW* 53
n.2.

9   **Eistedua Padric:** Lat. *Sedes Patricii*. There is no place of this
name now in St David's, but Porth Padrig and Carn Badrig
occur; see *LSD* 68–9, also *Y Genhinen* x, (1959–60), 243. From
the top of Carn Llidi (= *Llydu* 'monastery') (600 feet) the coast
of Ireland is visible on a clear day. The seat of Patrick may have
been near here, at a site on which a chapel to the saint was later
erected; but it appears that the spot from which Patrick was to
see Ireland was in the *valley*. Note the words of Giraldus Cambrensis: 'In clear weather the mountains of Ireland can be seen
from St David's' (*GW* 168).

There are only faint traces of Patrick's cult in Dyfed. We may
mention Capel Padrig in Nevern; also Patter Church (or Patrick
Church) once at Patter Dock (= Pembroke Dock).

Cf. *Eisteddfa Grannog*: 'a rock, resembling a large chair',
'above the little harbour or creek below the village (of Llangran-
nog)'. See *LBS* ii, 89; also *Eisteddfa Gurig*, ibid. 193, *Eisteddfa
Egwad*, ibid. 415–16.

14   **yr ys** 'for'; see *GMW* 142–3. Also 3.34 below.

pymthec mlyned 'fifteen years', but 'twelve' according to the
Latin: ante *duodecim* annos (*RLSD* 3).

Kruchier, in the Latin *Life* his name is not given in the earlier
versions, but in the Vespasian text it occurs as *Criumther*, probably an error for *cruimther* 'priest' (*Contrib.* 559). It is hardly
likely that this was originally a personal name. According to
Giraldus, the man's name was *Dunaudus* (*Opera* iii. 381).

15   **mynet a oruc Padric y Iwerdon,** 'P. went to Ireland'. In the
Vespasian text, but not in the earlier versions, it is said that he
got ready a ship in Porth Mawr: paransque navem in *Portu
Magno* (*RLSD* 3). According to Wade-Evans, '*Porth Mawr* is
now the Welsh name of the whole of Whitesand Bay, some mile
and a half to the N.W. of the Cathedral' (*LSD* 69). Nearby is
Carn Llidi (cf. 2.9 *Eistedua Padric* above). *Porth Melgan* is to
the north west of Porth Mawr (cf. 1.14 *Liton Mancan* above).
Here also possibly was St Patrick's chapel. Cf. Bowen in *SSSCL*
212: 'A well-known coastal chapel is that known as St Patrick's
chapel on the shore at Whitesands Bay near St David's in Pembrokeshire. Here a rectangular mound stood in a field known as
Parc-y-capel close to the shore'; further cf. *AC* lxxx (1925),
87–120. It was here apparently that Patrick embarked for
Ireland, at Porth Mawr 'extensively used by pilgrims and others
on their way to and from Ireland' (ibid.). According to the *De
Situ Brecheniauc*, it was from Porth Mawr that Marchell,
daughter of Tewdrig and mother of Brychan Brycheiniog, embarked for Ireland to marry Anlach, an Irish prince; cf. *VSBG*

p.   *l.*

2   313. Richard of Cirencester (fourteenth century) refers to Porth Mawr as the nearest crossing-point to Ireland; cf. D. W. James, *St David's and Dewisland* (Cardiff, 1981), 10.

17   **yr oed,** in the MS *r* is written above.

18   **yn kerdet ehun,** 'travelling alone'. Today *kerdet* means 'to walk', but earlier its meaning was more general; cf. *G* 134, *GPC* 465. In the Vespasian text (but not in the earlier versions) it is said that 'divine power sent Sant, king of the country of Ceredigion, as far as a community of the people of Dyfed' (*uirtus diuina misit Sanctum, regem Ceretiçę regionis usque ad plebem Demeticę gentis* (*RLSD* 3). According to Giraldus, they met in Pebidiog, the cantref within which St David's is situated; cf. *Opera* iii. 379.

     lleian yn, MS *leian yr.*

19   **ymauael a hi,** 'to seize her'. *ymauael* consists of *ym-* (reciprocal) + *gauael*. A verb containing this prefix is invariably followed by *a(c)*; cf. *ymwarandaw a* 'to listen to' *PKM* 1.11, *ymgael a* 'to reach' 1.15.

     dwyn treis arnei, 'to violate her', lit. 'to bring violation on her'; for other exs., see *B* xvi (1954), 9.

     a gafas beichogi 'conceived', lit. 'got conception'. Note here that there is no soft mutation of the object after the 3 sing. pret.; see *GMW* 18.

20   **Nonn:** Lat. *Non(n)ita* (*Nynnid*; cf. Eglwys Nynnid near Margam in Glamorgan); see *LSD* 70–1, *DWB* 686. In the calendar in Cotton Vespasian A xiv she is commemorated under March 2, and described as *Genetricis Sancti Dauid;* cf. *VSBG* ix.

     According to 'Bonedd y Saint' she was daughter of Cynyr of Caer Gawch in Mynyw (*EWGT* 54). On Caer Gawch/Gawg (for Gaeawg?) and its possible connection with Caeo in north-east Carmarthenshire, see *LSD* 71. The poet Ieuan ap Rhydderch in the fifteenth century refers to Nonn as Cynyr's daughter; see *IGE* 242. 17–18. *Cynyr* may well be the Irish *Conaire.* Nonn's mother was Anna, daughter of Uthr Pendragon, father of Arthur; see *EWGT* 39, 55.

     Llan Non is found at least five times in Wales, including one on the coast of Cardigan Bay (six miles to the north of Hen Fynyw). There is also a chapel on the edge of the cliffs, a little to the south of St David's, above St Non's Bay; see *SSSCL* 183. Here also we find Non's Well. The name is commemorated also in Cornwall (Alternon), Devon (Bradstone), and Brittany (Dirinon), where we find the *Life, Buez Santes Nonn;* see *RC* viii. 230–301, 406–91, *ChBr* 242–5.

     From an early period Nonn was thought of as a saint and as the mother of David, but the name may have originally been that of a monk, who was a contemporary of David and a companion of his,—a saint whose cult may be traced in Cornwall and

p.   *l.*
2
Brittany also, like some others of the saints of Wales during
these times. 'When the story of his life was forgotten, the resem-
blance of his name to the word nonna (nun) led to the invention
of the story of the violated nun, and the connection between
S. Nonna and S. Dewi were changed from that of companions
into that of mother and son' (*SN* 6). Similarly the tradition concerning Efrddyl, the daughter of Peibio and the mother of Dubricius; she also was a virgin who was violated, but the name may
have originally been that of a man who was a companion of
Dubricius: *LWS* 66.

20-1   **Dauid a rodet yn enw arnaw**, 'he was named Dafydd', lit.
'Dafydd was placed (as) a name upon him'. For other exs. of this
construction, where *dodi/rodi ar* is used to express the meaning
'to name', see *B* xvi (1954), 7.

22   **vedwl**, MS *ved|dwl*.
o vedwl a gweithret, 'in/as regards mind and deed'.

23   **o'r pann**, 'from the (time) when'; see *GMW* 242.

25   **namyn bara a dwfuyr**, 'except bread and water', a reference to
David's asceticism. He is described as *Aquaticus* in the *Life* of
St Paul Aurelian (*RC* v. 421). *Dyfrwr* 'Waterman' is an appell-
ation often found with his name, e.g. by Ieuan ap Rhydderch:

> Dewi *ddyfrwr* yw'n ddiwyd,
> Dafydd ben Sant bedydd byd. (*IGE* 229, 127–8).

'Dewi the waterman, true is he, Dafydd the chief saint of
Christendom.' See *LSD* 62–3, also *HW* i. 155; further *RC* xlv
(1928), 148–9, and also *EC* vii (1955), 340–7, where a different
interpretation is offered for the appellation *dyfrwr*. Of its use in
a Manual-Missal dated *c.* 1440, cf. *SDL* 35.
According to Giraldus (*Opera* vi. 104), 'Morgenau . . . was the
first Bishop of St David's to eat meat'; see *GW* 163.

27   **Gildas sant,** in the earlier versions of the Latin *Life* Gildas is
not mentioned by name, but referred to as 'a certain teacher'
(*quidam doctor*). However, in the Vespasian text he is described
as *Gildas, Cau filius* (*RLSD* 4), who was preaching 'in the time
of king Triphunus and his sons' (ibid.); likewise in his *Life* by
Caradog of Llancarfan, see *LSD* 46. *Triphunus* or *Tryffun* (in
the form *Trestin*) is named in an eighth-century Irish saga, *Indar-
ba inna nDési* (*EWGT* 4), a saga recording the wanderings of an
Irish tribe, the *Dési*, which eventually settled in Dyfed (*Cy* xiv.
101–35). Their first ruler in Dyfed was Eochaid, son of Artchorp
(or Eochaid Allmuir), whose descendants seem to have continued in Dyfed down till the tenth century. The Dyfed royal
pedigree is given in Harleian 3859 (*EWGT* 9–10). Here *Triphun*
is described as father of *Aircol*, father of *Guortepir*, but in the
version of the pedigree in Jesus College MS 20 *Erbin* comes
between *Gwrdeber* (*Guortepir*) and Aircol, son of Tryphun

(*EWGT* 45–6). *Aircol* is here described as *lawhir* '(with) long
hand', as he is in *LL* 125: *Aircol lauhir filio tryfun rege demetice.*
According to ibid. 118 he was a contemporary of Teilo. His son
Guortepir may well be the same as the *Voteporigis* (gen. sing.)
commemorated in the bilingual inscription (Ogam and Latin) at
Castelldwyran (Carm.); see *ECMW* 107, also p. xii above. With
him may also be identified *Vortipor(i)*, one of the five British
chieftains castigated by Gildas in his *De Excidio Britanniae* (*Gildas* i. 73). His hair was beginning to turn grey at the time Gildas
was writing (before 547), and it would seem, therefore, that his
grandfather Tryffun should be placed back somewhere in the
middle of the fifth century. Cf. *SC* xii/xiii (1977/8), 39–41. This
would appear to be too early a time for Gildas to be described as
preaching (see above).

Gildas may have hailed from the Old North, possibly from the
banks of the Clyde (from Arecluta). He was a man of considerable learning and talent, who is recorded as having been a disciple at Illtud's famous school. He must have been deeply influenced by Latin culture, but had scant regard for the native
British culture, which seems to have acquired new vigour after
the collapse of Roman rule. Although probably not a monk
himself, he seems to have been associated with the monastic
movement, which made such progress in the second half of the
sixth century, but like many a reformer, in the latter part of his
life, he seems to have looked with disfavour on some of the more
'extreme' tendencies in the movement; cf. *HW* i. 142–3. The
church in Britain described by him is ruled by bishops, and
monks are in a minority. He was in Ireland, and also in Brittany,
where he died in Ruys, in the monastery he himself founded.

He composed a treatise or letter, known as *De Excidio Britanniae* 'Concerning the Destruction of Britain', a work in many
ways reminiscent of the manner and outlook of Old Testament
prophets,—relentless denunciation of the evils of the age, and
severe condemnation of the political and ecclesiastical leaders of
the Britons (*Gildas* i. 148, ii. 149–252). But the monks are
commended for their godly living. He mentions by name five
chieftains, from the west and south west, and among them
Maelgwn Gwynedd, and Gwrthefyr (*Guortepir*, see above) in
Dyfed (*Gildas* i. 68–87). He is scathing also in his condemnation
of the enemies of the Britons, the Picts and Scots, and especially
the Saxons (cc. 19, 23).

According to the *De Excidio* (c. 26), he was born in the year of
the battle of Badon, which occurred in 516 according to *Annales
Cambriae* (see *N* 85). The Annals of Redon are wildly at vari-
ance with this date, and give 421 as the year of his birth; cf *SC*
xii/xiii (1977/8), 44. The latter date, namely 421, may ultimately
derive from a Breton source (ibid. 48).

From the evidence of most of the sources, he seems to have been a contemporary of David, but it does not appear that they collaborated at any time, or that they belonged to the same movement. David may have advocated standards of asceticism, regarded as excessive by Gildas in the latter part of his life; see *HW* i. 156. However, there must have been a strong tradition supporting Gildas's name and fame in parts of Britain and outside, or else there would not have been the desire to 'demote' him, as there is here. But it appears that the impact he made in areas of the west, such as Wales and Cornwall, was very slight; not a single church bears his name in Wales. According to the *Annales Cambriae* he died in 570; see *N* 85, and cf. *HW* i. 142 n.

Here it is instructive to note the reference in the Irish *Life* of Finnian of Clonard to that saint's visit to *Cell Muine*, where he met David, Gildas and Cathmael (Cadog). 'This was the cause of their being gathered together there—a contention for the headship and abbacy of the island of Britain between two of them, that is, between David and Gildas'. Finnian awarded David the island because of his *seniority*. Later, however, the British saints (including David and Gildas) through the wondrous offices of Finnian acquired land for the building of a church. 'Three monasteries were founded by them thereon. Of these is Lann Gabran to-day'. (Stokes, *Lives of Saints from the Book of Lismore*, Oxford, 1890, pp. 222–3). The place mentioned could well be Llancarfan. In the original Irish we find *Lann Gharban* (*no Gabran*) (ibid. 76). We find the same story in Caradog's *Life* of Gildas; see Mommsen, *Chron Min* iii. 106–10. Cf. also M. Miller, *SC* xii/xiii. 49.

Two *Lives* of him were written, the two being very different. The earlier (the more valuable and reliable), which may be assigned to the ninth century, was written in Ruys, Brittany. The other is later, probably mid-twelfth century, and was composed by Caradog of Llancarfan; see *Gildas* ii. 322–413, P. Grosjean, *Analecta Bollandiana* lx 35f.

The reference to him by name in the Vespasian text seems to be indicative of the influence on that text of traditions and texts derived from the south-eastern part of Wales; cf. xlii. He may well have been associated in the mind of the redactor with that area, and this more than the sixth-century situation may have prompted the author to emphasize David's superiority. He was anxious to promote the claims of St David's in opposition to those of Llandaff, or Llancarfan. Further evidence of Gildas's association with the south east comes from the *Life* of Illtud, where, as in the *Life* of St Paul Aurelian (see xvii), he is named as one of his disciples; see ibid. In that *Life* there is mention of a bell from Gildas, intended for David, but which is eventually presented to the master, Illtud (*VSBG* 222).

2

On him generally, see *Gildas* i and ii, *HW* i. 134–43, *LSD*
73–5, *DWB* 277–9, and also a valuable article by Mrs N. K.
Chadwick, *SGS* vii, 115–83.

28   **nys gallei,** 'he could not (do) it'. *nys* consists of the negative *ny*
+ *'s,* infixed pron. object 3 sing.; see *GMW* 55.

Gildas was unable to preach, because there was present someone greater than he, namely David, although he was as yet only
in his mother's womb. A version of this tale occurs in the *Life* of
Gildas by Caradog of Llancarfan; see *Gildas* ii. 398, 400, *LSD*
46–7. There the miracle occurred by the sea at a church in
Pebidiog. According to Giraldus, the church was in a place
called *Kanmorva* (or *Kairmorva*), *urbs maritima vel castrum*
(*Opera* iii. 381). According to Wade-Evans, 'doubtless the
"Morva" intended by Gerald is the well-known one, which lies
south of the Cathedral between Porthclais and St Non's Bay';
see further *LSD* 72–3.

Another version of the story (probably derived from
Rhigyfarch) is found in the *Life* of the Irish saint, Ailbe; see
VSH i. 153, also *LSD* 38–9. It is said that Ailbe found a saint
who could not say mass. He noticed among the congregation a
certain pregnant woman, and told the priest 'The reason thou
canst not offer is because this woman has in her womb a bishop.
He is David of *Cill Muni*. For a priest ought not to celebrate in
the presence of a bishop, except at his bidding'. According to
another version, 'The reason thou canst not speak is because
God hath willed that the fame of the infant, which that woman
has in her womb, should first be heard. For he shall be the elect
of God, and a renowned bishop, and will be called 'David'; see
LSD 39, and cf. *Slover* 91–3. In Ireland, according to the canons
attributed to Patrick, Auxilius and Iserninus (dating from the
sixth century), 'no priest might say mass in a church he had built
until the bishop of his *paruchia* had consecrated it; no stranger
might minister in the *paruchia* without the bishop's authority'.
Cf. *CEIS* 50.

The tradition was known to Geoffrey of Monmouth: *Menevia
pallio urbis legionum induetur et predicator Hybernie propter
infantem in utero crescentem obmutescet* (*HRB* 385). But the
predicator in this case was Patrick.

allann, MS *alla│ann.*

31   **y rwg,** *y rwng* 'between'. *g* is occasionally used for *ng*[ŋ], as
here; cf. *GMW* 8.

y rwg y dor a'r paret, 'between the door and the wall'. The
Welsh here agrees with the Vespasian text; cf. p. liii above.
There we find *inter ualuam et parietem*. The earlier versions have
Ego ... hic lateo 'I am here hiding'. Cf. *RLSD* 4.

32   **plwyf,** now it means 'parish', but earlier it meant 'people,
congregation', as here. It comes from Lat. *plēb-em*.

p.   l.
2

y le 'to his place'—*y* representing *y* 'to' + *y* 'his/her'. Cf. *y gyuoeth ac y wlat* 'to his domain and to his land' *PKM* 8.4–5. See under 2.6 *y duhudaw* above.

3   4   **Hep y Nonn,** 'Said Nonn': *y* is not the definite article, but rather belongs to the verb. The forms are *hebyr, heby, heb; heby* is here wrongly divided as *heb* (hep) and *y*. See *GMW* 154. Cf. *Heb y* Gildas yna.

Llyma vivi, 'Here am I!'. *Llyma* is from *syll yma* 'look here'; *GMW* 246.

4–5   **y mab yssy yg kroth y lleian honn,** for references to Irish unborn saints speaking from their mothers' wombs, cf. *LSBL* 232, 246, 343. On the loss of *-d* [ð] in *yssy,* cf. *issi, triti (trydydd* 'third') in the *Computus Fragment* in OW. See *B* iii (1927), 256. Also *eiste* 2.27 below.

5   **y vedyant,** 'his might, authority'. Here we have an example of a noun, preceded by a possessive pron., modifying the meaning of a preceding adjective. This is a common construction in Welsh; cf. *bychan y gorff* 'small in body' *B* ii. 23.13, *da eu diodef* 'good in suffering, long-suffering' 14.8 below. Here *voe y vedyant* means 'greater in might', lit. 'greater his might'; see *GMW* 37. On *moe/mwy* see ibid. 4.

5–6   **idaw ef ehun,** 'to him only'; see *GMW* 90.

6   **holl seint Kymry,** 'all the saints of Wales'. Cf. Lat. *cunctos Brytanniȩ doctores (RLSD* 5), although the sentences in the two versions do not correspond exactly. As for the use of *Britannia* for Wales, cf. Wade-Evans, *VSBG* viii.

In MW the one form *Kymry* means both Wales and Welshmen.

8   **hwy,** 'longer', here used adverbially. Cf. y drigyaw *a vo hwy* 12.12–13 below, where a relative construction (*a vo*) is used to denote the adverbial use of the comparative, see *GMW* 229. Later the most common construction is to employ *yn* (the adverbial particle) with the comparative.

10   **ynys arall,** both *Lives* agree that he went to Ireland; see *HW* i. 142. Cf. the *Life* of Gildas by Caradog of Llancarfan: *Unde contigit, quod sanctissimus praedicator Gildas transivit ad Hiberniam* 'Then it happened that the most holy preacher Gildas crossed to Ireland' (*Gildas* ii. 400). There 'he converted countless people to the Catholic faith'. *ynys* and the Lat. *insula* can also mean 'monastery'; see Taylor *LSSD* 26. In the *Life* of Cadog he is mentioned as having arrived from Ireland—*ab Hibernensium finibus (VSBG* 84).

Note also the tradition linking Gildas with Brittany, where he is supposed to have died; cf. 2.27 *Gildas sant* above; also *HW* i. 143.

11   **ef a,** here used as a pre-verbal affirmative particle; see *GMW* 172. Also 3.15, 12.15 below.

p.   l.

3   15   **pann vedydywyt,** in the Latin *Life* it is said that he was baptized by the Irish saint Ailbe, the patron saint of Munster; see *VSH* i. 46–64. There was a church dedicated to him in Pebidiog, namely Llan*eilfyw* (Llan*eilw*, St *Elvis*), some four miles east of St David's; also Fagwr *Eilw* two miles to the north, in Llanhywel parish. In the *Life* of St Ailbe (*VSH* i. 53) it is said of the infant David that 'his father gave him to St Ailbe to bring him up to God' (*LSD* 39).

According to Giraldus (*Opera* iii. 383), he was baptized in Porth Clais, a harbour a mile to the south west of St David's, where the river Alun enters the sea. Ailbe had arrived there from Ireland by divine providence. In the tale *Kulhwch ac Olwen* we are told that the Twrch Trwyth landed there from Ireland: Disgynnu a wnaeth twrch trwyth ym *porth cleis* yn dyuet 'Twrch Trwyth came ashore at Porth Cleis in Dyfed' (*WM* 500. 36–8). It was here also that Gruffudd ap Cynan landed with a fleet from Waterford in 1081; see *HGVK* 13, 73. Cf. further *LSD* 77.

16   **ffynnyawn,** consonantal *i* (here -*y*-) is sometimes found in positions where it appears to have no phonological justification; cf. *GMW* 6n.

Cf. the reference by Browne Willis to a spring near the harbour: 'near the Key stands *Capel-y-Pistyll*, which has its name from a Spring that runs under it, into a Cistern at the East End, under the Pinion'. (*Survey* 55, 52).

A fountain also appeared when Cadog was baptized; see *VSBG* 30.

dall, 'a blind (man)'. Lat. *Moui ceci oculos* 'the eyes of blind Movi' (*RLSD* 6). Doubtless we are here again reminded of links with Ireland, whence probably came the blind man. *Movi* may be equated with the Irish *Mobi*, of Glasnevin, who also was 'flat-faced'; see *MOC* 216, 222, 224.

17   **daly** 'to hold'. The -*y*- is non-syllabic, deriving from original *g*; see *GMW* 10. ModW *dal(a)*. Cf. under 1.10 *hely* above.

19   **y ganet** 'he was born'. *y* consists of the particle *y* and the infixed pronoun object 3 sing. *y*; see *GMW* 55.

20   **wynebclawr** 'flat-faced', without nose or eyes. It consists of *wyneb* 'face' + *clawr* 'face, surface, lid, cover, board' = Ir. *clár*.

Cf. Gwynfardd Brycheiniog (*c.* 1180):

> Pan deuth o Freinc Franc o'e erchi,
> Yechyd rac clefyd rac clwyf delli,
> *Wynepclawr* ditawr dim ny weli,
> Pesychwys, dremwys drwy vot Dewi. (*HGCr* 48. 158–61)

It appears, as Henry Lewis suggests (*HGCr* 192), that with the reference to *Franc* and *Freinc* a different incident is referred to

p.   *l.*
3

here. But the reference by ? Iolo Goch (*c.* 1340–98) is to the same incident as here:

> Eilwaith y rhoes ei olwg
> I'r claf drem rhag clefyd drwg,
> Ei dad bedydd, dud bydawl,
> Dall *wynepglawr*, mawr fu'r mawl.   (*IGE* 101. 6–10)

Cf. Irish *clár-enech*; see *CIL* 381, *clár aighthe* in the *Life* of Máedóc (Aidán), *BNE* i. 185. 11–12. In another version of the *Life* of this saint, we find the following: *Do bi neach ele i mBretnaibh 'gá raibhe a acchaid 'na haon clár uile, gan súil, gan sróin, do bi marsin aga breith. Ruccadh go Maedhócc é da leicches* 'There was another among the Britons whose face was one surface, without eye, without nose, and he had been born like that. He was brought to Máedóc to be cured' (*BNE* i. 210). In the Latin version of this *Life* we find, *Vir quidam in Brittania, tabulatum faciem habens, id est sine oculis et naribus ex utero natus, adductus est ad Sanctum Moedhog causa curandi* (*VSH* ii. 146). Cf. also *LSD* 36–7.

It is likely that this reference to the curing of a blind man, and the appearance of a spring is derived from an Irish source. A similar incident is recorded in a version of the *Life* of Patrick: *Ó rogenair iarom intí noem Patraic issed rucad cusin mac ndall claireinech dia baitsiud* 'Then when holy Patrick was born, he was brought to the blind flat-faced youth to be baptized' (*TLP* 8). No water was available, and the blind youth made the sign of the cross with the infant's hand above the earth, so that there sprang forth a fountain of water. He washed his face with that water, and was cured (ibid.); also *LSBL* 150–1, where the flat-faced youth is named Gornias. See *AC* 1920, 224–50, *RC* xlv (1928), 146–8, also *LSD* 77, *SEBC* 142.

One of the miracles attributed to Brigit was that 'she blessed the blind table-faced man, and gave his eyes to him' (*LSBL* 197).

y olwc a gauas, 'he got his sight'. Note the order: *Object + a + Verb*, another possible variant of the Abnormal Sentence; see *GMW* 179–80, and cf. 1.7 *Keredic vrenhin a wledychawd* above.

20–1   **a chwbl o'r a berthynei arnnei** 'and all that appertained to it', lit. 'and all of that which …'. For *cwbl* 'the whole, all', see *GMW* 100–1. *o'r a* consists of the preposition *o* 'of' + *ar*, a demonstrative which serves as antecedent to a relative clause (*GMW* 70–1), + *a*, relative pronoun. The preposition *ar* is commonly used with *perthynu* 'to relate, appertain (to)' in MW; see *B* xv (1952), 10.

21   **dylyynt,** 'they ought': 3 pl. imperf. of the verb *dyly-u*. The stem is *dyly* (cf. Irish *dlig-im*, *L&P* 30); see *GMW* 151–2.

p.   l.

3   22   **Y lle:** MS *Yny lle.*

Vetus Rubus, cf. Giraldus (*Opera* iii. 284): qui et Kambrice *Hen-meneu* Latine vero *Vetus Menevia* vocatur 'which is called in Welsh *Hen Meneu* (Hen Fynyw), but in Latin *Vetus Menevia*'. *Henllwyn* is but a translation of the Latin. It is difficult to determine which place is meant, either Hen Fynyw in Ceredigion, a little to the south of Aberaeron (see *LSD* 78–9, 83–5), or some other unidentified place much closer to St David's, but a little to the north of it; see below. In 9.8, 11.22 below *dinas Rubi* occurs for St David's; see further 9.5 *Mynyw yn y deheu* below.

23   **seilym,** old pl. of *salym* 'psalm', a learned borrowing from the Lat. *psalma.* Note the occurrence of the epenthetic *y* in *seilym*; see *GMW* 12–13, also 1.1 *talym* above.

Of the essential role of the Scriptures in Celtic Christianity, cf. *CCB* 29–51.

24   **colomen,** a dove was present when Samson was ordained deacon, and bishop; see *LSSD* 19–20, 45; also the *Life* of Illtud, *VSBG* 214.

26   **Odyna yr aeth Dewi,** .... It appears that we have here an attempt to reconcile two different traditions about David's education; see *HW* i. 54. Another version is found in the *Life* of St Paul Aurelian, and in the *Life* of Illtud, where Dewi is named among the latter's disciples; see *RC* v. 421, *VSBG* 208.

Paulinus, a saint from the north east of old Carmarthenshire, and possibly to be identified with Saint Paul Aurelian of Brittany (a fellow-pupil of David; see p. xvii), whose cult seems to be centred on St Pol de Léon. We meet him again in the account of the synod of Brefi, pp. 8–11. In the *Life* of St Paul Aurelian by Gourmonoc (*c.* 884) it is said that he hailed from a place called *Brehant Dincat*, probably Llandingad, the parish in which Llandovery is situated; see *LWS* 147, 150–2, *Doble* i. 12, 33–4, *SSSCL* 175–8 (Earlier in the *Life* there is mention of *Penn Ohen, RC* iv. 418; cf. *LWS* 147–9).

There are traces of his cult in the neighbourhood of Llandovery. Two chapels are dedicated to him in the parish of Llandingad, at Capel Peulin and at Nant-y-bai; there is also a holy well called Ffynnon Beulin. The parish church of Llan-gors, east of Brecon, is dedicated to him, and there is also a chapel called Llan*beulin*. The name occurs in a number of inscriptions of the fifth and sixth centuries (*LHEB* 323), the most interesting of which from our point of view is the one in Caeo, to the north west of Llandovery. This belongs to the first half of the sixth century, and it contains the words, HIC PAVLINVS IACIT 'Here lies Paulinus'; see *ECMW* 107, *LWS* 155. But, as Doble suggests, 'it does not necessarily follow that this stone commemorates our saint . ... The inscription . . . sounds more

p.   l.
3   like the epitaph of a virtuous and pious layman' (*LWS* 155). See
             further *Doble* i. 10–60, *LWS* 146–61.

             It is stated here that he was a disciple of a saintly bishop from
             Rome (3.27). According to the Latin *Life*, he was a disciple of
             Germanus, the famous saint from Auxerre, who twice visited
             Britain, in 429 and sometime in the 440s, to help with the
             struggle against the Pelagian heresy.

             In the *Life* of Teilo (*LL* 99; see also *LWS* 154, 168–71) it is
             said that that saint also was a disciple of Paulinus (*Poulinus*).
             Llandeilo Fawr, a little to the south of Llandovery, was Teilo's
             centre. Doble maintains that Paulinus's first monastery was at
             Llanddeusant, seven and a half miles south east of Llandovery;
             see *LWS* 150–2. In the Vespasian text of the Latin *Life* of David
             we are told that Paulinus was 'in a certain island' (*in insula
             quadam RLSD* 6), which could well mean 'monastery'. Both
             David and Teilo may thus have been together as disciples at
             Llanddeusant. Note also the references in the *Lives* of St Paul
             Aurelian and St Illtud to Paulinus and David as disciples of
             Illtud (see *RC* v. 421, *VSBG* 208), in which case Paulinus could
             hardly have been David's teacher. But the tradition represented
             in the *Life* of David and elsewhere seems to be more consistent
             with verifiable evidence. The tradition connecting Paulinus with
             Whitland is certainly late; see *HW* i. 151.

28   **athro,** cf. the Vespasian text: *quoque eum docuit in tribus
             partibus lectionis donec fuit scriba* 'and who taught him in the
             three parts of reading, until he was a *scribe*' (*RLSD* 6).

             Cf. Kathleen Hughes in her discussion of Irish law: 'The high
             rank of *scriba*, or *suí* (sage, *sapiens*), is indicated in the secular as
             well as in the ecclesiastical laws. His presence indicates a school
             of Latin learning and his prestige was analogous to that of the *fili*
             who professed secular learning.' (*CEIS* 136).

30   **colli o athro Dewi y lygeit,** 'that David's teacher lost (the sight
             of) his eyes'. The whole clause is the subject of the verb
             damweinawd '(it) happened', and it consists of the verbal noun
             colli, followed by the subject *athro Dewi*, which is preceded by
             the preposition *o*,—a common construction for denoting the
             subject of the verbal noun in MW; see *GMW* 161, and cf. 2.1
             ethol ohonaw above.

32–3   **y'm poeni,** '(they are) causing me pain'. Here *y* is used with the
             infixed pron. genitive 1 sing. before the verbal noun, to form a
             present participle in the periphrastic construction; see *GMW*
             199, and Arwyn Watkins, *B* xviii (1960), 362–72.

34   **yr ys,** 'for, since', with a noun denoting a period of time; cf.
             GMW 142–3. Also 2.14 above.

35   **y'th wyneb di,** = *yn dy wyneb di* 'in thy face'. On the use of *y* =
             yn before a noun with a possessive pronoun 1 or 2 sing. or pl.,
             cf. Arwyn Watkins, *B* xvii (1957), 137–58.

p. l.
3   35   **ryuedu,** 'to wonder at'. In MW, unlike ModW where *at* is used with it, the verb is used with a direct object: *Ryuedu* hynny yn uawr a wnaeth 'He wondered greatly at that' *PKM* 59.15. See further *LlC* v (1959), 117.

36   **kewilyd,** 'modesty'. Cf. Vespasian text: *nimiam uerecundiam admirans illius* 'wondering at his excessive modesty' *RLSD* 7. But the meaning in 5.32 below is 'shame, insult' (Vespasian text: *intolerabilem iniuriam* 'unbearable insult' ibid. 10).

4   3   **o** 'with, by, by means of': *o* is often used in MW to denote manner; see *GMW* 204.

3-4   **ynn ysgriuennedic,** MS *ynny* | *ysgriuennedic.*

4   **dedyf,** Vesp. text *testamento* 'testament' *RLSD* 7. Note the use of the epenthetic vowel *y*; see *GMW* 12, and cf. 1.1 *talym*, 3.23 *seilym* above.

7   **ysyd dyghetuen y gan Duw idaw y wnneuthur,** 'which are destined by God for him to do'. Here we should expect *y mae* and not *ysyd*, at the beginning of the relative clause, where the relative depends on a verbal noun; see *CFG* 86–91. Note also that the possessive pron. *y* before the verbal noun *(g)wnneuthur* is 3. sing. masc. (as is shown by the following soft mutation), despite the fact that the antecedent to which it refers is plural. There are other exs. of this in M and ModW, and it is still found in the spoken language; see *BD* xl, *TC* 162–3, *GMW* 65n.

A noteworthy feature of Irish *Lives* is the departure of a disciple from a monastic school, after he has shown by a notable miracle that he has acquired great sanctity; cf. *Doble* iii. 125.

The itinerary here described is indicative more of Rhigy-farch's aims and motives than of the movements of the historical David. It commences from Somerset, across Mercia, as far as Crowland, then back to Repton and down through Elfael (in Powys) to Leominster, and then to Gwent; thence westwards through Llangyfelach and Cydweli (? and Meidrim), back to Hen Fynyw. Rhigyfarch clearly was anxious to show that the privileges and claims of St David's extended over areas of England; he may possibly have been asserting a claim to metropolitan rights over these parts; cf. *LSD* 80–1. David was thus shown to have a widespread *paruchia*.

8   **Glastynburi,** Glastonbury in Somerset. This is what Silas Harris has to say of the tradition linking David with that foundation:

There is no inherent reason why David should not have had something to do with the monastic foundation at Glas-tonbury, as Rhygyfarch and Giraldus assert that he had, and it is certainly the most reasonable explanation of the early appropriation of his name by that abbey. Already in the eighth century Glastonbury was claiming 'the blessed David' as its chief patron after our Lady, and in the next

century asserted itself (albeit falsely) to be in possession of
his relics. This considerably antedates Rhygyfarch, as does
the liturgical witness to the cultus of St David at Glastonbury. (*SDL* 71).

It must have been one of the earliest centres of Christianity in
Britain, but one must have misgivings about any suggestion that
David had something to do with its foundation. However,
British Christians may well have regarded it as their centre, in
opposition to Canterbury. William of Malmesbury visited it in
1125, and wrote an account of its history.

    adeilawd, 'built': 3 sing. pret. with the ending *-awd*; see
GMW 125. The stem was *adeil-* (*ad* + *eil-*), and the verbal noun
adeil-at; see *GMW* 158. Later the form of the verbal noun was
adopted as stem, with the personal endings added to it. And a
new form of the verbal noun was produced, *adeilad-u*.

12   **yr Enneint Twymynn,** 'the Hot Bath': Bath, in Somerset.
Ptolemy (*c.* 150) calls it ὕδατα θερμα 'hot springs'. In the *Anto-
nine Itinerary* it is referred to as *Aquae Sulis* 'The waters of Sul'.
In the *Anglo-Saxon Chronicle* it is *Bathan ceaster*, with which
may be equated Welsh *Caerfaddon*.

    enneint means 'bath'; see *PKM* 138, *G* 479, *GPC* 1218. As for
the term *enneint twymyn*, cf. Brut y Brenhinedd: A'r gvr hunv
[namely Rhun, son of Bleiddudd] a adeilvs *Caer Uadon* ac a
wnaeth yr *enneint twymyn* yr medeginyaeth y rei marwavl 'And
that man built Caerfaddon, and made the hot bath for healing
the mortally sick' *BD* 25.31–26.2; see also note on p. 216.

13   **Krowlan,** Crowland, in the extreme south of Lincolnshire,
founded by St Guthlac (d. 714); cf. Farmer, *The Oxford Dic-
tionary of Saints* (Oxford, 1978), 184–5, *ASC* 43.

    Repecwn, Repton, in the south of Derbyshire, near Lichfield.
A monastery existed there as early as the seventh century; see
LSD 81–2.

14   **Collan,** 'Colva, Radnorshire, now a chapel of ease
[St David's] under Glascwm' *LSD* 82.

    Glascwm, Glasgwm, in Elfael (south Radnorshire); one of the
most important of the churches dedicated to David; see *HW*
i. 254–5. Giraldus mentions a bell possessing miraculous
powers, which belonged to this church:

> In the church at Glascwm, in Elfael, there is a handbell
> which has most miraculous powers. It is supposed to have
> belonged to Saint David and it is called a 'bangu'. In an
> attempt to liberate him, a certain woman took this handbell
> to her husband, who was chained up in the castle of Rhaiadr
> Gwy, in Gwrthrynion, which castle Rhys ap Gruffydd had
> built in our time. The keepers of the castle not only refused

to set the man free, but they even seized the bell. That same night God took vengeance on them, for the whole town was burned down, except the wall on which the handbell hung. (*GW* 79).

The poet Gwynfardd Brycheiniog (*c.* 1180) also refers to the bell, and connects it with Glasgwm; see *HGCr* 45.54–8.

Note also the reference in a grant of the 'vill of Glascum' to St David's (1215–22) to 'sufficient proof that the church of St David's from of old was in possession of the vill of Glascom'; cf. *EAWD* i. 352, *St Bk of St David's* (A), 138–9.

15   **Llannllieni,** MS *lann llieni*: Leominster in Herefordshire; on the banks of the river Lugg, not the Severn, as is stated here. A mandate by the bishop of St David's (1204–14) informs that all who do injury to the church of Leominster be excommunicated; see *EAWD* i. 342.

16   **Pebiawc,** *Pepiau* in the Vesp. MS and in some of the later MSS of the Digby recension; see *RLSD* 34. *Pe(i)piau* is mentioned in *LL* 72–6, 78–9. Here in the *Life* he is described as blind, and is cured by David. In *LL* 78 he is *clavorauc* 'drivelling, foaming, leprous'. His father was Erb, and his daughter Efrddyl, the mother of Dubricius, Dyfrig. When the father saw that she was pregnant, he sought to destroy her, but in vain. He was cured of his disease by the touch of the infant Dubricius's hand; see *LL* 79. Peibyaw occurs as a name in *Kulhwch ac Olwen* (*WM* 480–1); note also Garth*beibio* in Montgomery, and Ynys *Beibio*, near Holyhead.

J. W. James has pointed out that the form found in the other Latin texts, those of Nero, the earlier Digby MSS, and Giraldus (the passage does not occur in the Irish recension) is *Proprius*, which must be regarded as the earlier, though not necessarily the more correct reading; see *RLSD* 8.33–4n.

Ergyng, Archenfield. Cf. J. E. Lloyd:

> Erging was bounded by the Wye, the Worm and the Monnow, though so close to the gates of Hereford, it was a stronghold of Welsh customs and ideas as late as the end of the twelfth century. The Welsh Saints were honoured throughout the district, and among them St David had a great church at Much Dewchurch, and Dyfrig, who was (if we may believe his legend) by birth and residence a man of Erging, a group of churches which commanded the allegiance of the dwellers along the winding banks of the Wye (*HW* i. 280).

This ancient cantref was the subject of contention between Llandaff and Hereford in the twelfth century, as is evidenced in the *Book of Llan Dâv*; cf. *EAWD* i. 120–1, 150. It was eventually retained within Hereford; ibid. 180. It is noteworthy that Rhigyfarch should here wish to associate David with this area in south-west Hereford, where the cult of Dubricius (the founder saint of Llandaff) was so much in evidence.

See also *G* 485. In the MS the line is repeated and underlined, but with the omission of *yg Gwent*, and with a double *n* in *raclann*.

17   **Gwent,** the country between the rivers Usk, Wye, Monnow and the sea. It consisted of two cantrefs separated by a great forest, Gwent Is Coed and Gwent Uch Coed. To the west lay the cantref of Gwynllŵg. After the Act of Union (1536), Gwynllŵg and Gwent were joined together, to form Monmouthshire.

Raclan, Rhaglan in Gwent Uch Coed. The church is now dedicated to St Cadog.

18   **Llanngyfuelach,** Llangyfelach in Morgannwg, a little to the north of Swansea. It must have been an important centre of David's cult, and may well have been founded by him. It was here that the gifts awarded to him by the Patriarch of Jerusalem arrived, conveyed by angels; see *RLSD* 21, 43.

19   **Gwyr,** Gower, the country between the rivers Loughor and Tawe, from the foot of the Black Mountains to the end of the peninsula extending westwards from Swansea; see *HW* i. 269. As for the form, cf. *Guhir LL* 35.1, *Guher* 41.2, *Guoher* 42.16, *Goher* 55.24.

20   **Kedweli,** Vesp. text *in prouincia Cetgueli*, a commote which originally consisted of the whole country between the rivers Loughor and Tywi; later the western part of the area was known as Carnwyllion. Along with Gwyr (and later Carnwyllion) it formed the cantref of Eginog, one of the seven cantrefs of Ystrad Tywi; see *HW* i. 269.

This sentence (lines 20–21) is found in the Vesp. text, but does not occur in the earlier recensions.

Boducat a Nailtrum, nothing is known of either of these two names.

Boducat, the second element must be *cat* 'battle, army'; cf. Dina*cat EWGT* 10. As for the first element, cf. *Bodgu* 'Boddw' ibid. 12, *bodu CA* 18.438, *Bodv*oci on the Margam Mountain inscription, *ECMW* 146. It occurs as second element in a number of forms: Art*bodgu EWGT* 12, El*bodgu* ibid. El*bodugus*, Elu*od Ll* 179.27 (see *G* 467), Guru*odu* ibid. 179.13, 190.18, Guor*uodu* ibid. 191.25. *Catuodu* occurs in Breton; see *ChBr* 110. Cf. Irish *bodb* 'a scald-crow', according to *CIL* 234; also *Bodb* as a personal name (*AO* 50). On the Celtic root *boduo-*, see *ACS* 461, *GPN* 151.

Nailtrum, Vesp. text *Martrun*, or *Maitrun*. It is difficult to make anything of these forms. Perhaps the name intended was

p.   *l.*

4   that of *Meidrim*, a place to the west of Carmarthen, where the church is dedicated to David. Cf. also Gwynfardd Brycheiniog:

A Dewi bieu bangeibyr yssyt
Meitrym le a'e mynwent y luossyt.   (*HGCr* 46. 89–90).

22   **ymhoelawd,** 'returned', apparently written *ymhoelawt* originally, but later corrected. *-es* is the ending usually found in MW with verbs where the stem contains *-o-/-oe-*; see *GMW* 122. Here we have *-awd*, the ending which became general later with all types of verbs. Its use here indicates that it was already beginning to encroach upon *-es*; see ibid. 125, also *B* xvii (1958), 260.

   y lle a elwit Vetus Rubus, 'the place which was called *Vetus Rubus*'. Rhigyfarch wants to show that it was here David had intended to settle, before he received a strong hint from the angel to move elsewhere.

23   **Goeslan,** Lat. *Guisdianus*, etc. Vesp. text. *Guistilianus*; see *RLSD* 8n. He may have been David's teacher in Hen Fynyw or *Vetus Rubus*; see *HW* i. 154. Wade-Evans suggests that David took him with him to Glyn Rhosyn, *LSD* 85–6. It appears that there was a tradition associating him with David. In MS Vespasian A xiv, in the Calendar of the saints of Wales he is included under March 2; see *LBS* i. 66.

   Another form was *Gwes(t)lan* 6.23, 6.27 below.

   brawt ffyd, 'brother (in the) faith', clearly a mistranslation of the Lat. *fratruelis* 'father's brother's son'. But Wade-Evans (*LSD* 86) suggests that it could mean 'father's brother' or 'uncle'. That is how the relationship is described by Giraldus, *avunculus* (*Opera* iii. 386).

24   **Angel yr Arglwyd a dywot y mi,** 'the angel of the Lord told me'. There are many references in the *Life* to a visit by the angel, who brings with him a message or instruction: 1.9, 16, 2.6, 4.5, 24, 9.3, 12.3. Paulinus says that an angel was constantly with David as companion: 8.22–29. According to the *Life* of Patrick by Muirchú, the saint had an angel as guide throughout his life; *SEBC* 140–1.

25   **A dangosses y mi le arall,** 'And he showed me another place', by which must be understood Mynyw or St David's. In the Vespasian text we have *Ostenditque mihi locum* 'And he showed me a place' (*RLSD* 9), but in earlier versions we find *est autem alius prope locus* 'but there is another place *near*' (ibid.).

26   **nyt a neb y vffern,** 'no one will go to hell': an echo of an early primitive belief that the sanctity of a place ensures salvation; see *VSH* i. xciii. Note the angel's words to St Cadog: *omnesque uestri familiares amici, qui in hoc loco defuncti fuerunt, a gehennalibus erunt extorres suppliciis* 'and all your familiar friends, who shall have died in this place, will be liberated from the sufferings of hell' (*VSBG* 60, 61). In the *Life* of the Irish saint,

Bairre, after referring to the fixing of the boundaries of the graveyard of his church, it is declared: *Omnis quicumque in humo huius cimiterii sepultus fuerit, infernus super eum post diem iudicii non claudetur* 'Whosoever will have been buried in the earth of this graveyard, hell will not be closed over him after the Day of Judgement'. (*VSH* i. 71). Also the *Life* of Senán (*LSBL* 67. 2242–3): '*Roir Dia duit*', *or in t-aingel*, '*ni ba hithfer-nach iar mbrath anti dara ragha úir na hinnsi-si*' 'God has granted to thee,' said the angel, 'that over whom the mould of the island shall go, shall not be after Judgement an inhabitant of hell'. We learn that Brendan and Jarlath composed a hymn on Tuam, in which there is a promise that no one buried there should go to hell; cf. *LBS* i. 235. Note Kathleen Hughes's comment on this feature in the saint's *Life* (*CEIS* 225): 'Like other saints' Lives, it stresses the spiritual advantages which accrue from burial in the saint's cemetery, and burial . . . brought substantial fees to the monastery'. Enda requested before he died that 'no one dying in true contrition and buried in his churchyard should go to hell'; see *Doble* iii. 121. Ciaran made a similar request; cf. ibid. iv. 11. Ciaran is said to have come to Aird Manntain, beside the Shan-non, a delightful place, 'but few souls will go hence to heaven'. He came to another place: 'Here then we will stay, for many souls will go to heaven hence.' (*LSBL* 275). Cf. further *CCB* 164.

The *Lives* of the saints (Welsh and Irish) are full of primitive and pagan concepts and beliefs; see *VSH* i. cxxix–clxxxviii. An attempt is sometimes made to give the belief a more Christian look. Here this is done by adding that good faith and belief are also necessary. Gwynfardd Brycheiniog (*c.* 1180), however, is more primitive. He says that anyone who goes to the grave of David's cemetery will not go to hell and its suffering:

A el y medrawd mynwent Dewi,
Nyd a yn uffern, bengwern boeni.   (*HGCr* 48.166–7)

Also a later poet (? fourteenth century):

I bwll uffern ni fernir
Enaid dyn; yn anad tir,
A gladder, diofer yw,
Ym mynwent Dewi Mynyw.   (*IGE* 102.27–30)

In attributing special sanctity to Glyn Rhosyn, Rhigyfarch's in-tention was doubtless to show its superiority over another centre to the north, *Vetus Rubus* or Hen Fynyw; cf. *SEBC* 156–7.

o'r a, See *GMW* 70–1; also under 3.20 a *chwbl o'r a berthynei arnnei* above.

28   **dydgweith,** 'one day': *dyd* 'day' + *gweith* 'time', cf. un*weith* 'once'.

4   **Aedan,** also *Maydawc* (7.21): founder and bishop of Ferns in
Co. Wexford, and one of the Irish saints who had been disciples
of David (cf. 6.30–7.21, also p. 13 above). There are many references to David in his *Life*; see *VSH* ii. 144–7, also *LBS*
i. 116–26. An early recension of his *Life (Vita S. Aidui)* occurs in
Cotton Vespasian A xiv, where we also find the Latin text of the
Life of David. For other versions of his *Life*, see *SEHI* i. 449. He
was succeeded at Ferns by Senán, who is also reported to have
been with David; cf. *LSBL* 208–9.

Aedan is Irish, consisting of *aed* 'fire', and the diminutive
ending *-án* (**-agnos*). A hypocoristic form of his name is *Maedóc*
(Welsh *Maydawc*), formed from the stem *aed*, the prefix *mo*
'my', and the ending *-óc*. The latter, according to Thurneysen,
may be equated with the ending *-awc* (ModW-*og*) in Welsh: it
occurs in the names of Irish saints from the sixth century on; see
GOI 173–4. It is difficult to determine the relation between
Maeddog and Madog. The latter may well represent a different
saint, a Welsh saint venerated in Dyfed, who may have
collaborated with David. He has two churches on St Bride's
Bay. He is also remembered in Llanmadog in Gower, Llan-
fadog in Brecknock and at Capel Madog in the Elan valley; see
further *SCSW* 97, *SEBC* 189.

Aeddan has dedications at Llanhuadain (Llawhaden), Nol-
ton, Harolston West and Solfach (some three miles east of
St David's), in Pembrokeshire, see *SCSW* 97; also Tref Aeddan
(colloquially *Trefeiddan*), a farm between Clegyr Fwya and
Porth Stinan to the west of St David's, and Ffynnon Faeddog,
some 500 yards from the beach at Whitesand Bay, and a mile and
a half north west of St David's. We are told by John of Tynemouth
that in his time the feast of Aedan was observed at St David's; cf.
LBS i. 125.

29   **Eliud,** Eludd or Teilo. For the first element in the name, cf.
*El*bodgu 'Elfoddw', *El*ci, *El*cu, *El*gnou, *El*guarui, *El*guoret, *El*-
hebarn, etc, also *Ell*tud (the Welsh form of *Illtud*). *el* (Irish *il*)
means 'many' (<**pelu-s*), and is found only in compound forms;
see *B* viii (1935), 30–1. The second element is *udd* (<**iud*) 'lord',
cf. Marge*tiud* > Mared*udd*, Grip*iud* > Gruff*udd*; see *L&P* 14,
(*iud* represents an earlier orthography for *udd*). The hypocoristic form of this saint's name was *Teiliaw*, later *Teilo*. It was
formed from the first element *el*, with the prefix *ty* 'your' and the
ending *-(i)aw* (**-awo-*): thus *Ty-e(i)liaw* > *Te-e(i)liaw* >
Te(i)liaw, and through loss of consonantal *i* (a feature of south
Wales dialects, *Teilaw, Teilo*. For a similar formation, cf. *Ty-sul-
iaw/-io*; see *A Bret* x. 67, *AC* xii (1895), 37–8; Vendryes, *Choix
d'études linguistiques et celtiques* (Paris, 1952), 182–95.

Teilo is widely venerated in south Wales and in Brittany. His
centre was Llandeilo Fawr in the vale of Tywi, and most of his

churches belong to the south west. There are references to him
in marginal notes in the Book of St Chad, a manuscript now in
Lichfield Cathedral, which must have belonged at one time to
Llandeilo Fawr. This constitutes evidence of an active cult in the
ninth century. His *Life* was written by Geoffrey Stephen,
brother of Urban (d. 1134), bishop of Llandaff. He sought to
promote the claims of that diocese, and the name of Teilo was
linked with Llandaff, where he was claimed as the second of its
bishops. A version of his *Life* (clearly influenced by that of
David) occurs in *LL* 97–117; here he goes to Dol in Brittany (to
escape the Yellow Plague), and is made a bishop there. Another
Life corresponding closely with this (but containing a number of
significant omissions) occurs in BL Cotton Vespasian A xiv.
Geoffrey of Monmouth refers to him as Samson's successor as
archbishop of Dol; cf. *HRB* 458, also *BD* 161, where Samson is
described as 'archescob Caer Euravc' (*York*); note ibid. 272. He
returned to Wales after the Yellow Plague had abated, and
remained there till the end of his life. Three churches claimed his
body, Penally, Llandeilo Fawr and Llandaff.

    See further Loth, *ABret* ix. 81–5, 278–86, 438–46, x. 66–77,
and Doble, *LWS* 162–206; also *LSD* 87–9.

    Here Eludd is referred to as a disciple of David, likewise also
in 6.23–4 below. Rhigyfarch associates him with David, apparently in order to refute Llandaff's claim to Teilo churches. Giraldus (*Opera* vi. 102) makes him archbishop of St David's.

    Ysmael, little is known about him. In the *Life* of Teilo in *LL*
(115) we are told that it was he who succeeded David as bishop
of St David's. There are a number of churches bearing his name
in the south west; also Llanismel, near Cydweli (Carm.). His
cult probably flourished mainly in Dyfed. *Eglwys Ismael* (St Ish-
mael's on Milford Haven) is listed as one of the 'seven bishop-
houses in Dyfed', *LlB* 84.12.

30   **Hodnant,** Gwynfardd *Hotnant* (*HGCr* 50.228). Cf. Corn.
Hethenaunt; see *RC* xxxvii. 162. It must have been in common
use for *Vallis Rosina* (the only name used by Rhigyfarch) among
the Welsh. Cf. Vespasian text: *Rosinam Vallem, quam uulgari
nomine Hodnant Brittones uocitant* 'Rosina Vallis, which the
Britons [i.e. Welsh] call by the common name Hoddnant'
(*RLSD* 9). It occurs as the name of a valley in the *Life* of Illtud
(*VSBG* 200, 202, *LWS* 106, 126), where it is said that it means
uallis prospera in Latin; there Llanilltud must be the place
meant. It occurs as the name of a small stream (in former
Radnorshire) in Powys (*EANC* 151–2); also Blaen Porth *Hodnant* in Ceredigion (*BTy RB* 90); *HW* ii. 434n., *BTy Pen 20*[1]
168).

    Nant could formerly mean 'valley', and *Hodnant* is the name
of the valley, rather than of the small river which flows through

p.   l.

4   it. The first element is *hawdd* (*hodd*) in the meaning of
        'pleasant'. *Hodnant*, therefore, means 'pleasant valley'. In the
        Latin *Life* it is said that Patrick recognized that it was a *pleasant*
        place (*gratum* agnoscens locum *RLSD* 2).

31   **Kyntaf lle,** this must be taken as a reflection, at least in part, of
        the struggle between the missionaries of the new faith and the
        ministers of the old pagan religions. The latter were dislodged by
        the 'Saints', but not at once. For a period there must have been
        considerable confrontation, and also probably a measure of co-
        existence and co-operation. Eventually the old order ceased,
        but some of its features survived in the new. The 'Saints'
        inherited some of the customs and rights of the old orders, and
        also their lands. It is significant that many of the troubles we hear
        of are concerned with rights to land. Confrontation between a
        saint and a secular leader is not infrequently recorded, and the
        Life of a Welsh saint had to show him measuring his strength
        against the powers of this world and miraculously defeating
        them. In the *Life* of Cybi king Ethelic seeks to eject from his land
        the saint and his monks (*VSBG* 236). Also the *Life* of St Brynach
        (ibid. 8), where the ruler Clechre expresses concern at seeing
        smoke rising from a place where he knew there was no *tref* or
        farm; cf. *LBS* i. 323.

        The Irish *Lives* contain many references to such confronta-
        tions. Often, as here, the clash is occasioned by the saint lighting
        a fire. His authority extended as far as the smoke would reach.
        Also, the act of lighting a fire in a particular place signified
        settlement in it, and a claim to possession of it. See *VSH*
        i. clxv–clxvii, *RC* xlv (1928), 155–6.

        The account given here should be compared with the account
        of the dispute between Patrick and the wizards of king Loegaire.
        The night before Easter after landing in Ireland, he and his
        companions lit the Paschal fire in Magh Bregh. The fire was seen
        from Tara, and the king along with some of his men and his
        wizards sought to destroy Patrick, but he was overcome by the
        superior magic of the saint; see *LSP* 104–6, also 302–3, and
        LSBL 158, *IER* lxx (1948), 680–6. Likewise David here; it is not
        because of his superior saintliness, but rather because of his
        superior magic that he succeeds in worsting Boia.

32   **y kylchynawd y mwc hwnnw,** this is clearly designed to
        impress upon people the superiority of David as the greatest
        saint in these islands; cf. also 11.5–19.

5   1–2 **y bore glas,** 'early in the morning'. *glas* has various meanings,
        the colours 'blue, green, grey', also 'fresh, young'; see *GPC*
        1401–2.

    2   **pryt gosper,** 'evening': *pryt* 'time', *gosper* 'evening, evening
        prayer, vespers' from the Lat. *uesper(um)*; see *GPC* 1509.

    3   **Boya,** Lat. *Quidem . . . Baia uocatus* 'A certain man named

p.   *l.*
5

Baia' (*RLSD* 9), Vesp. text: *Quidam ... satrapa magusque, Baia uocatus* 'A certain chieftain and druid named Baia' (*VSBG* 155). Gwynfardd and Giraldus *Boia* (*HGCr* 50.229, *Opera* iii. 387). The name *Boia* was known in Cornwall in the tenth century, because it occurs as the name of a witness on several pages of the Bodmin Gospels; see Förster, *Miscellany offered to Otto Jespersen* (Copenhagen, 1930), 88, 92, 93, 94. *Boius* is the name of one of St Paul Aurelian's companions (*Doble* i. 19); see Rhys, *AC* xii (1895), 20–1, Vendryes, *RC* xlv (1928), 141–72, also *G* 70.

Boia is referred to in the *Life* of Teilo, but is not named. He is described as a prince of the Picts (*picti*), who had come to Britannia from Scythia. After causing slaughter, destruction and sacrilege, he settled in Mynyw and built his *palatium* there. Eventually, after unsuccessful encounters with Teilo, David, 'and the other servants of God who lived with them in the same place', he 'and all his house ... received the Catholic faith, and were baptized' (*LSD* 54–5; see also *LWS* 170–2). A variant of Boia is Bwya, which occurs in the name *Clegyr Fwya*, a rock about half a mile south west of St David's. It may be that this was the high rock on which Boia was sitting, see *LBS* ii. 298. This was excavated twice, in 1902 and 1943, and was found to contain a post-Roman Iron Age fort (possibly Boia's fort) and foundations of two Neolithic buildings; see *AC* iii (1903), 1–11, cii (1952), 20–47. According to the Latin *Life*, he was within the 'ramparts of his fortress' (*arcis menibus RLSD* 9). The fort meant may have been one originally known as *Caer Fwya*, later *Castell Pen-lan*, overlooking the Alun, and less than half a mile south west of St David's; see *LSD* 90–1. It was probably here that he met his death (6.12–14 below).

Yscot, 'Irishman': Vesp. text *Scottus*, but not in the earlier versions. For exs. of the use of *Yscot* for Irishman, see *HGVK* lxxix–lxxx. Also the *Life* of Beuno (*VSBG* 17): Gwydelwernn y lle a gauas y enw ygann yr *Yscot* 'Gwyddelwern, the place which got its name from the Irishman'.

4   **o lit,** 'in anger, angrily'. *o* 'of' is commonly used in MW to denote manner or cause; *GMW* 204.

5   **medrawd arnaw,** 'came upon'. *medru ar* is used in the sense of 'to meet, or come across, by chance'.

6   **Dyoer,** 'Indeed!' From *Dyw a wyr* 'God knows' (> *Dïwyr* > *Dïoer* > *Dioer*—monosyllabic; see *G* 363).

10   **Yr wyt yn ynvyt,** 'You are mad'. According to the Welsh version, Boia is the one who is mad. But, according to the Vesp. text, *Cui coniunx in insaniam versa, 'Surge,' inquit* 'To whom (his) wife having become mad [lit. 'having been turned to madness'] said, "Arise"' (*VSBG* 155). Thus it is the wife who has become mad. I feel tempted to suggest that the Welsh originally

5   read, *Heb y wreic a yrrwyt yn ynvyt kyuot* 'Said the wife who
was driven mad, "Arise"' (*gyrru* 'to drive'). In other Latin
versions the expression *in insaniam uersa* occurs later. In the
earlier versions it is found in ch. 18, immediately before the
reference to her disappearance; see *RLSD* 11, *LSD* 92.

         y vynyd, 'up', consisting of *y* 'to' and *mynyd* 'mountain'. Cf.
Un a gyuodes *y uynyd* 'One rose up' *PKM* 9.19–20.

13   **ysgiweryeit,** pl. of *ysgwier* 'esquire', a borrowing from
English *esquire* (< OF *esquier*); see *EEW* 149; also *ysgwiereit*.

         ar vedwl, 'with the intention of', *ar* 'on' + *medwl* 'mind'. Cf.
dyuot *ar uedwl* medi honno 'he came with the intention of
reaping that one' *PKM* 59.18; see *GMW* 185.

14   **y disgyblon,** 'to his disciples'. *y* consists of *y* 'to' + *y* 'his';
see *GMW* 53n.2, and cf. 2.6, 32.

19   **ry,** an affirmative pre-verbal particle (Ir. *ro*), commonly
employed in the earlier period, but less frequently in late MW;
see *GMW* 166–9. In this text only two exs. are found (here and
in 6.15), and in both it occurs with a verbal noun.

         ysgrybyl, a collective noun, denoting all the animals, as is
explained here. A borrowing from Latin; cf. *scrīpulum*,
scrūpulus (*EL* 13–14). *scribl* occurs in Old Welsh; see *B* v
(1931), 234–5. Cf. further *LlB* 177, *HGVK* 96.

20   **greoed,** pl. of *gre* 'stud'. See *G* 587, *LlB* 213–14, *GPC* 1527.

23   **hoyw:** *B* has *heb wy* 'said they', which seems to be the better
reading.

         yn y, in the MS the second *y* is inserted above between *yn*
and *wattwar*, apparently by the original copyist.

24   **Sef y cawssant wy yn y kyngor** 'this is (how) they found (it)
in the/their deliberation(s),' meaning 'this is how they
decided', the content of the decision being expressed by a
following verbal noun, *gwediaw y sant* 'to pray to the saint'.
Cf. *Sef a gahat* yn y *kynghor*, rodi Branwen y Vatholwch
'What they decided was to give Branwen to Matholwch' *PKM*
30.28.

         Sef consists of *ys* '(it) is and *ef* 'it'. It occurs at the beginning
of a sentence, and refers to something which follows, and
which may be expressed by a noun or verbal noun. *Sef* itself
may be substantival, adjectival or adverbial. Here it is adverbial, with *y* following it before the verb, in which case it often
has meanings such as 'thus, now, then'.

29   **llawuorynyon,** 'handmaidens'. Lat. *ancillis* (abl. of *ancillae*
'maid-servants, female slaves').

30   **diosglwch awch dillat,** 'take off your clothes'. The girls are
sent naked to David and his men, in order to try and make
them leave. We find other references to action of this kind
taken by druids and hostile chieftains; see *VSH* i. clxvi n. 2. In
Irish tales mention is made of naked women being used as

p.   *l.*

5   defence against the enemy, and Caesar speaks of something
           similar among the Gauls; see *RC* xlv (1928), 159–64.

           According to the *Life* of Teilo in *LL*, it was Boia who caused
           his wife to send her handmaidens to the saints, and it is said that
           they became mad (*LL* 100, *LSD* 55). According to Gwynfardd
           Brycheiniog, they went to their death:

           Ellygwys gwraget eu gwrecysseu,
           Rei gweinyon noethon aethan uateu.
           Y gwerth eu gwrthwarae gwyrth a oreu,
           Kertassant gan wynt ar hynt agheu.   (*HGCr* 51. 233–6.)

           'They proceeded with the wind on the path of death'.

33   **allwnn,** MS *aallwnn*.

34   **dywaut,** MS *dywant*.

35   **Ponyt,** '*nonne*?', in MW introducing a question which expects
            an affirmative answer, later *oni*(*d*); see *GMW* 175–6.

38   **Alun,** Alun, now a winding stream, some six miles long, which
            flows through Vallis Rosina and enters the sea at Porth Clais; see
            LSD 91–2, *DPGOH* I. 99–100, *DS* 33.

6   3   **dihaedaf,** probably consisting of *di-*, an affirmative prefix (<*
            dē) and *haed*, as in *haeddu*, *cyrraedd*. Here it appears to mean
            'examine', a meaning suggested by the reading in the Vesp. text:
            uolo enim cirros tuos leniter inuestigare 'for I wish gently to
            examine your locks' (*RLSD* 11). For references in Irish litera-
            ture to examining a head, see *RC* xlv (1928), 168.

       5   **llad penn y uorwyn santes,** an example of *llad* with the
            meaning 'cut off'; also 6.14. Cf. *Ac yna y peris Bendigeiduran
            llad y benn* 'And then Bendigeidfran caused his head to be cut
            off' *PKM* 44.28.

            It may well be that this action by Boia's wife was intended as a
            sacrifice to appease the wrath of the gods; see *LBS* ii. 297, *RC*
            xlv (1928), 164–9.

       6   **yd ymdangosses ffynnyawn,** 'there appeared a fountain'. For
            other references to the appearance of a fountain with healing
            properties at the place where a virgin had been decapitated, note
            the story of Gwenfrewi/Wenefred in the *Life* of Beuno and the
            Life of St Wenefred; see *VSBG* 18–19, 290–2; also *Ffynnawn
            Digiwc* in the *Life* of Beuno, ibid. 20. For a further reference, cf.
            LSD 50–1 (*Life* of St Justinan); also *LBS* i 186 (St Aude).

     7–8   **Fynnawn Dunawt,** Vesp. text. *Martirium Dunawt* 'Merthyr
            Dunawd'. Neither name is known in the vicinity of St David's,
            although the well was clearly thought of as being in this area;
            HWW 41.

            Dunawt comes from Dōnātus or Dōnāta, and occurs quite
            commonly as a personal name; for exs. see *G* 396. According to
            Giraldus, *Dunaudus* was the name of the man raised from the
            dead by Patrick; see 2.14 above.

p.   l.
6   10   **drycaruaethu,** MS *dryc aruaethu.* This is obviously for
             drygyruerthu. The forms are not infrequently confused in the
             MSS; cf. *G* 392. The meaning is 'cry, wail, lament, groan'.
     12   **sef y,** *sef* is here adverbial. Cf. 5.24 *Sef y cawssant* . . . above.
     13   **y elyn,** 'his enemy'. In the Vesp. text his name is given as *Lisci,*
             the son of *Paucaut (RLSD* 11), Giraldus *(Opera* iii. 389) *Leschi.*
             Porth Lisci is an inlet on the coast, west of Porth Clais; see *LSD*
             93, also *AC* xii (1895), 20.
  14–15   **y doeth tan o'r nef,** 'there came fire from heaven'. See *VSH* i.
             cxxxviii for references in the *Lives* of the Irish saints to the
             bringing of fire from heaven. Not infrequently we learn of places
             being consumed by fire from heaven; cf. *ASC* 39. In the *Life* of
             St Germanus fire falls from heaven, and burns the forests of the
             tyrant Benlli; cf *N* 68. In the case of Vortigern also we are told
             that his fortress was destroyed by fire sent from heaven. But
             'others say that the earth opened up and swallowed him up on
             the night when his fortress was burnt about him'. Cf. ibid. 33, 73.
     16   **Satrapa y wreic,** 'Satrapa his wife'. The author of the Welsh
             Life has misunderstood the Latin, and has taken *satrapa*
             'chieftain' (used to describe Boia: *Quidam* . . . *satrapa magus-*
             que VSBG 155, *Baia satrapa* 156) as the name of his wife. He
             clearly thought that it suited her, and that she should not remain
             nameless! But in none of the Latin texts is she named. The Vesp.
             text here reads: *Nemoque dubitet quod Dominus propter Dauid*
             seruum suum percussit Baiam et uxorem eius 'Let no one doubt
             that the Lord for the sake of David, his servant, struck down
             Baia and his wife' *VSBG* 157.
     17   **adeilawd Dewi,** 'David built'. *adeilawd* is not normally used
             without an object, and one would here expect a noun, such as
             manachlawc 'monastery', to follow *Dewi.* As has already been
             observed (p. xlviii), the Welsh version merely mentions the
             foundation of St David's, omitting entirely the detailed descrip-
             tion of the life of the community, found in the Latin version; see
             RLSD 12–14, 35–8.
     18   **Glynn Hodnant,** see under 4.30 *Hodnant* above.
             onnyt chydic o dwfyr, MS *onnyt chydic onny dwfyr.* Note the
             form *chydic* 'a little', which is rare; usually *ychydic.* For the
             textual variants, see *BDe* 10. Cf. the Vesp. text here; '*Locus*
             iste', *inquiunt,* '*hyeme habet aquas, sed estate uix tenui riuulo*
             fluuius illabitur'. 'This place', they said, 'in winter has waters,
             but in the summer scarcely does the river flow in a tiny stream.'
             (*VSBG* 159).
     20   **ffynnawn eglur,** 'a clear fountain'. Giraldus (*Opera* iii. 390)
             speaks of the springing up of a fountain in St David's. And in his
             Itinerary he says, 'Two stories worth mentioning, or so I think,
             are first that, in our own lifetime, when David 11 was Bishop, the
             River Alun ran with wine, and secondly that the Pistildewi, that

p.   l.

6   is Saint David's Spout, a spring which flows through a narrow
            channel into the churchyard from the east, several times ran with
            milk' (*GW* 168); see also *LSD* 100–1, and *LL* 103 (*Life* of
            Teilo).
                There are many references in the *Lives* of the saints to the
            welling of fountains or springs, resulting in most cases from the
            saint (or someone else) striking the earth or the rock with the
            end of his staff; see *VSBG* 88, 94, 180, 212, 244, 282, also *LBS*
            i. 172, ii. 182, *VSH* i. cl, and cf. *LSBL* (*Life* of Senán) 218. Not
            infrequently we are told of the water turning into wine or milk;
            see *VSH* i. ci, also 9.23 below. In the *Life* of Brynach (*VSBG*
            14) the saint draws wine from the torrent Caman. Columb Cille
            blesses the water, and it turns into wine, *LSBL* 173.

22   **y'r ryw wr hwnnw,** 'to such a man as that'; see *GMW* 90–1.

23   **Gweslan escob,** see under 4.23 *Goeslan* above.
            brawt, MS *brawp*, but corrected to *brawt* by the rubricator.

24   **Eliud,** see under 4.29 *Eliud* above.
            dyrwestassant, MS *dyrwestassassant*, but with *-ssa-* apparently
            crossed out before *-ssant*.

25–6   **rac sychet yr amsser,** 'because the weather was so dry'. On the
            use of *rac* with the equative adjective, see *GMW* 43. *amsser* here
            means 'weather'; cf. Irish *aimsear* and Breton *amzer*.

27   **Ffynnawn Gwestlan a Ffynnawn Eliud,** no wells with these
            appellations are now known in the vicinity of St David's; see
            LSD 101, *HWW* 208. They are not mentioned in the Latin *Life*,
            where there is only a general reference to 'other springs of fresh
            water which were bestowed by disciples after the father's
            example, which proved of service to men for daily use and for
            health' (*RLSD* 38).

30   **Aydan sant,** see under 4.28 *Aedan* above. In the Latin *Life*
            we learn of incidents relating to him which happened when he
            was at St David's; see *RLSD* 38–9. Also in his own *Life*; cf. *LSD*
            34–8.

31   **Gwernin,** in the MS it could be read as *gweruin*, Ferns in Co.
            Wexford. In the Latin *Life* it is said that Aydan built a monastery
            there after he had completed his studies, and gone to Ireland:
            Sanctus autem Aidanus, ad plenum eruditus, uirtutibus pluri-
            mum excoctis ad purum uitiis pollens, Hiberniam petit, con-
            structoque ibi monasterio quod Hibernensi lingua Guernin
            uocatur, sanctissimam duxit uitam 'Now St Aidan completed his
            studies, and his virtues perfected and his faults suppressed to the
            degree of purity, he went to Ireland, where he built a monastery
            called Guernin in the Irish tongue; and there he lived a most holy
            life' (*RLSD* 16, 39).

7   4   **Neur,** consisting of *neu* + *ry*, two affirmative particles; see
            GMW 170.
            deryw, 3 sing. pres. indic. of *daruot* 'to happen', with perfect

7   meaning; see *GMW* 145–6. The prep. *y* 'to' is used with it to
denote the logical subject, the subject according to meaning; the
grammatical subject is the verbal noun *gwnneuthur*; see *B* xvi
(1955), 83. With the particle *neur* (which appears to have survived longer with this verb than with others), *deryw* serves
chiefly as an auxiliary to denote a perfect meaning: 'three of his
community here have plotted against him'.

6   **o'e vwytta,** 'to eat (it)'; see *GMW* 53 n. 2.

8   **pa delw,** '(in) what manner/way, how?' (*delw* 'image, form,
mode, manner', Irish *delb*). Cf. *pa delw y gellit dy lad ditheu?*
'how could you be killed?' *PKM* 86.24.

9   **y mae,** read *yma* (Cf. Lincoln MS. 149 below). The whole
sentence should read as follows: *ac yma nyt oes long yn barawt*
'and here there is no ship ready'. In Lincoln MS 149 we find,
Nulla enim hic navis parata est 'For here no ship is ready';
CLIGC ix (1955/56), 12.

11   **Scuthyn,** Scuithin, another Irish saint who had been a disciple
of David. In the Latin *Life* the form is *Scut(h)inus*, but it is said
that he had also another name, *Scolanus* (*RLSD* 16); with the
latter cf. *Bed Yscolan*, l. 19 below.

12   **druod,** an adverbial form of *trwy/drwy*, which in MW can
have the meaning 'over, across'; see *GMW* 212, *PKM* 185. Cf. *Y
chwedyl . . . a aeth drwy yr holl ynys honn* 'The news went over
all this island'. 11.28 below.

   yr oedit yn y erchi idaw, 'what was being asked of him': a
relative clause without an expressed antecedent; see *GMW* 72.

13   **cherdet,** in the MS all the letters apart from *-et* are difficult to
identify.

14   **anghenuil,** in the MS *an-* not distinct.

14–15 **anghenuil o'r mor,** 'a monster from the sea': Lat. *belua*; see
LSD 103. In the *Life* of Aidan it is said that that saint crossed the
sea back to Ireland from St David's on the back of a monster
(*magnum animal*), after he had been visiting David before his
death. David ordered him to go on the back of the first animal he
met on the shore; see *VSH* ii. 153. In a note in *MOC* (40) there is
a reference to Scuthyn walking on the sea; see *Slover* 109. In the
Life of St Bairre, Bairre returns to Ireland from St David's on
the back of David's horse; see *VSH* i. 69, also *LSD* 104.

16   **dyw Pasc,** on *dyw* 'day', see *GMW* 33, also *L&P* 171.

19   **Bed Yscolan,** nothing is known of this place. On *Yscolan*, see
B vi (1933), 352, *GDG* 486–7, *YB* x. 51–78, *LlDC* lx, 55.

20   **mynet dwylaw mynwgyl idaw,** 'to embrace, greet', common in
MW. *mynwgyl* means 'neck'. Note the epenthetic vowel
between *g* and *l*; see *GMW* 12–13.

22   **daruot,** see *GMW* 145–6. Here it means 'happen', and *y* 'to' is
used with it. The grammatical sub. is a vn; cf. *deryw*. It can also
mean 'finish', e.g. 7.27.

p.   *l.*

24   **a megys,** MS A megys | A megys.

26   **diolwch,** 'thanks'. This is the earlier form, consisting of *di-* (affirmative prefix <*dī* <*dē*) + *golwch* 'praise'. Later it became *diolch*; cf. *onid* > *ond, myned* > *mynd, llonaid* > *llond,* and see *WG* 55–6.

28   **a wassannaethei,** MS *awnna awassannaethei.*

32   **synnyaw arnaw,** 'to wonder, be surprised', also 7.39, 12.9 below. On this verb, its meaning and construction, see *B* i. (1922), 107, xv (1952), 11. Note that the logical subject is governed by the prep. *ar.*

gwydyat, 'he knew': 3 sing. imperf. For the ending -(*y*)*at,* see *GMW* 122.

36   **allmarw,** MS *a* | *allmarw.*

y bu allmarw, Vesp. text: *misera morte uitam finiuit* 'it ended his life with a wretched death' (*RLSD* 6). For *allmarw,* cf. a'e dyfwrw a gaflach blaenllym a'e uedru yn y lygat, hyt pan aeth y'r gwegil allan, ac ynteu yn *allmarw* y'r llawr 'And he took aim at him with a sharp-pointed spear and hit him in the eye, so that it went out through the nape of the neck, and he *stone-dead* to the ground' (*WM* 124. 33–6).

37   **y trawyt yr amrant ar y llall,** 'the (one) eyelid was struck against the other'. Other exs. are found in MW, where the first alternative is expressed by the noun only; see *GMW* 86n.

a thorri . . . a syrthaw, note the use of verbal nouns instead of finite verbs; see *GMW* 161.

8   1–2   **y rwng y ffreutur,** 'between the refectory . . .'. I suggest that this represents the original reading. In all the texts *y rwng* is omitted, probably because the eye of an early copyist leapt from one *y* to the other (the one before *ffreutur*), leaving out *rwng.* Cf. Vesp. text: *Misitque Dauid agius alteram partem coruo, qui erat in nido suo in fraxino quę erat inter refectorium et amnem ad australem plagam* 'And holy David threw the second part to a raven, which was in its nest in an ash tree, which was between the refectory and the river towards the south side' (*RLSD* 16).

9   **rodi ar,** *rodi ar* A, *dodi ar* C, D. It appears that *gwedi* 'prayer' should be read after *rodi, rodi gwedi* 'to pray'. Cf. *dodi gwedi ar* yr Arglwyd yn y megys hwnn 'to pray to the Lord in this way' (*YCM* 59.14).

9–10   **hyt na,** '(in order) that . . . not', denoting purpose; see *GMW* 238.

11–12   **holl lauurwyr yr hynys hon,** 'all the labourers of this island'. The 'labourers' as such are not mentioned in the Latin *Life;* cf. *RLSD* 21.

12   **sened Vreui,** 'The synod of Brefi'. On the soft mutation in *Breui,* a proper noun in a genitival relationship after a fem. sing. noun, see *GMW* 14.

8

In the Latin *Life* the synod is associated with the revival of the Pelagian heresy, *RLSD* 21.

Further, in the Latin *Life* there is mention of a subsequent synod, called the Synod of Victory, ibid. 24.

In the *Life* of Cadog it is stated that David, who is described as *uerus Dei confessor atque pontifex*, assembled the synod after having been commissioned by an angel. It was held while Cadog was away on pilgrimage! *VSBG* 60–2, also *LSD* 39–41. In the *Life* of Cynnydd we are told how David (along with Teilo and Padarn) sought (unsuccessfully) to bring that infirm saint to the synod; see *NLA* ii. 108–9, also *LSD* 41–2. In the *Life* of Samson, we are told that that saint was invited to a synod, where he was appointed abbot and ordained bishop; see *LSSD* 43–6.

Germanus of Auxerre visited Britain twice, in 429, and later in the 440s; cf. *BEH* 24–32. He may well have been engaged in repelling the Pelagian heresy, as well as in helping the Britons to withstand their enemies; cf. *LWS* 3n. The mention of these two synods by Rhigyfarch can hardly be based on historical fact, and here it is pertinent to quote Mrs Chadwick: 'We must insist that our only authority for such synods is the late eleventh-century work of Rhigyfarch, which here reads suspiciously like an echo of Constantius's *Life of St Germanus*, a work by which Rhigyfarch would seem to be directly influenced' (*SEBC* 139). Cf. further Molly Miller, who suggests that 'since the synod is not mentioned in AC [*Annales Cambriae*], it seems very likely that it had not been invented by c. 955' (*SC* xii/xiii (1977/8), 58–9).

Breui, the name of a small stream, some five miles long, which flows westwards into the river Teifi. In the Latin *Life Breui* is the name of a place (*loco cui nomen Breui RLSD* 22); cf. the *Life* of Cadog; *magnam sinodum in Ciuitate Breeui VSBG* 54. See further *G* 73, *LSD* 108–9, *EANC* 129–30. It is worth noting that this situation on the banks of the Breui is quite near the important Roman fort of Llanio, a location as Professor Bowen properly remarks, 'fully accessible to the whole of Wales in Roman and sub-Roman times'; cf. *DS* 59.

escyb, 'bishops', 118 of them according to the Latin *Life*; cf. *RLSD* 21.

14   **kreuydwyr,** 'clerics, men in orders'; see *G* 171, *GPC* 588.

15   **heb allu rif arnadunt,** 'without a count being possible on them, without it being possible to count them'.

16   **amot,** 'agreement' here. Now the usual meaning is 'condition'; see *GPC* 97, *CA* 75.

18   **gadv:** + *hwnnw* in other MSS.

pennadur, 'chief, chieftain': Lat. *metropolitanus archiepiscopus*.

p.   *l.*

8   **Yny[s]**, in the MS -*n*- is blotted out.

19   **bop eilwers,** 'in turn, alternately', lit. 'every second time'.
        gwers 'a while'; cf. *GMW* 98, 227.

22-3   **a allo pregethu,** 'who can preach'. There is often no soft
        mutation of the object in MW after the 3 sing. pres. subj.; see
        TC 187, 213, *GMW* 18.

25-6   **ac y,** '(so) that', denoting result after an equative adjective
        (*mor deilwng*); see *GMW* 41-2.

26   **y'r hwnn yniuer yma,** Llanstephan MS 27 *y'r niuer hwnn*
        yma, apparently the better reading. On the use of *yma* 'here'
        with *hwnn* etc., cf. *GMW* 84-5.

        On the prosthetic *y-* in *yniuer* in this text, cf. *GMW* 12.

28-9   **ketymdeith,** 'companion', ModW *cydymaith*. It consists of
        two elements, *ket-/kyt-* (ModW *cyd-* 'co-, fellow-') and *ym-*
        deith (see *GMW* 156). The -*d*- [ð] was later lost in this word,
        as in the expression (*y*) *ymdeith* > *ymeith* (5.33 above)
        'away'; see *GMW* 222-3.

9   2   **ac yn Rufein a vrddwyt yn archescob,** 'and in Rome was
        ordained archbishop'. In the various versions of the Latin *Life*
        it is stated that the Patriarch of Jerusalem made David arch-
        bishop in Jerusalem (*RLSD* 20), where he had gone on a pil-
        grimage with Teilo and Padarn. However, in MS Lincoln 149
        Paulinus, as in the Welsh *Life*, states that he went to Rome
        and was ordained archbishop there: *ac deinde Roman pergens*
        ibi archiepiscopus ordinatus est (*CLlGC* ix. 14). In a letter,
        sent by the chapter of St David's to Pope Eugenius III in
        1145-7, it is stated that, after the synod of Brefi, where he
        defeated the Pelagian heresy, he was given the pallium by the
        Roman pope in the presence of Teilo and Padarn; see *EAWD*
        i. 262. Gwynfardd Brycheiniog refers to visits to Rome and
        to Jerusalem, but there is no mention of his being ordained:

        A chyrchu *Ruvein*, rann gyreifyeint.
        A gwest yn *Efrei*, gwst diamreint.   (*HGCr* 44. 21-2.)

        Likewise also Ieuan ap Rhydderch (*IGE* 243. 15-18,
        243.27-244.6). On the significance of some conflict of evi-
        dence from various sources, note Mrs Chadwick's observa-
        tions in *SEBC* 151-3. Cf. further *Doble* iv. 57: 'Pilgrimages to
        Rome and Jerusalem are ... a characteristic feature of Lives
        of Celtic saints composed in the twelfth century'.

        3   **angel yn dyuot attaw,** see 4.24 above.

        4   **y wlat,** 'to his country'. For *y*, see 2.32 *y le* above.

        parchassei, 'had kept, reserved'. *parchu* now means 'to
        respect', but earlier it carried meanings such as 'to keep,
        spare'. It comes from the Lat. *parc.o*; see *EL* 44.

        5   **Demetica,** Dyfed, in the south west, consisting of former
        Pembrokeshire and part of west Carmarthenshire. It was

p. *l.*
9   divided into seven cantrefs; cf. *PKM* 1.1–2, also note, ibid. 93.

Mynyw yn y deheu, 'Mynyw in the south', doubtless a reference to St David's. The old name was *Mynyw* (Lat. *Menevia*), which is commonly found in the *Brut* and the *Annales Cambriae*. *Menevia*, however, is not used by Rhigyfarch, who calls the place *Vallis Rosina* (see 1.15 *Glynn Rosin*). *Mynyw* seems originally to have been the name of another place, possibly Hen Fynyw; see 3.22 *Vetus Rubus*. That was the place to which David returned after his itinerary, according to the Welsh *Life*, see 4.22–5. In the Latin *Life* it is said that 'he then returned to the place which he had left behind, when setting forth on his journeying' (*RLSD* 34). Whether Hen Fynyw (a little to the south of Aberaeron) is meant or not, it is suggested to David by the angel that he should seek another place (4.25 *A dangosses y mi le arall*), which must mean St David's. In the Latin *Life* this place is described as being 'near by' (*est autem alius prope locus RLSD* 9). It has been maintained that it must therefore be in the vicinity of St David's, and that Hen Fynyw, near Aberaeron, is too far away. However, as Hen Fynyw is not so very far from St David's, which is after all to the south of it, and as no other place bearing the name *Mynyw* has been found to the north of St David's, it must be conceded that Hen Fynyw has a stronger claim than any other place to be recognized as the original Mynyw. It is in Ceredigion, the kingdom to which David belonged. 'It would seem therefore that the name Mynyw was transferred to *Vallis Rosina* in Dyfed from an original Mynyw, which later came to be called *Hen Fynyw*' (*SEBC* 155). Note further Doble: 'It is interesting to compare other place-names with *Hen* "old" as a first element; *Henllan* "Old church", common in Wales and Cornwall. In Celtic times the sites of monasteries, schools and churches seem to have been not infrequently abandoned, and new sites sought, for reasons which were afterwards forgotten.' (Doble, *LWS* 67).

The form *Mynyw* is of interest. In OW we find most often *miniu* (*N* 88, 90, *LHEB* 378, also *mineu* ibid.). In the *Annales Cambriae s.a.* 601 we read, 'Dauid episcopus *moni* iudeorum' (*Cy* ix. 156, *N* 86). Loth suggested that we should read *moniu deorum*, and further that *deorum* is for *desorum*, Lat. gen. pl. of *Dés(s)i*, the name of the Irish tribe which came to Dyfed in the late fourth century; see *RC* xx (1899), 206, xxxvii (1917/9), 315–16, also under pp. xii–xiii above (for another interpretation, see E. W. B. Nicholson, *ZCP* vi (1908), 447–8). We thus may have another form, *Moniu*. The Latin *Menevia* is a formation based on the Welsh word.

The Latin *Rubus* does not occur for St David's, although *dinas Rubi* is found in the Welsh *Life*, 9.8, 11.22. Cf. also *Vetus Rubus* 4.22–5. *Rubus* is but a translation of the Welsh *mynyw*; as for its meaning, see *L&S* 'a bramble-bush, a blackberry-bush,—a blackberry', also *LTBL* 275 '*Ensemble d'arbrisseaux à tiges épineuses non culturés*'. *mynyw* as a common noun is not attested, but in Irish we find the common noun *muine*, which corresponds to our *mynyw* according to Loth (*RC* xxxvii. 315). On the Irish word, see *Contrib*. M 189 'A brake or thicket, generally applied to thorn-brakes or bushes, occas. of groves of trees'. *Muine* occurs as a gloss on *rubus* (*Ir.Gl.* 81), and it corresponds to *rubus* in *Lat. Lives* 18. The name for St David's in the *Lives* of the Irish saints is *Cell Muine* 'The cell (or church) of Mynyw'; see *BNE* ii. 14, 17, 178, 180, 201, 205, 223. Giraldus also gives *Kil-muni* as the Irish for St David's, and maintains that 'this place took its name from the Irish *muni*, which means *rubus* 'grove' (*Opera* iii. 384).

The etymology of *mynyw* presents difficulties. Jackson is uncertain (*LHEB* 378), but he suggests the ending -*ouiā*, and British **Monouiā*. We ought also to consider the suggestion of Mr R. J. Thomas (*B* viii. 37–8) that it can be connected with names such as *Manaw* (and *Manaw Gododdin, Mon, Menai*, and *Mynwy*; also the names of the tribes *Menapii* (from the land of Gallia Belgica), and *Menapioi* (south-eastern Ireland); see *ACS* 543–7. We understand from Ptolemy that the *Menapii* were in Ireland before the Christian era. They probably crossed over from Britain, and it may be that the names *Mynyw* and *Mynwy* are reminiscent of their occupation at some time of these parts; see *IW* 21, 42–3.

8   **dinas Rubi,** St David's. See above l.5 *Mynyw yn y deheu*.

11   **Nyt af vi . . . yno,** 'I will not go there'. Cf. the reluctance of Cuthbert to attend the synod, where he was elected bishop of Lindisfarne, *Life of Cuthbert* ch. 24.

13–14   **a rodes gynt,** MS *arodes gynt | Arodes*.

14   **kyduundeb,** 'agreement': ModW *cytundeb*, in which the two *u* vowels have coalesced to form one; cf. *yn gytuun* 'united, agreed' 11.5 below, *duunaf* 'I will agree' *PKM* 23.13, *duunaw* '(they) agree(d)' 53.5. The form contains *cyd* + *duundeb* 11.30 (<*dy*- + *undeb* 'unity, union'; on *y . . . u* > *u . . . u*, see *GMW* 3).

15   **y deu sant bennaf,** 'the two chief saints'. In MW the adjective constantly undergoes the soft mutation after the dual, even when the noun is masculine, e.g. deu varch *u*awr 'two big horses' *SGr* 88.35; see *GMW* 19, *TC* 61–2.

Deinyoel, Deiniol, the patron saint of Bangor, and the founder of a number of monasteries, including possibly Bangor-is-coed (Bangor on Dee). According to *Bonedd y Saint* (*EWGT* 56), he was a son of Dunawd Fawr, son of Pabo Post Prydein. According to the *Annales Cambriae* (*N* 86) he died in 584, but this date may be too late. It is said in *LL* 71 that it was Dubricius who consecrated him bishop. See *LSD* 109–10, *DWB* 166–7.

p.   l.

9   Deiniol is associated mainly with Gwynedd, but as the Revd
Silas Harris has shown (*JHSCW* v. 5 foll.), he had connections
with Dyfed also. He is commemorated in Llanddeiniol
(Ceredigion). His brother was Cynwyl, commemorated in Cynwyl Gaeo and Cynwyl Elfed (Carmarthen).

16   **Dubricius,** Welsh *Dyfrig*. He must have been earlier than
David. Along with Illtud and Cadog, he belonged to the earlier
generation of saints. He is connected with the south east, more
especially with Archenfield, where the churches dedicated to
him are mostly grouped. He may well have been the product of
Romano-British Christianity.

He is mentioned in the *Life* of Samson (beginning of the
seventh century), where he is referred to as a bishop and connected with Llantwit Major and Caldey Island. Three *Lives* of
him have survived, the earliest of which is that found in *LL*,
where he is connected with the diocese of Llandaff, and described as Archbishop. We are told of his miraculous birth in a
place called *Matle* (Madley in Herefordshire), a son of Efrddyl,
daughter of Peibio, king of Ergyng (see 4.15 *Pebiawc* above).
He founded a monastery and famous school at *Hennlann*
(Hentland-on-Wye, near the old Roman settlement, *Ariconium*,
Ergyng). Then, at the end of seven years, he moved to his native
district, to *Mochros* (Moccas), where he remained for many
years. Towards the end of his life he retired, a hermit, to
Bardsey, and was buried there. His remains were removed to
Llandaff in May, 1120. On him, see Doble, *LWS* 56–87. Accord-
ing to a later tradition, he was a disciple of St Germanus of
Auxerre. There is also a tradition which makes him a descendant
of king Erb.

Sometime between 1124 and 1130 the chapter of St David's
sent a letter to Pope Honorius II, claiming metropolitan status
for the church, and appealing to history. The church had been a
metropolitan see from the time Christianity was first introduced
into Britain. St David, it is maintained, was made archbishop by
the whole kingdom of western Britain, and consecrated by his
predecessor, St Dubricius; see *SEBC* 207–8, 241. Geoffrey
makes Dubricius archbishop in Caerleon-on-Usk (*HRB* 413,
BD 129), where he was succeeded by David (*HRB* 458, *BD* 161).
Giraldus tells the same story. After the synod of Brefi, David
was with acclaim elected archbishop. 'What is more, as I have
already told you, Saint Dyfrig, in his archiepiscopal court at
Caerleon, had only recently resigned this honour to him, naming
him personally and appointing him as his successor. As a result
the metropolitan see was moved from Caerleon to St David's.'
(*GW* 179). It appears that there were two traditions relating to
David's election as archbishop. Dubricius figures in both, but in
different roles.

9   16   **kynn,** MS *honno.*

Dewi, Dewi, MS, *dewi. Adewi.*

17   **gwybydwch chwi y daw kennadeu yma avore,** the saint knows beforehand of the coming of the messengers. There are plenty of references to such foreknowledge in the Irish *Lives,* e.g. *VSH* i. 72 (Bairre), 161 (Cainnech), 249, 252 (Coemgen); and ibid. clxx.

20   **vrthv[nt],** in the MS it occurs at the end of the line.

22-3   **a'r dwfyr a aeth yn win ar hynt,** 'and the water straightway became wine'. In the *Life* of St Sezni it is related that that saint made the sign of the cross over some jars of water in the monastery, and the water was changed into wine. This was on the occasion of a visit to the monastery by Saint Patrick. See *Doble* ii. 7. In the *Life* of Cuthbert (ch. 35) likewise, water is turned into wine. And in the *Life* of Ciaran we are told that the saint blessed a vessel full of water, 'and it was turned into choice wine, and was dealt out to the monks' (*LSBL* 276, also ibid. 280).

Cf. Kathleen Hughes's reference to St Brigit: 'Several of the miracles told of St Brigit show her entertaining guests, and demonstrate clearly that good entertainment was expected from a saint with a reputation to maintain.' (*CEIS* 148).

27   **y'th aros** 'waiting for thee'. Here note the use of *y* (with infixed pronoun) as a predicative particle before a verbal noun. See *GMW* 199, also Watkins, *B* xviii (1960) 362-72, and 2.31-2 *y'm poeni* above.

28   **haedu,** here the meaning is 'obtain, incur'. Cf. gwae a *haed* meuyl yr bychot 'woe to him who incurs shame (in exchange) for a little' *EWGP* 28.3. The more general meaning later is 'merit, deserve'.

29-30   **ketymeithonn,** 'companions'. On the sing. *ketymdeith* see 8.28 above. The pl. *ketymdeith(y)on* became *ketymeith-(y)on(n),* through loss of *-d-* [ð]; cf. (*y*) *ymdeith > ymeith.* The weak syllable immediately before the accent was lost, thus yielding *cydmeith(y)on.* This represents a common tendency in words of four syllables; cf. *Cristionogion > Cristnogion.* Then finally *cymdeithion* was produced by metathesis. This would be helped by the evidence of forms such as *ymdeith, ymdaith, ymdeithio* 'journey' (verb and noun).

Note in the form *ketymeithonn* the loss of consonantal *i* (*y*), a feature found in MW prose, and in the spoken language of south Wales today; *GMW* 6.

10   1   **y hun mab,** 'her only son'. In the earlier Latin versions we are told, cui barbara imperitia *magnum* nomen dederat (*RLSD* 23). Some four Digby MSS have, *magna* nomen dederat (ibid.), while two MSS of the Vespasian recension read, qui *Magnus* uocabatur (ibid.). To translate *magnum nomen* as 'a lengthy name' (as in *RLSD* 45) seems hardly right. *magnum, magna* and

p.   l.

10   *magnus* seem intended to represent a personal name. In the
     Welsh *Life* the name is not given, but it is worth noting that
     Maen occurs as a personal name in Welsh. It is the name of one
     of Llywarch Hen's sons (*CLlH* 7.42a, *EWGT* 86). It is suggested
     in *LSD* 111 that the name occurs in Llandyfân, the name of a
     church and district near Llandeilo Fawr in the Tywi valley (with
     Tyfân a colloquial form of *Tyfaen*, a hypocoristic form of *Maen*
     with the prefix *Ty-*; see also *LBS* ii. 394, *LWS* 206n. *Magna* is the
     form given by Gwynfardd Brycheiniog:

     A Dewi a'e goruc, gwr bieifyt,
     Magna uab yn vyw a'e uarw deudyt.   (*HGCr* 47. 124–5).

     Also Ieuan ap Rhydderch:

     Da y gwna *Fagna* â'i fagl
     O farw yn fyw o firagl   (*IGE* 244.15–16).

     For another instance of restoring an only son to life, cf. the *Life*
     of Senán, *LSBL* 208.
9–10 **ti a disgynneist,** 'thou who didst descend'. The influence of
     Latin syntax accounts for concord in person here between verb
     and antecedent. As a rule, the verb is 3 sing. in an affirmative
     relative clause, where the relative pron. is subject; see *GMW* 61.
12   **y eneit,** MS *yny eneit.*
15   **mal bei atuei,** 'as if he were'. *bei* is 3 sing. imperf. subj. of the
     verb 'to be', used here as a conditional conjunction; see *GMW*
     242–3. *atuei* is 3 sing. imperf. subj. of *aduot* 'happen, be'; ibid.
     145.
16   **y vam,** 'to his mother'; see 2.31 *y le* above.
19   **o'r a welsant,** '(of those) who saw'; see *GMW* 70–1. Note that
     the verb is pl., whereas it is usually sing. in a clause of this kind,
     where the relative pron. is subject; see *GMW* 61, and cf. 10.9–10
     ti a disgynneist above.
22   **gwell,** MS *gwe|ell.*
22–3 **A chyuarch gwell . . . a syrthyaw . . . ac erchi,** note the series of
     verbal nouns, and cf. 1.9 *dywedut* above.
24   **buassei bregeth,** note the soft mutation of the subject after the
     3 sing. plup.; see *GMW* 18.
25   **ar dalym o enkyt,** 'for a short while'. On *talym*, see 1.1
     above. *enkyt* 'a short while'.
29   **y benn y brenn,** 'to the top of the mound'. According to the
     Latin *Life*, this mound was 'piled up with garments' (*RLSD*
     45). It is not said that he declined to ascend the mound. How-
     ever, according to the Vespasian text (ibid. 23), he did refuse,
     and ordered the boy restored to life to spread his handkerchief
     (*sudarium*) under his feet.
30–1 **pregethu . . . o,** cf. 1.1 *traethu o* above.
31   **megys llef kornn eglur,** Ieuan ap Rhydderch (*c.* 1430–70) tells

10   us that he was clearly heard 'like a bell' (*mal cloch*) in Llandu-
            doch, St Dogmael's, on the Cardigan coast, close to Cardigan
            town, and a good way from Llanddewibrefi!

> Clywad ef, clau wawd ofeg,
> Mal cloch yn Llandudoch deg.   (*IGE* 244. 25–6).

36   **y kyuodes y llawr hwnnw**, 'that ground rose'. There is refer-
            ence to a similar incident in the *Life* of Kentigern, *SEBC* 318.
            megys, MS *megys megys*, with a line through the first *megys*.

11   1–2   **yr hwnn yssyd etwo yn vrynn vchel**, the church of Llanddewi-
            brefi stands on a hill above the river Teifi.

4   **Llanndewivreui**, in Ceredigion, some seven miles north east
            of Lampeter.

5   **kytuun**, 'united, agreed': *cyd + duun* (<*dy + un*); see 9.14
            kyduundeb above. Cf. *duhun* 11.6.

6–13   **gann dywedut . . . Ynys Prydein**, this section does not occur in
            the Latin *Life*.

9   **yr adar**, in the MS the *r* of *yr* has been written above, between
            y and *adar*.

10   **hwnn**, MS *hwnnw*, with -*w* crossed out.

11–12   **Martin**, Martin of Tours (316–97). He was the founder of the
            monastic movement in the West, inspired by St Anthony's
            monastic settlement in Egypt. About 372 he was consecrated
            bishop of Tours, but chose to live in a cell outside the city walls.
            Pupils came to him from far and near, and his influence spread
            throughout Gaul. One of his pupils was Ninian, the first to estab-
            lish monasticism of this kind in Britain. He built a stone church
            at Candida Casa (Whithorn in the west of Galloway), which in
            the time of Bede was dedicated to St Martin.

            Martin's *Life* was written by his disciple, Sulpicius Severus.

12   **Sampson**, St Samson of Dol in Brittany. His *Life* was one of
            the earliest to be written (possibly in the first half of the seventh
            century), and many later *Lives* seem to have been modelled on
            it. See R. Fawtier, *La Vie de Saint Sampson* (Paris, 1912); also
            T. Taylor, *The Life of St Sampson* (London, 1925).

            He was born around 486 in south Wales. His father hailed
            from Dyfed and his mother from Gwent. When he was very
            young, he was sent to Illtud's school, and there ordained deacon
            and priest by Dubricius. Then he went to the monastery of Piro
            (on Caldey Island, opposite Tenby, on the south Pembroke
            coast), and became abbot there after Piro's death. It is said that
            he visited Ireland, and after returning sent his uncle Umbraphel
            there to take charge of a monastery which had been given him.
            He retired for a while to a cave near the Severn, and then there
            came a request for him to visit a synod, where he was con-
            secrated bishop. Subsequently, he was instructed in a vision to
            leave his monastery. He went to Cornwall, where he remained

p.   *l.*

11   for a period, and then crossed to Brittany. There he founded the monastery of Dol, which became a centre of missionary activity over the whole of Brittany. He made several journeys to Paris. He was present at councils held there in 553 and 557, when we find him signing the decrees as *Samson peccator episcopus*. He died at Dol, and was buried there.

The cult of Saint Samson became very popular in the Celtic countries (and outside) soon after his death. Dol became the centre of the church in Brittany, a church which preserved its independence from the sixth century till the ninth, despite attempts by Tours to bring it under its authority. Not before 1199 did the Pope (Innocent III) proclaim his decision finally rejecting the claim of St Samson's church to metropolitan status. Its circumstances and problems were therefore quite similar to those of St David's. See Taylor, *LSSD* xxx–xxxiv. In the second half of the eleventh century the *Chronicle of Dol* was written to defend its claims.

According to the letter addressed by the chapter of St David's to Honorius II (1124–30), Samson was David's successor. Fleeing from the plague; he took his pallium to Brittany, where he founded the archbishopric of Dol; see *EAWD* i. 250. But, according to the summary of the *Life* of Samson in the *Book of Llandaff*, he had never been an archbishop before he crossed to Brittany; see *LL* 6–24.

15   **am,** MS *a│am*.

16   **yn yr honn,** in the MS *r* is added above, after *y* and before *h-*. **allawd,** MS *aallawd*.

pop kyuryw dyn, 'every (kind of) man'; see *GMW* 92.

o'r a '(of those) who'; see *GMW* 70–1, and note other exs. in 3.20, 4.26, 11.21, 22, 13.10.

23–4   **o Dyfi hyt ar Deiui,** 'from Tywi as far as Teifi'. *Dyfi* seems to be an error for *Dywy* (Tywi). Gwynfardd Brycheiniog defines the boundaries in more detail; see *HGCr* 48.140–7, also the note by Henry Lewis, 191–2. In the *Life* of Cadog the saint asks king Maelgwn 'that refuge should be granted him in the community of Gwynlliog from himself and from his posterity like to the *refuge of saint David in Vallis Rosina*' (*VSBG* 137).

This section, dealing with the right of sanctuary, is only found in the Vesp. texts of the Latin *Life*, but they do not mention the boundaries.

24   **a vo moe,** 'farther'. Note the use of a relative construction to denote the adverbial meaning of *moe* 'more'; see *GMW* 229. On *moe/mwy*, see ibid. 4.

26   **lauasso,** in the MS a solitary 6 (=*w*) occurs between *lauasso* and *na*.

30   **duundeb,** 'agreement'; see 9.14 *kyduundeb* above.

31   **y neb a dorrei nodua Dewi sant,** 'he who would breach the

62

THE WELSH LIFE OF ST DAVID

p.   l.
11   protection of Dewi Sant'. Breaching David's protection, or right
            of sanctuary, meant interfering with a person or with property in
            the care of a church or monastery, which was associated with his
            name and cult.
                Cf. the *Life* of Cadog (*VSBG* 78), where Rhun, son of
            Maelgwn, tells Cadog: *Si quis . . . refugium tuum infregerit, sit
            excommunicatus* 'If anyone shall infringe thy refuge, let him be
            excommunicate'. Note further *WEMA* 137, 167–8.
12   5   **pann y mynnych,** 'when you desire it'. *y* here represents the
            infixed pron. object of *mynnych* (see *GMW* 55). *mynnych* is the
            2 sing. pres. subj. of *mynnu* 'to want, desire'.
       7   **ythagneued,** for *y'th dagneued* '(in)to thy peace'; on *-th d->th*,
            see *GMW* 17.
       10   **yn yng ar hynny,** 'close on that'.
       13   **a uo hwy** 'longer', adverbial; cf. 11.24 *a vo moe* above.
       15   **ef a,** cf. 3.11 *ef a* above.
    15–16   **naw rad nef y gyt ac ef, a decuet y dayar,** Lat. *multa constipatus
            angelorum militia* 'accompanied by a great host of angels'
            (*RLSD* 25). On the apparent soft mutation of *rad* (*grad*) after
            naw 'nine', cf. *WG* 168, *TC* 137, also *BT* 4.4–5 naw rad nef.
            References to the *naoi ngradhe nimhe* are frequent in Irish
            Lives, and elsewhere in Irish literature; cf. *LSBL* cv.
       16   **a eilw,** MS *ael aeilw*.
    16–19   **ac a eilw . . . y gyt a thi,** there is nothing corresponding to this
            in the Latin *Life*.
       18   **croessan,** 'buffoon', also 'a lewd or obscene person'—the
            most probable meaning here (despite what I said in *BDe* 56). Cf.
            Irish *crosán, Contrib. C Fasc. 3* (1974), 550 'buffoon, jester,
            reviler'.
       19   **hynny,** demonstrative, pl. here meaning 'those', 'they'. More
            commonly, however, the pl. is expressed by *y rei hynn/hynny*;
            see *GMW* 84.
       20   **kymein hun,** for *kymeint* 'as much/many' + *un* 'one'. It means
            'all, every one', and as here is used in apposition after a pl. noun
            or pronoun; see *GMW* 95. For the change *kymeint un > kymein
            hun,* cf. *canant wy >* (colloquial) *canan hw* 'they sing'.
       28   **yr holl ynys honn,** Lat. *per totam Brytanniam* (*RLSD* 26),
            where *Brytannia* apparently means Britain, rather than Wales.
       30   **pann yw,** 'that (it is)', used to introduce a noun clause; *GMW*
            80.
       31   **hwnn yma,** cf. *GMW* 84–5.
       34   **disgyblonn,** in the MS *b* has been crossed out between *b* and *l*;
            the *-y-* appears to be written over *l*.
       35   **personnyeit,** Vesp. *peregrinorum*.
13   5   **y brenhined yn cwynaw eu brawt,** Vesp text: *reges enim ut
            arbitrum lugebant* (*RLSD* 27). It appears from this that 'judge-
            ment' and not 'brother' is meant by *brawt* in the Welsh *Life*.

p.   *l.*

13   6   **yr hyneif yn cwynaw eu mab,** Vesp. text: senores ut *fratrem* (brother) plangebant *RLSD* 27, but earlier in ch. 62 (and in most MSS), senes ut *filium* (son) lugent. Ibid. 26, *VSBG* 167.

    7–8   **A'e gyuryw,** 'and the like of it'. *kyfryw* 'such' consists of *kyf* + *ryw*. Here it is used with the infixed possessive pronoun 3 sing. masc.; see *GMW* 91–2.

    8   **gwedy ef,** 'after him'. In MW (but not in ModW) (*g*)*wedy* may be used with a personal pronoun. In the MS another *ef* follows, with a line drawn through it.

    8–9   **Nys gwelas,** here a proleptic infixed pron. 3 pl. *'s* is used before the verb, with the object following in the form of a noun, *y sawl dynyon* 'so many people'. This is found not infrequently in MW; see *GMW* 56–7.

    10   **a'r,** MS *ac*.

    10–11   **o'r a,** '(of those) who'; see *GMW* 70–1, and note other exs., cf. 11.21 above.

    aeth, MS *a*.

    byth bellach nyt ymwelwn ni, 'never again shall we see each other'. Two MSS (D and Pen 225) add *yny byt hwn* 'in this world', which reminds us of the reading of the Vesp. text: *In hac terra nunquam nos amplius uisuri sumus* 'On this earth we shall never again be seen' (*RLSD* 26).

    Words such as these are found in the Vesp. text, but not in the earlier versions; see p. xli. Nevertheless, it is interesting to observe that Rhigyfarch himself in his 'Lament' uses language which echo some of the words here: *Cur non terra uorat, non mare mergit?* 'Why does the earth not consume us, nor the sea swallow us?' (*SC* viii/ix. 88).

    23   **ynkylch canu y keilyawc,** 'about cock-crow'. Lat. *ad pullorum cantus* (*RLSD* 26).

    26   **vawrhydri,** MS *va⎮wrwrhydri*.

    28–31   **y gyt a … am y byt,** there is nothing in the Latin *Life* corresponding to this section.

    32–14.17   **ac y dugant y'r lle y mae goleuni … Amen.** Cf. p. li. This section is not found in the Latin *Life*, but it resembles the final passage in the *Life* of Cybi; see *VSBG* 248–51, *CLlGC* ix (1955/6), 19.

    a gorffwys, MS *argorffwys*.

    33   **lauur,** MS *lauuryei*.

    anuundeb, 'discord, disagreement'. *an-* (neg. prefix) + *duundeb*; see 11.30 above.

14   8   **da eu diodef,** lit. 'good their suffering', i.e. 'long-suffering'; *GMW* 37, and 3.5 above.

    12   **Pawl,** in the MS followed by *gwyr*, which has been crossed out.

    13   **Ieuan,** 'John'; see *EL* 12.

    14   **Judea,** MS *yjudea*.

14   19   **bo, grymhao,** exs. of the pres. subj. expressing wish; see
             GMW 113.

      20   **ar gaffel,** 'in order to obtain'. *ar* can denote purpose or inten-
             tion with verbs of asking, seeking, etc.; see *BD* li, *CFG* 135–6. A
             liturgical original may lie behind these final words, with their
             reference to the saint's intercession; cf. *SDL* 16.

ABBREVIATIONS

(a)	*Bibliographical*
A	Jesus College MS 119 or Llyvyr Agkyr Llandewivrevi (Bodleian Library, Oxford)
AB	*Analecta Bollandiana.*
ABr	Edward Lhuyd, *Archaeologia Britannica* (Oxford, 1707).
ABret	*Annales de Bretagne.*
AC	Archaeologia Cambrensis.
ACS	A. Holder, *Alt-Celtischer Sprachschatz* (Leipzig, 1891–1913).
AI	Sean Mac Airt, *The Annals of Inisfallen* (Dublin, 1951).
ALKA	W. H. Stevenson (ed.), *Asser's Life of King Alfred* (Oxford, 1904).
AO	Francis Shaw, *Aislinge Oengusso* (Dublin, 1934).
AP	Ifor Williams, *Armes Prydein* (Caerdydd, 1955).
AP[1]	Ifor Williams, *Armes Prydein* English edn. with additional notes, Rachel Bromwich (Dublin, 1972).
ASC	G. N. Garmonsway (trans.), *The Anglo-Saxon Chronicle* (Everyman's, 1953).
AU	W. M. Hennessy, *The Annals of Ulster* i (Dublin, 1887).
B	Llanstephan MS. 27 or The Red Book of Talgarth (NLW).
B	*The Bulletin of the Board of Celtic Studies.*
BD	Henry Lewis, *Brut Dingestow* (Caerdydd, 1942).
BDe	D. Simon Evans, *Buched Dewi* (Caerdydd, 1959, 2nd edn. 1965).
BEH	*Bede's Ecclesiastical History of the English Nation* (Everyman's, London, 1954).
BL	British Library.

BLSM	W. Stokes, *The Birth and Life of St Moling* (Paris, 1906).
BNE	Charles Plummer, *Bethada Náem n Érenn* 2 vols. (Oxford, 1922).
BT	J. G. Evans, *The Book of Taliesin* (Llanbedrog, 1910).
BTy Pen 20[1]	Thomas Jones (trans.), *Brut y Tywysogyon or The Chronicle of the Princes Peniarth MS. 20 Version* (Cardiff, 1952).
BTy RB	Thomas Jones, *Brut y Tywysogyon or The Chronicle of the Princes Red Book of Hergest Version* (Cardiff, 1955).
BWP	Ifor Williams, *The Beginnings of Welsh Poetry*. Trans. and ed., Rachel Bromwich (Cardiff, 1972).
C	Llanstephan MS 4 (NLW).
CA	Ifor Williams, *Canu Aneirin* (Caerdydd, 1938).
Card	A Cardiff manuscript, in the Cardiff Central Library.
CCB	L. Hardinge, *The Celtic Church in Britain* (London, 1972).
CEIS	Kathleen Hughes, *The Church in Early Irish Society* (London, 1966).
Celtica	Dublin Institute for Advanced Studies (1946–).
CFG	Melville Richards, *Cystrawen y Frawddeg Gymraeg* (Caerdydd, 1938).
ChBr	Joseph Loth, *Chrestomathie Bretonne* (Paris, 1890).
ChO	Ifor Williams, *Chwedlau Odo* (new. edn. Caerdydd, 1958).
Chron Min	T. Mommsen, *Chronica Minora iii—Monumenta Germaniae Historica, Auctores Antiquissimi* xiii (Berlin, 1894–8).
CIL	Kuno Meyer, *Contributions to Irish Lexicography* (Halle a.S., 1906).
CLlGC	*Cylchgrawn Llyfrgell Genedlaethol Cymru—The National Library of Wales Journal.*
CLlH	Ifor Williams, *Canu Llywarch Hen* (3rd edn. Caerdydd, 1970).
Contrib.	*Contributions to a Dictionary of the Irish Language* (Royal Irish Academy, Dublin).
Councils	Haddam & Stubbs, *Councils and Ecclesiastical Documents relating to Great Britain and Ireland* 3 vols. (Oxford, 1869–78. Reprinted 1965).
CS	W. M. Hennessy, *Chronicum Scotorum* (London, 1866).

Cy	*Y Cymmrodor.*
D	Cotton MS D xxii (BL).
Di	A text of the Digby recension (see p. xxxix).
Doble	G. H. Doble, *The Saints of Cornwall* (1923–4; reprint in 5 vols. Truro, 1960–70).
DPGOH	H. Owen, *The Description of Pembrokeshire by George Owen of Henllys.* Notes by E. Phillimore. 4 vols. (Cymmr. Rec. Series: London, 1892, 1897, 1906, 1936).
DS	E. G. Bowen, *Dewi Sant/Saint David* (Cardiff, 1983).
DWB	*A Dictionary of Welsh Biography down to 1940* (London, 1959).
E	NLW MS 5267B or Y Casgliad Brith (NLW).
EANC	R. J. Thomas, *Enwau Afonydd a Nentydd Cymru* (Caerdydd, 1938).
EAWD	J. C. Davies, *Episcopal Acts and Cognate Documents relating to Welsh Dioceses, 1066–1272* 2 vols. (Hist. Soc. Church in Wales Pubns. Cardiff, 1948, 1953).
EC	*Études celtiques.*
ECMW	V. E. Nash-Williams, *The Early Christian Monuments of Wales* (Cardiff, 1950).
EEW	T. H. Parry-Williams, *The English Element in Welsh* (London, 1923).
EHR	*English Historical Review.*
EL	H. Lewis, *Yr Elfen Ladin yn yr Iaith Gymraeg* (Caerdydd, 1943).
EWGP	K. H. Jackson, *Early Welsh Gnomic Poems* (Cardiff, 1935).
EWGT	P. C. Bartrum, *Early Welsh Genealogical Tracts* (Cardiff, 1966).
Flor. *Wigorn.*	*Florentii Wigorniensis Monachi Chronicon ex Chronicis.* Ed. B. Thorpe *English Hist. Soc.* 2 vols., London 848–9, Trans. T. Forester in Bohn's *Antiquarian Library* (London, 1854).
G	J. Lloyd-Jones, *Geirfa Barddoniaeth Gynnar Gymraeg* (Caerdydd, 1931–63).
GDG	T. Parry, *Gwaith Dafydd ap Gwilym* (new edn. Caerdydd, 1963).
Gildas	H. Williams, *Gildas: The Ruin of Britain* 2 vols. (London, 1899, 1901). Also M. Winterbottom, *Gildas: the Ruin of Britain and Other Works* (Phillimore, 1978).

GMW	D. S. Evans, *A Grammar of Middle Welsh* (Dublin, 1964).
GO	E. Bachellery, *L'Oeuvre Póetique de Gutun Owain* (Paris i. 1950, ii. 1951).
GOI	R. Thurneysen, *A Grammar of Old Irish*. Trans. D. A. Binchy and O. Bergin (Dublin, 1946).
GPC	*Geiriadur Prifysgol Cymru—A Dictionary of the Welsh Language* (Caerdydd, 1950–).
GPN	D. E. Evans, *Gaulish Personal Names* (Oxford, 1967).
GW	Lewis Thorpe (trans.), *Gerald of Wales: The Journey through Wales/The Description of Wales* (Penguin Books, 1978).
HASD	W. E. Jones & E. A. Freeman, *The History and Anti- quities of St. David's* (London, 1856).
Hav	A Havod manuscript, in the Cardiff Central Library.
HGCr	H. Lewis, *Hen Gerddi Crefyddol* (Caerdydd, 1931).
HGVK	D. S. Evans, *Historia Gruffud vab Kenan* (Caerdydd, 1977).
Historia	*Eadmeri Historia Novorum in Anglia*. Ed. Martin Rule. R. S. London, 1884. Trans. G. Bosanquet (London, 1964).
Hist. Reg.	*Historia Regum*, vol. ii of Symeon of Durham's works. Ed. T. Arnold. R. S. (London, 1885).
HRB	A. Griscom, *The Historia Regum Britanniae of Geof- frey of Monmouth* (London and New York, 1929).
HW	J. E. Lloyd, *A History of Wales from the Earliest Times to the Edwardian Conquest* 2 vols. (London, 1911).
HWW	F. Jones, *The Holy Wells of Wales* (Cardiff, 1954).
IER	*Irish Ecclesiastical Record*.
IGE	H. Lewis, T. Roberts, I. Williams, *Iolo Goch ac Eraill* (Caerdydd, 1937, reprint 1972).
IHS	*Irish Historical Studies*.
Invect.	*De Invectionibus*. Ed. J. S. Brewer. R. S. 1963.
IrGl	W. Stokes, *Irish Glosses, a medieval tract on Latin declension* (Dublin, 1860).
IW	C. O'Rahilly, *Ireland and Wales* (London, 1924).
JHSCW	*The Journal of the Historical Society of the Church in Wales.*
JRSAI	*Journal of the Royal Society of Antiquaries of Ireland.*
L	A text of the Vespasian recension, as found in the Lincoln Cathedral Library MS. 149 (see p. liv).

L&P	H. Lewis and H. Pedersen, *A Concise Comparative Celtic Grammar* (Göttingen, 1937, 1961).
L&S	Lewis and Short, *A Latin Dictionary* (Oxford).
Lat Lives	E. Hogan, *The Latin Lives of the Saints* (Dublin, 1894).
LBS	S. Baring-Gould & J. Fisher, *The Lives of the British Saints* 4 vols. (London, 1907–13).
LCBS	W. J. Rees, *Lives of the Cambro-British Saints* (Llandovery, 1953).
LHEB	K. H. Jackson, *Language and History in Early Britain* (Edinburgh, 1953).
LL	J. G. Evans & J. Rhys, *The Book of Llan Dâv— Liber Landavensis* (Oxford, 1893—Facsimile edn. Aberystwyth, 1979).
LSBL	W. Stokes, *Lives of Saints from the Book of Lismore* (Oxford, 1890).
LSD	A. W. Wade-Evans, *Life of St. David* (London, 1923).
LSP	J. B. Bury, *The Life of St Patrick* (London, 1905).
LSSD	T. Taylor, *The Life of St. Samson of Dol* (London, 1925).
LTBL	J. Andrew, *Lexique des termes de botanique en Latin* (Paris, 1956).
LWS	G. H. Doble, *Lives of the Welsh Saints* Ed. with introduction and notes, D. Simon Evans (Cardiff, 1971).
LlA	J. Morris-Jones & J. Rhŷs, *The Elucidarium and Other Tracts from Llyvyr Agkyr Llandewivrevi* (Oxford, 1894).
Llan	A Llanstephan manuscript, in the National Library of Wales.
LlB	S. J. Williams & J. E. Powell, *Cyfreithiau Hywel Dda yn ôl Llyfr Blegywryd* (Caerdydd, 1942).
LlC	*Llên Cymru.*
LlDC	A. O. H. Jarman, *Llyfr Du Caerfyrddin* (Caerdydd, 1982).
MOC	W. Stokes, *The Martyrology of Oengus the Culdee* (London, 1905).
MT	R. I. Best & H. J. Lawlor, *The Martyrology of Tallaght* (London, 1931).
N	A text of the Nero recension (see p. xxxix).
N	J. Morris (ed. & trans.), *Nennius* (Phillimore: London & Chichester, 1980).
NLA	C. Horstman, *Nova Legenda Anglie* 2 vols. (Oxford, 1901).

NLW	National Library of Wales.
Opera	J. F. Dimock, *Giraldi Cambrensis Opera* 8 vols. (R. S. London, 1861–91).
Pembroke-shire	See *DPGOH*.
Pen	A Peniarth manuscript, in the National Library of Wales.
PKM	I. Williams, *Pedeir Keinc y Mabinogi* (Caerdydd, 1930).
PMR	H. J. Lawlor, *The Psalter and Martyrology of Ricemarch i* (London, 1914).
RC	*Revue celtique.*
RLSD	J. W. James, *Rhigyfarch's Life of St. David* (Cardiff, 1967).
RMWL	J. G. Evans, *Report on Manuscripts in the Welsh Language* 2 vols. (London, 1898–1910).
SC	*Studia Celtica.*
SCSW	E. G. Bowen, *The Settlements of the Celtic Saints in Wales* (Cardiff, 1956).
SDL	S. M. Harris, *Saint David in the Liturgy* (Cardiff, 1940).
SEBC	N. K. Chadwick (ed.), *Studies in the Early British Church* (Cambridge, 1958).
SEHI	J. F. Kenney, *The Sources for the Early History of Ireland Vol i Ecclesiastical* (New York, 1929).
SG	M. Miller, *The Saints of Gwynedd* (The Boydell Press, 1979).
SGS	*Scottish Gaelic Studies.*
SGr	R. Williams, *Y Seint Greal, Selections from the Hengwrt MSS. Vol. i* (London, 1876).
SH	*Studia Hibernica.*
SILH	J. Carney, *Studies in Irish Literature and History* (Dublin, 1955).
Slover	C. H. Slover, 'Early Lit. Channels between Ireland and Wales' (*U. of Texas Bulletin, Studies in English, No. 7*, 1927).
SN	G. H. Doble, *Saint Nonna* (Liskeard, 1928).
SPAI	J. H. Todd, *St. Patrick Apostle of Ireland* (Dublin, 1864).
SSSCL	E. G. Bowen, *Saints, Seaways and Settlements in the Celtic Lands* (Cardiff, 1969).
Studies	An Irish quarterly review. Dublin.
Survey	Browne Willis. *A Survey of the Cathedral Church of St. David's* (London, 1717).

TC	T. J. Morgan, *Y Treigladau a'u Cystrawen* (Caerdydd, 1952).
TCAS	*Transactions of the Cardiganshire Antiquarian Society.*
TLP	W. Stokes, *The Tripartite Life of Patrick Part i* (London, 1887).
TLlM	G. J. Williams, *Traddodiad Llenyddol Morgannwg* (Caerdydd, 1948).
V	A text of the Vespasian recension (see p. xl).
V¹	BL MS. Vespasian A XIV (see p. xlii).
VSBG	A. W. Wade-Evans, *Vitae Sanctorum Britanniae et Genealogiae* (Cardiff, 1944).
VSH	Ch. Plummer, *Vitae Sanctorum Hiberniae* 2 vols. (Oxford, 1910).
WCCR	G. Williams, *The Welsh Church from Conquest to Reformation* (Cardiff, 1962).
WCO	A. W. Wade-Evans, *Welsh Christian Origins* (Oxford, 1934).
WEMA	W. Davies, *Wales in the Early Middle Ages* (Leicester, 1982).
WG	J. Morris-Jones, *A Welsh Grammar* (Oxford, 1913).
WHR	*Welsh History Review.*
WLC	K. Hughes, *The Welsh Latin Chronicles: Annales Cambriae and Related Texts*—The Sir John Rhŷs Memorial Lecture (London, 1973).
WM	J. G. Evans, *The White Book Mabinogion* (Pwllheli, 1907). Now see reprint with a new introduction by R. M. Jones (Caerdydd, 1973).
YB x	J. E. Caerwyn Williams, *Ysgrifau Beirniadol, Cyfrol x* (Dinbych, 1977).
YCM	S. J. Williams, *Ystorya de Carolo Magno* (2nd edn. Caerdydd, 1968).
ZCP	*Zeitschrift für celtische Philologie.*

(b)   *Linguistic*

abl.	ablative
adj.	adjective
adv.	adverb
adverb.	adverbial
affirm.	affirmative
affix.	affixed
art.	article
comp.	comparative
conj.	conjunction
conjunct.	conjunctive
consuet.	consuetudinal
Corn.	Cornish
def.	definite
dem.	demonstrative
equat.	equative
fem.	feminine
fut.	future
gen.	genitive
imper.	imperative
imperf.	imperfect
impers.	impersonal
indep.	independent
indic.	indicative
infix.	infixed
interj.	interjection
interr.	interrogative
Ir.	Irish
Lat.	Latin
masc.	masculine
ModW	Modern Welsh
mut.	mutation
MW	Middle Welsh
neg.	negative
nn.	noun
obj.	object
OF	Old French
OW	Old Welsh
part.	particle
pass.	passive
pers.	personal
pl.	plural
plup.	pluperfect

poss.	possessive
predic.	predicative
prefix.	prefixed
prep.	preposition
pres.	present
pret.	preterite
pre. verb.	pre-verbal
pron.	pronoun
reduplic.	reduplicated
rel.	relative
sing.	singular
spir.	spirant
sub.	subject
subj.	subjunctive
superl.	superlative
var.	variant
vb.	verb
vn.	verbal noun

(c)	*Miscellaneous*
c.	*circa*, about
c(c). ch.	chapter(s)
ex(s).	example(s)
ibid.	in the same place
l.	line
lit.	literally
MS(S)	manuscript(s)
n.	note
op. cit.	work cited
p(p)	page(s)
rev.	revised
s.a.	*sub anno*

PROPER NAMES

n. after a reference indicates that the form is discussed in the notes.

Aaron 14.9.
Abel 14.5.
Abraham 14.7.
Achaia 14.14.
Aedan 4.28n, 7.4, Aydan sant 6.30;
    Maydawc 7.23, Maydawc sant 7.21,
    25.
Auallach 1.5n.
Alexandria 11.11, 14.15.
Amguoel 1.4n.
Amweryt 1.4n.
Andreas 14.15.
Arglwyd (yr) 1.18, 2.5, 7, 4.24, 6.18,
    7.1, 8, 10.11, 12.7, 31, 13.1.
Arglwyd Duw (yr) 6.16, 10.9, 12.5.
Arglwyd Grist (yr) 2.5, A. Iessu Grist
    12.12, 13.25.
Asia (yr) 14.13.

Bed Yscolan 7.19n.
Boducat 4.20n.
Boya 5.3n, 13, 18, 22, 25, 26, 29,
    37, 6.10, 11, 13, 14, 16.
Breui 8.12n, 15, 9.36.

Kaerussalem 11.11.
Kedweli 4.20n.
Keredic 1.2n, 7.
Keredigyawn 1.8n.
Collan 4.14n.
Kreawdyr 14.20.
Krist 9.7, 10.31, 11.11, 14.2; also
    Iessu Grist.
Krowlan 4.13n.
Kruchier 2.14n.
Kuneda 1.2n.
Kymraec 3.22.
Kymry 3.6.

Chwefrawr, mis 12.1–2.

Dauid, the king 14.9.
Dauid 2.20, 4.28, 7.3, 28, 8.32, 9.21,
    10.20, 21, 11.12, 12.4, 11; Dauyd
    1.2, 3.32, 33, 4.2, 6, 6.11, 9.23,
    12.14.
Deil 1.3n.
Demetica 9.5n.
Dewi 1.1n, 2.12, 23, 25, 26, 3.11, 15,
    17, 22, 25, 26, 27, 31, 4.22, 23, 24,
    etc.
Deynioel 9.15n.
Dubim 1.4n.
Dubricius 9.16n.
Dunawt 6.8n.
Duw 2.10, 3.9, 21, 4.7, 29, 6.22, etc.
Dwuyn 1.3.
Dyd Brawt 1.13, 3.7, 4.11–12.
Dyfi 11.23n.

Edern 1.2.
Euegyl 10.31.
Eistedua Padric 2.9n.
Eliud 4.29n.
Enneint Twymynn (yr) 4.12n.
Enoc 14.6.
Ergyng 4.16n.
Eudoleu 1.5n.
Eugen 1.5n.

Ffreinc 11.12.
Fynnawn Dunawt 6.7n.
Ffynnawn Eliud 6.27n.
Ffynnawn Gwestlan 6.27n.

Gildas 2.27n, 27, 28, 30, 3.4.
Glasgwm 4.14n.
Glastynburi 4.8n.

VOCABULARY

n. after a reference indicates that the form is discussed in the notes.

a interr. part. 2.30, 8.25, 25.

a rel. pron. sub. 1.18, 3.12, 16, 5.9, 11, 6.10, 7.32, 35, 8.1, 2, 22, 11.31, 12.8, etc.

a rel. pron. obj. 1.12, 14, 17, 2.4, 8, 9, 11, 14, 15, 18, 19, 20, 20, 23, 26, 29, 33, 3.3, etc.

a affirm. part. 1.7, 10, 10, 16, 17, 2.5, 5, 6, 7, 9, 10, 10, 16, 19, 27, 3.11, 12, etc.

a(c) conj. *and* 1.7, 8, 8, 9, 10, 11, etc.; *but* 2.29, 6.10, 9.31.

a(c) prep. *with* 2.18, 19, 3.12, 19, 5.18, 7.15, 19, 21, 12.33; *as* 7.9, 10.32, 33, 12.37, *that* 8.25.

a dan prep. *under* 11.18–19.

a uo hwy (*for*) *longer* 12.13n; **a uo moe** *farther* 11.24n.

ac y conj. *that* 8.25.

ach *pedigree* 1.1.

adar *birds* 11.9.

adaw vn. *leave* 5.35, also **ydaw**; imper. sing. 2 **adaw** 1.16.

adeilat vn. *build*; pret. sing. 3 **adeilawd** 4.8, 15, 17, 6.17.

adeiladeu *buildings* 6.15.

adnabot vn. *know*, *recognize*: pres. sing. 1 **adwen** 8.29.

adref adv. (motion) *home* 5.17, 26, 27.

adaw vn. *promise*: pres. sing. 2 **edewy** 9.25.

adef vn. *acknowledge* 11.6.

adoli vn. *worship* 11.18.

adwyn adj. *fine, gentle, virtuous* 8.28.

auon *river* 1.12, 5.30, 8.2, 10.7.

auory *tomorrow* 1.10, 7.6; **avore** 9.18.

agoret adj. *open* 5.21, 6.14.

angel *angel* 1.9, 16, 2.6, 6, 4.5, 6, 24, 6.31, 7.4, 24, 8.28, 9.3, 12.3, 4, 14, 29, 29, pl. **engylyon** 13.23, 32, 14.16.

anghenuil *monster* 7.14n.

anghev *death* 6.10, 13.21.

alusen *alms, charity, blessing* 9.34.

allann adv. *out* 2.28, 7.35.

allmarw 7.36n.

am prep. *for, concerning* 3.30, 7.21, 8.6; *because of* 11.15; **am hynny** *because of that* 3.7.

amdiffynn nn. *defence, protection* 11.20, 23.

amen 14.17.

amled *abundance* 13.33.

amlwc adj. *clear* 10.32, 11.2.

amot 8.16n.

amouyn vn. *enquire* 7.20.

amrant *eyelid* 7.37.

ams(s)er *time* 4.6; *weather* 6.26n.

an poss. pron. prefix. pl. 1 *our* 5.20, 20, 20, 20, 10.11, 13.14, 20, also **yn**; **y an llosci ni** *to burn us* 13.19.

anawd adj. *difficult* 5.32.

anuon vn. *send*: pres. sing. 1 **anuonaf** 7.9; pret. sing. 3. **anuones** 2.6, 7, 7.39, 9.8; impers. pass. **anuonet** 9.14; imper. sing 2 **anuon** 7.6, 10.

aniueil *animal*: pl. **anyueileit** 5.27.

aniweir adj. *unfaithful, indecent, obscene* 5.31.

annobeith *despair, despondency* 12.36.

anryded *honour* 13.29.

anryued adj. *wonderful* 9.26.

ansawd *condition, state* 7.21, 22.

anuundeb *discord, dissension* 14.3–4.

anwyt nn. *cold* 13.30.

ar prep. *on, over* 2.14, 3.9, 4.1, 2, 5.12, 34, 6.19, 7.15, 28, 8.1, 9, etc; *to*

14.20 n; sing. 3 masc. **arnaw** 2.21,
5.5, 6.21, 8.5, 32, 9.3, fem. **ar(n)nei**
2.19, 21; pl. 3 **arnadunt** 8.15, **arnunt**
7.39, 12.9; **ar dal y deulin** *on her
knees* 10.4–5, **ar dal y glinyeu** 10.23;
ar eu glinnyeu *on their knees* 11.18.
ar dalym o enkyt *for a period of time, a
short while* 10.25.
ar vedwl 5.13n.
ar hynt adv. *straightway* 9.23.
ar y geuyn *on its back* 7.15.
ar neilltu *on one side* 7.23.
ar warthaf prep. *on top of, on* 10.35.
ar y dechreu *at the beginning* 9.1.
arall adj. *(an)other* 3.10, 11, 15, 4.25,
7.16.
archangel *archangel*: pl. **archengylyon**
14.16.
archescob *archbishop* 9.2.
arffet *lap* 6.2, 4, 10.10.
arganuot vn. *discover*; pret. sing. 3
argannuv 5.3.
arglwyd *lord* 3.33, 12.31; pl **arglwydi**
13.12.
arogleu *smell, odour* 12.10.
aros vn. *wait for* 9.27, 10.21.
at prep. *to* 1.16, 4.5, 9.14, 16, 29,
12.31; sing. 2 **attat** 2.7, 3.34; 3 masc
attaw 2.6, 3.29, 7.23, 9.3; pl. 2
attawch 9.6.
atteb nn. *answer* 9.10, 13; vn. pret.
sing. 3 **attebawd** 8.27.
athro *teacher* 3.26, 28, 28n, 29, 32, 33,
35, 7.3, 16, 9.2; pl. **athrawon** 8.13.
awch poss. pron. prefix. pl. 2 *your*
5.30.
awr *hour* 3.11, 19, 7.35, 8.2, 13.25; **yr
awr honn** *this hour, now* 1.12, 2.2, 8,
12.7.
awyr *air, sky* 4.31.

bara *bread* 2.24, 25, 7.5, 5, 7, 7, 29, 34,
36, 8.1, 3, 4.
barwn *baron*: pl. **barwneit** 8.14.
bedyd *baptism* 3.18.
bedydyaw vn. *baptize*; pret. impers.
pass. **bedydywyt** 3.15.
beidyaw vn. *dare*; imperf. sing. 3 **beidei**
10.26.
bendigaw vn.*bless*; pret. sing. 3
bendigawd 4.3, 11, 8.4; imper. sing.
2 **bendicka** 4.1.

ben(n)dith *blessing* 4.3, 9.28, 13.10,
11.
beth *what?* 13.4.
beth bynnac *whatever, whatsoever*
2.10–11.
bieiuyd 1.13n.
blew *hair* 7.36.
blinder *weariness, fatigue, affliction*
13.30, 14.4.
blwydynn *year* 3.23; pl. **blwyn(n)yded**
10.18, **blyned** (with numerals) 2.14,
17, 3.34.
bop eilwers 8.19n, **pob eilwers** 8.23.
bot/vot vn. *to be* 3.17, 5.20, 7.19, 8.29,
30, 10.5, 11.6, 12, 19, 13.16; indic.
pres. sing. 1 **wyf** 2.30, 5.7, 39, 2 **wyt**
5.10, 3 **yw** 3.9, 23, 4.6, 9.5, 11.22,
23, 25, **y mae** 3.36, 7.9, 12.5, 13.32n,
14.1, 2, 5, 6, 7, 8, 8, 9.9, 10.10, etc.,
that it is 4.24, 8.31, 9.7, **oes** 3.7, 8.22,
ys 7.2, 9.11, **ys(s)y(d)** (rel.) 2.8, 3.4,
5, 5.30, 9.6, 11.2, 12.30, pl. 2 **ywch**
8.21, 3 **y maent** 3.32; fut. sing. 1
bydaf 4.1, 2 **bydy** 2.9, 3 **byd** 2.10,
7.31, 11.23, 24, 12.37; imperf. sing.
3 **oed** 2.14, 17, 20, 21, 30, 3.12, 16,
18, 20, 26, 27, 4.10, 16, 20, 23, 23,
5.3, etc., **yttoed** 3.14, 31, pl. 3 **oedynt**
10.26, etc., impers. **oedit** 10.21;
consuet. past sing. 3 **bydei** 10.33, pl.
3 **bydynt** 5.17; pret. sing. 3 **bu** 1.18,
2.16, 21, 3.13, 28, 4.31, 5.32, 6.20,
21, 7.15, 36, 9.2, 10.17, 34, pl. 1
buam 5.23, 3 **buant** 4.2; plup. sing. 3
buassei 2.33, 3.16, 10.24; subj. pres.
sing. 3 **bo** 4.26, 11.22, 24, 26, 12.13,
14.19; imperf. sing. 3 **bei** 10.33;
imper. sing. 2 **byd** 2.7, 3 **poet** 13.15,
pl. 2 **bydwch** 12.24, 13.12.
bod *will, favour* 5.25.
bore *morning* 4.32, 5.1, 4, 6.12, *early*
13.25.
brat *treachery, betrayal* 7.5.
bran *crow, raven* 8.1.
brawt 13.5n.
brawt ffyd 4.23n, 6.23.
breint *privilege* 3.6.
brenhin *king* 2.18, 4.16, 11.25, 26; pl.
brenhined 8.13, 11.17, 30, 12.36,
13.5, 14.10, 17.
brodyr *brethren* 7.18, 38, 8.5, 7, 8,
9.24, 33, 12.20, 24, 13.12.

bronn *breast*: pl. **bronnev** 13.4.
brynn *hill* 10.24, 11.2, **brenn** 10.29.
buched *life* 1.1, 16, 14.18.
budugolyaeth *victory, triumph* 13.29, 14.1.
bugeil *shepherd*: pl. **bugelyd** 5.18–19.
bwrd *board, table* 9.22.
bwy *who?* 12.33; also **pwy**.
bwyt *food* 2.24, 25, 5.5, 6, 9.25, 34, 13.22.
bwytta vn. *eat* 7.6; pret. sing. 3
  bwytaawd 8.4; imper. pl. 2
  bwyttewch 9.23.
bychein adj. pl. *small* 13.13.
byt *world* 6.9, 10.10, 11.9, 12.31, 13.31.
byrr adj. *short* 7.9.
byth adv. *ever* (with neg.) 13.8; **byth bellach** *(not) ever/never again* 13.16.
byw adj. *alive* 5.27, 14.6.

kadarnnhav vn. *strengthen, safeguard* 8.11.
cadw vn *keep*: imper. pl. 2 **kedwch** 12.25, 13.13.
cael vn. *get, obtain* **caffel** 6.13, 7.10, 14.20; pres. sing. 2 **keffy** 1.10; imperf. pl. 3 **keffynt** 6.28, 8.10, impers. pass. **keffit** 4.3; pret. sing. 3 **kauas** 2.19, 3.17, 20, 6.6, 11.28, 28, (+ **beichogi** *became pregnant*), 2.19–20, 23 pl. 3 **cawssant** 5.24, 27, 8.26.
calan *first day* 13.28.
can(n)horthwy nn. *help* 3.30, 9.32.
canhorthwyaw vn. *help*; imper. sing. 2 **canhorthwya** 12.22, 36.
canhorthwywr *helper* 14.19.
kannvet *hundredth, one in a hundred* 8.20.
cannyat *permission* 5.12.
kannhlyn vn. *follow* 10.17.
kan(n)ys *because, for* (**kann** + **ys** *it is*) 2.9, 3.5, 36, 6.8, 11.27, 28, **kanyt** *because . . . not* (**kan** + **nyt**) 6.25.
cant *100* 4.25.
canu vn. *sing*: pret. sing. 3 **canawd** 13.7.
canu y keilawc *cock-crow* 13.23n.
cardawt *alms, charity* 9.34; pl. **cardodeu** 13.30.
kared *sin, crime* 7.32.

caryat *love* 2.1, 10, 9.12, 29.
carrec *stone* 3.12.
caru vn. *love* 8.30, 9.6; pres. sing. 3 **car** 8.30; imperf. sing. 3 **carei** 2.5, 7.21.
karw *deer, stag* 1.11n.
ketymdeith *companion* 8.28–9n; pl. **ketymeithonn** 9.29–30n.
keuyn nn. *back* 7.15.
keissaw vn. *seek* 3.30, 5.24, 25, 38, 6.24; pret. sing. 2 **keisseisti** (+ affix. pron.) 12.4.
kenedyl *species* 11.8.
kennat *permission, leave* 11.23; *messenger* 7.6, 9, 18, 22; pl. **kennadeu** *messengers* 9.8, 10, 15, 16, 17, 20, 35, 10.3, 20.
kennadwri *message* 7.24.
kerd *song*: pl. **kerdeu** 13.24, 14.4.
kerdet vn. *travel, go, proceed* 2.18n, 5.39, 7.13; pres. sing. 1 **kerdaf** 9.31, 13.14, 3 **kerdha** 5.9; pret. sing. 3 **kerdawd** 5.10, 10.20.
cerubin *the cherubim* 14.16.
kewilyd *modesty* 3.36n; also **kywilyd**.
kinyaw *dinner* 9.21.
cladu vn. *bury*: plup. impers. pass. **kladyssit** 2.14; subj. pres. impers. pass. **cladher** 4.27.
claerder *brightness, clearness* 14.1.
claf *ill, sick*: pl. **cleiuon** 6.28, 13.1.
clot *fame, renown* 10.4.
klywet vn. *hear*: pres. sing. 3 **clyw** 8.20, impers. pass **clywir** 13.8; imperf. sing. 3 **clywei** 8.17, 12.3, pl. 3 **clywynt** 12.10, 13, impers. pass. **clywit** 13.17; pret. sing. 3 **kigleu** 9.9, pl. 2 **klywyssawch** 12.25, 13.13, 3 **klywyssant** 12.20, impers. pass. **clywysbwyt** 13.8; plup. sing. 3 **klywssei** 10.4.
kneu *nuts* 5.38.
coffau vn. *commemorate*: pret. pl. 1 **coffayssam** 14.18.
colomen *dove* 3.24.
colli vn. *lose* 3.28.
corff *body, corpse* 10.7, 8.
kornn *horn* 10.31.
kret *belief, creed* 4.26, 8.11, 13.13.
kreuydwr *cleric*: pl. **kreuydwyr** 8.14n.
creic *rock* 5.4.
croen *skin* 7.37.
croessan 12.18n.

croew adj. *fresh, clear* 6.25.
kroth *womb* 3.4.
crupl *cripple*: pl. **crupleit** 6.28.
kryt *fever* 5.15.
cwbl *everything* 3.20n.
kwyn *lament, complaint* 12.35, 13.5.
kwynaw vn. *lament, moan* 12.21, 13.5, 6, 6; **kwynnvan** 5.22, 13.1, 17.
kyt ac prep. *along with* (**a ch.**) 13.26.
kyduundeb *agreement* 9.14n.
kyuanhedu vn. *inhabit, settle* 9.4.
kyuarch gwell vn. *greet* 10.22.
ky(f)uaruot vn. *meet* 2.18, 5.18, 7.19.
kyfeir *place, spot* 6.5.
kyfulawn adj. *complete, full* 3.18.
kyuot vn. *rise* 9.35; **kyfuodi** *rise* 5.8, 7.28, 29, 10.14, 15, 13.17, *raise* 2.13, 10.16; pret. sing. 3 **kyuodes** 4.32, 6.19, 10.21, 36, impers. pass. **kyuodet** 10.16; imper. sing. 2 **kyuot** 5.10, 38.
kyuoethawc *rich*: pl. **kyuoethogyon** nn. 14.2.
kyurann *share, part* 8.10.
kyurannawc adj. *partaking of, sharing in* 8.31.
kyfuredec vn. *gather together, assemble* 12.32.
kyureith *law* 10.31.
kyuryw *such*: **a'e gyuryw** *and the like of it* 13.8n.
kyffredin adj. *common, general* 8.17, 13.10, 17, equat. **kyffredinet** 10.33; nn. *the assembly in general* 8.20, 10.28.
kyngor 5.24n.
kylchynu vn. *encircle* 5.8; pret. sing. 3 **kylchynawd** 4.32.
kyllell *knife* 6.4.
kymein hun 12.20n.
kymenn adj. *accomplished* 6.3, 8.29.
kymryt vn. *take* 3.18, 7.15; pres. pl. 1 **kemerwn** 9.23; pret. sing. 3 **kymerth** 7.34, 8.2, 4, 10.28, 13.28, 31; subj. pres. pl. 2 **kymeroch** 9.33; imper. sing. 2 **kymer** 5.11, 12.7, 12.
kynn prep. *before* 3.7, 9.16, 36; **kynn noc ef** *before it* 13.8, **kyn no hynny** *before then* 10.24.
kynn adv. *as* + equat. adj. 12.37.
kynneu vn. *kindle*: pret. sing. 3

kynneuawd 5.9, 11, pl. 3
kyn(n)euassant 4.31, 32.
kynnhewi vn. *become quiet* 7.15.
kynntaf *first* 2.23, 4.31, 8.33, 12.15, 13.28.
kynnulleidua *assembly, gathering* 8.16, 20; **kynnulleit(t)ua** 9.36, 11.1.
kysgu vn. *sleep* 6.13, 10.15.
kysseuyll vn *stand, halt, stop* 12.3.
kyssegredic adj. *consecrated, sacred* 11.26.
kytdisgybyl *fellow-disciple* 7.10–11; pl. **kytdisgyblon** 3.24.
kytuun adj. *united, agreed* 11.5n.
kywilyd *shame, disgrace* 5.32.
kywilydus adj. *shameful* 5.31.

'ch pers. pron. infix. obj. pl. 2 *you* 9.33; infix. gen. pl. 2, 13.13.
chwaer *sister*: pl. **chwioryd** 13.12.
chwedyl *story, news* 12.28.
chwi pers. pron. indep. simple pl. 2 *you* 9.31; affix. simple pl. 2, 8.25, 9.17, 12.31.
chwitheu pers. pron. affix conjunct. pl. 2, 9.31, 33.
chydic *a little* 6.18n.
chynt spir. mut. of **cynt** adv. *before* 2.21.

da nn. *possession, benefit, good thing*; adj. *good* 4.26, 6.3, 21, 13.33; **da eu diodef** 14.8n; comp. **gwell** 5.35, 9.11.
dagreu *tears* 13.4, 18.
dangos vn. *show* 2.7; pret. sing. 3 **dangosses** 4.25.
daly vn. *hold* 3.17n, 18.
dall (*a*) *blind* (*man*) 3.16, 17, 19, 4.16; pl. **deillonn** 6.28.
damunaw vn. *desire, wish* 3.2.
damwein nn. *incident, event* 8.7; **damweinaw** vn. *happen*; pret. sing. 3 **damweinawd** 3.28, 6.12.
dan prep. *under* 10.36.
daruot vn. *happen* 7.22n, 13.11, *end, finish* 7.27, 13.9; pres. sing. 3 **deryw** 7.4; pret. sing. 3 **daruu** 10.14.
darparv vn. *prepare* 7.2.
datkanu vn. *declare* 7.24.
dayar *earth* 3.16, 10.13, 11.8, 12.16, 13.16, 18, 14.19.

dechreu nn. *beginning* 9.1, vn. *begin* 10.30; pret. sing. 3 **dechreuawd** 2.27, 6.10, 8.18–19.

dedyf *law* 4.4n.

deueit *sheep* (pl) 5.20.

dec ... ar hugein(t) *thirty* 2.2–3, 17; **deg ... ar hugein** 2.17.

decuet *tenth* 12.16.

deg *ten* 3.34.

deheu nn. *south* 8.2, 9.5; adj. *right* 10.15.

deissyuyt adj. *sudden, immediate* 7.14.

deu *two* 1.13, 3.13, 4.20, 9.15, 24, 12.8.

di pers. pron. affix sing. 2 2.9, 3.2, 35, 4.1, 7.3, 30, 9.27, 10.13, 12.7, 15.

diagon *deacon* 7.28.

diannot *without delay* 6.14, 19.

diawt nn. *drink* 5.5, 6, 9.25, 34, 13.22.

didan adj. *pleasant* 12.10.

didanu vn. *comfort* 12.23.

digoned *abundance, plenty* 9.22.

digrifwch *pleasure, delight* 13.24.

dihaedaf 6.3n.

dillat *clothes* 5.30.

dim *any* 5.15, 6.18; *anything* 6.25, 8.21.

dinas *city* 6.25, 30, 12.11, 13.24, 24; pl. **dinassoed** 5.8.

diodef vn. *suffer* 5.32, 34, 12.33; pres. sing. 2 **diodeuy** 2.10.

diolwch *thanks* 7.26n.

diosglwch imper. pl. 2 *take off* 5.30.

disgybyl nn. *pupil* 3.26, 6.23, 7.21, 22, 23; pl. **disgyblon** 3.30, 4.21, 28, 5.14, 16, 31–2, 6.11, 12, 9.17, 21, 12.34.

disgyn (nu) vn. *descend*: pret. sing. 2 **disgynneist** 10.9–10n.

disgyryaw vn. *shout, scream* 10.2.

ditheu pers. pron. affix. conjunct. sing. 2 9.25.

diwed nn. *end* 13.32, 14.5.

diweir adj. *chaste, clean* 2.21, 6.3, 8.30.

diwethaf superl. adj. *last* 3.31, 12.1.

dodi vn. *place, put* 7.5, 10.8.

dolur *disease, pain* 3.29, 14.3.

dor *door* 2.31, 8.12.

dracheuen adv. *back, again* 10.12.

dros prep. *over* 3.13, 13.19, *on behalf of* 8.19; pl. 1 **drossom** 13.1.

drwc adj. *evil* 5.34, 6.9, 14.2; nn. *harm* 5.15, 11.21; pl. **drygeu** 12.13.

druod adv. *over* 7.12n., 15.

drws *door* 7.35.

drwy prep. *through* 2.1, 10.17, 12.20, 28, *in* 13.22.

drycaruaethu 6.10n.

drygyruerth *wailing, lamentation* 10.3.

duhudaw 2.6n.

duhun *united, agreed* 11.6.

duundeb *agreement, concurrence* 11.30.

duw *day* (with names of days, feasts, etc.) 12.1; also **dyw**.

dwf(u)yr *water* 2.24, 25, 3.19, 4.10, 11, 6.18, 18, 25, 25, 7.13, 14, 9.22, 23; **dyfuwr** 9.18; **dwfuyr bedyd** *water of baptism* 3.19.

dwy *two* (fem.) 5.38, 8.26.

dwyn vn. *carry, take, live (a life)* 1.15; **dwyn treis** *violate* 2.19; pret. sing. 3 **duc** 6.10, pl. 3 **dugant** 13.32; imper. pl. 2 **dygwch** 9.18.

dy poss. pron. prefix. sing. 2 3.2, 33, 5.11, 12, 12, 6.2, 7.3, 7, 10, 10.13, 12.7, 15, **de** 4.1, **di** 6.3.

dyd *day* 7.16, 9.20, 11.17, 20, 12.14, 26, 28, 13.27.

dydgweith *one day* 4.28.

dyuot vn. *come* 2.32, 6.12, 7.1, 13, 17, 26, 9.3, 16, 25, 36, 10.1, 7, 22, 12.30, 33, 13.25; pres. sing. 3 **daw** 9.17, 12.15, 19, 13.19, 19; pret. sing. 1 **deuthum** 3.34, 3 **deuth** 4.8, 10, 13, 14, 28, 7.14, 10.21, **doeth** 1.16, 2.32, 3.12, 4.5, 5.13, 6.14, pl. 3 **deuthant** 5.27, 8.12, 9.20, **doethant** 5.14, 6.1; imper. sing. 2 **dabre** 9.27.

dygwydaw vn. *fall*: pret. sing. 3 **dygwydawd** 6.5, pl. 3 **dygwydassant** 5.14–15.

dylyet 1.12n.

dylyynt 3.21n, 7.27.

dyn *man, person* 8.20, 32, 10.32, 11.25; pl. **dynyon** 6.6, 11.9, 29, 12.9, 13.9.

dyoer interj. *indeed* 5.6n, 7.3.

dyrchauel vn. *rise, ascend* 10.23,
raise 12.6; pret. pl. 3 **dyrchauassant**
12.21.
dyrwest *abstinence, fasting* 13.30.
dyrwestu vn. *fast*: pret. pl. 3
dyrwestassant 5.36, 6.24.
dysgu vn. *teach* 3.25, 9.9, *learn* 3.34,
8.33; pres. sing. 3 **dysc** 12.35; pret.
sing. 3 **dyscawd** 3.27, 8.33, 9.1;
impers. pass **dysgwyt** 3.22, 23.
dyw *day* (with names of days, feasts,
etc.) 13.7, 21, 21, 27; also **duw**.
dywedut vn. *say, speak* 1.18, 3.36, 4.5,
5.16, 18, 23, 6.2, 7.1, 26, 30, 8.19,
22, 10.9, 25, 29, 11.7, 12.3, 6, 11, 14,
35, 35, 36, 13.18; imperf. sing. 3
dywedei 12.29; pret. sing. 3 **dywaut**
5.34, **dywot** 4.24, 24, **dywat** 2.6, 28,
5.29, 37, 8.19, 22, 9.16, 20, 23, 24,
12.23, 13.11, pl. 3 **dywedassant** 5.19,
33, 12.22; imper. pass. **dywetpwyt**
1.14, **dywedwyt** 10.35; plup. sing. 3
dywedassei 7.24; imper. pl. 2
dywedwch 5.31.

ebostol *apostle* 2.9; pl. **ebestyl** 14.11.
edrych vn. *look (at), examine* 3.33,
5.34, 8.5, 11.1; pret. sing. 1
edrycheis 3.34; imper. sing. 2
edrych 3.32, pl. 2 **edrychwch** 8.25.
ef pers. pron. indep. simple sing. 3
masc. 1.10, 13, 2.15, 18, 29, 3.8,
10, 36, 4.8, 5.7, 7, 9, 13, 26, 7.2,
etc. affix. simple sing. 3 masc. 1.7,
3.6, 11, 23, 24, 4.2, 5.9, 25, 6.21,
7.6, 22, 8.29, 9.7, 10, 10, 17.
ef a affirm. part. 3.11n, 15, 12.15.
euo pers. pron. indep. reduplic. sing.
3 masc. 2.30.
eglur adj. *clear* 2.33, 6.20, 10.32,
13.27; equat. **egluret** 10.32.
egluraw vn. *illuminate, make bright*
13.27.
eglwys *church* 2.26, 28, 30, 32, 3.3,
4.9, 17, 18, 6.30, 7.17, 12.26.
eil *second* 2.26, 7.39; **eilweith** *second
time, again* 9.12, 12.11, 13.
eirawl vn. *pray, intercede* 14.20.
eiroet adv. *ever* 3.16, 13.9.
eisseu *need, lack* 6.21.
eissoes adv. *nevertheless, however*
2.5, 6.12, 9.30, 10.28, 12.28.

eisted vn. *sit* 2.33, 5.4, 7.32, **eiste** 6.1,
7.27.
eistedua *seat* 2.8.
elchwyl adv. *a second time, again*
2.29.
emelltith nn. *curse* 8.9, 9.28.
enkyt *moment, (short) while* 7.36,
10.25.
eneit *soul, life* 10.12, 12.12, 13.28,
32.
enw *name* 2.15, 20, 21, 6.8, 10.13.
erbyn prep. *by* 10.15; **erbyn hanner
dyd** *by mid-day* 7.16.
erchi vn. *ask, request, command*
7.11, 9.4, 10.23, 26; pres. pl. 2
erchwch 9.30; imper. sing. 2 **arch**
2.32, 3.33, 7.7.
escob *bishop* 2.16, 4.23, 6.23, 8.27,
11.27; **escob sant** 3.27; pl. **escyb**
8.12, 14.9.
escor vn. *be delivered* 3.14.
escussaw vn. *excuse (oneself)* 10.25.
et(t)wo adv. *still, yet, again* 1.13, 17,
3.35, 11.2.
ethol vn. *choose, select* 2.1.
eu poss. pron. prefix pl. 3 5.16, 20
(**ac eu**) 21 (**ac eu**) 8.8, 9.21, 12.21,
23, 13.4, 4, 5, 6, 14.8.
eur *golden* 3.25.

val hynn *like this, thus* 4.5, 12.4–5,
6–7.
val y(r/d) conj. *as* 2.17, 33, 3.21,
5.17, 7.17, 12.1, 14.18; *how* 12.29,
(*so*)*that* 7.10, 8.17, 10.12; **val na** *so
that . . . not* 6.21; **val pei atuei** *as if
he were* 10.15.
velle adv. *thus, so* 3.36, 5.17, 11.9,
14.19.
vi pers. pron. indep. sing. 1 12.12;
affix. sing. 1 9.11, 13.4.
vivi pers. pron. indep. reduplic. sing.
1 3.4.
vy poss. pron. prefix. sing. 1 3.32,
4.1, 1, 9.17, 10.9, 12.12, 23.

ffo vn. *flee*: imperf. sing. 3 **ffoei**
11.21; pret. sing. 3 **ffoes** 6.9;
imper. pl. 1 **fown** 5.33.
fford *way* 3.8, 5.9, 13.14.
ffreutur *refectory* 8.2.
ffyd *faith* 4.26, 8.11, 13.13.

ffynnawn *well, spring* 6.7, 20, 20, 26,
28, 9.19, 22, ffynnyawn 3.16, 6.6,
ffynnyaon 3.16; pl. ffynnhonnev
6.25.

gadaw vn. *leave* 3.10; pret. sing. 3
gedewis 2.12; plup. sing. 3
gadawssei 13.26.
gadv vn. *leave, allow* 8.18; imper.
sing. 2 gat 12.12.
galw vn. *call* 3.29, 31, 7.23, 9.3; pres.
sing. 3 geilw 12.16; impers. pass.
gelwir 2.8, 4.12, 17, 18, 30, 6.7, 27,
7.19, 8.33; imperf. impers. pass.
gelwit 2.18, 3.22, 26, 4.20, 22, 23,
5.3, 6.24, 10.7; imper. pl. 2 gelwch
3.3, 9.6.
gallel vn. *be able (to do)* 3.31, gallu
8.15; pres. sing. 1 gallaf 9.31, pl. 1
gallwnn 5.33; impers. pass. gellir
9.26; imperf. sing. 3 gallei 2.28, 29,
10.26, 12.33, pl. 3 gellynt 5.15; pret.
sing. 2 gelleisti (+ affix. pron.) 3.1,
3 gallawd 11.16; subj. pres. sing. 3
gallo 8.22, 26; impers. pass. galler
7.10.
gan(n) prep. *with, by* 10.34, 11.2,
12.29, 32, 13.5, 17, + vn. 10.23,
11.6, 12.23; sing. 1 gennyf 9.11,
12.25, 13.14, 3 masc. gantaw 4.26,
7.29; pl. 3 gantunt 5.32.
gast *bitch* 7.35, 36.
gawr *cry, shout* 13.17.
geir *word*: pl. geireu 5.16, 31.
geir bronn prep. *before* 14.20, ger
bronn 9.22.
gelyn *enemy* 6.13, 10.11.
geneu *mouth* 10.8, 8.
geni vn. *be born*: pres. impers. pass.
genir 2.2; pret. impers. pass. ganet
1.17, 2.2, 20, 3.11, 19.
ger prep. *by, beside* 1.10n.
ger llaw prep. *beside* 5.30.
glann *bank* 4.15.
glas *early* 4.32, 5.2.
gleissat *(young) salmon* 1.11.
glin(n)yeu *knees* 7.14, 11.18.
gloyw adj. *bright, clear* 9.19.
glyn *valley* 6.1.
gobrwy *reward, payment*: pl.
gobrwyeu 14.5.

gouyn *ask*: pret. sing. 3 gouynnawd
2.29–30, 3.1, 5.6.
gogonyant *glory* 14.4.
golchi vn. *wash* 3.19.
goleuni *light* 13.32.
golwc *sight* 3.17, 20.
gollwng vn. *let (go on), drop, shed*
10.3, 13.4.
goreugwr *nobleman*: pl. goreugwyr
8.14.
gorffen vn. *finish, complete*: imper. pl.
2 gorffennwch 12.25.
gorffwys nn. *rest* 13.33.
gormod adj. *excessive* 3.29, 8.6.
goruc 1.17n, 2.4, 15, 19, 29, 33, 3.15,
29, 32, 35, 5.22, 26, 6.1, 3, 4, etc.;
pl. gorugant 11.5.
gorwagrwyd *vanity* 14.4.
gorwed vn. *lie* 8.1.
gossot vn. *set, place*: pret. sing. 3
gossodes 11.29.
gostwng vn. *go down*: pret. pl. 3
gostynghassant 11.18.
grad *order, grade* 12.15, 13.26.
gras *grace* 7.27, 8.24, 9.7.
greoed 5.20n.
griduan vn. *groan, moan* 4.22.
grymoccau vn. *avail*: subj. pres. sing.
3 grymoccao 14.19.
grymus adj. *powerful, mighty* 13.15.
gwaet *blood* 6.5.
gwaelawt *bottom* 6.1.
gwahawd vn. *invite*: pret. pl. 3
gwahawdassant 9.13.
gwar adj. *gentle, meek* 6.3.
gwaran(n)daw vn. *listen* 2.26–7, 3.2,
12.2, 8.
gware vn. *play* 3.25.
gwaret vn. *cure* 4.16, 6.7, 28.
gwarthec *cattle* 5.20.
gwas *servant, youth* 1.18, 8.28, 9.9,
12.7; pl. gweisson 5.11, 13.3.
gwassan(n)aethu vn. *serve* 2.1,
7.28–9, 10.18, 12.2; pres. sing. 2
gwassanaethy 7.30; imperf. sing. 3
gwassannaethei 7.28.
gwassanaethwr *server* 7.31.
gwastat adj. *continual, constant,
steadfast* 8.28, 12.24, nn. *level
ground, floor* 10.30, 13.20.
gwastatir *plain, level ground* 11.2.
gwattwar vn. *mock* 5.16, 23.

gwedy prep. *after* 2.16, 6.13, 7.17, 18, 22, 27, 27, 8.11, 10.1, 13.9, 21, 29; gwedy ef *after it* 13.8; (g)wedy hynny *after that, afterwards* 2.17, 9.1, 35; adv. *after* 2.21, 3.7.

gwedi *prayer* 10.14.

gwediaw vn. *pray* 5.24, 6.31, 9.9, 11, 10.9, 12.27, 13.22; pres. sing. 1 gwediaf 9.33, 3 gwedia 13.1; pret. sing. 3 gwediawd 6.19; imper. pl. 2 gwediwch 9.32.

gwedw adj. *widowed* 10.1, 12.

gweidi vn. *cry, shout* 10.2.

gweith *time* 9.14.

gweithret *deed* 2.22, 10.17; pl. gweithredoed 14.18.

gwelet vn. *see*: pres. sing. 2 gwely 2.9, pl. 1 gwelwnn 8.24; imperf. sing. 2 gwelut 12.31, 3 guelei 7.18, pl. 3 gwelynt 9.36; pret. sing. 1 gweleis 5.7, 9.3, 3 gwelas 3.24, 10.2, 13.9, pl. 2 gwelsawch 12.24, 13.14, 3 gwelsant 7.38, 10.19, 22.

gwely *bed* 6.14.

gwell comp. adj. *better* 5.35.

gwen(n)wyn *poison* 4.10, 7.5, 7.

gwenwynaw vn. *poison* 8.8.

gwen(n)wynic adj. *poisonous* 7.29, 34.

gwin *wine* 6.21, 21, 9.23.

gwir adj. *true* 14.20.

gwiryon adj. *innocent* 12.17.

gwlat *land, country* 9.4.

gwledychawd 1.7n.

gwn(n)euthur vn. *do, make* 4.6, 7, 5.15, 7.5, 11, 10.26; pret. sing. 3 gwn(n)aeth 2.23, 26, 3.11, 21, 5.23, 10.5; pl. 3 gwnaethant 6.1; impers. pass. gwnaethpwyt 8.16, 11.14; subj. pres. sing. 2 gwnelych 2.11, imperf. sing. 3 gwnnelei 11.21; imper. pl. 2 gwnewch 13.13.

gwr *man, husband* 2.14, 15.21, 5.8, 6.22; pl. gwyr 8.9, 14.12, 12, 13, 13, 14, 15, 15.

gwrda *nobleman* 7.1.

gwreic *woman, wife* 5.5, 10, 18, 22, 29, 37, 6.16, 10.1, 1, 2, 4, 11; pl. gwraged 5.34.

gwrthot vn. *refuse* 10.29.

gwybot vn. *know*: pres. sing. 1 gwn(n) 7.3, 8.28, 30, 31, 9.7; 2 gwdosti (+ suffix. pron.) 7.2, pl. 2

gwddawch 8.25; imperf. sing. 3 gwydat 7.32; pret. sing. 3 gwybu 3.17, 6.9; imper. sing. 3 gwybydet 6.15, pl. 2 gwybydwch 9.17, gwybydwchwi (+ affix. pron.) 12.29.

gwynuydedic adj. *blessed* 7.2.

gwyrth *miracle* 2.23, 26, 3.11, 15, 11.3.

gwyryf *virgin*: pl. gwerydon 13.2, 14.11.

gyt a(c) prep. *along with* 14.7, 9, 10, 11, also y gyt a(c).

gyfuerbynn a adj. *opposite* 3.12.

gyluin *beak* 8.3; g. eur *golden beak* 3.25.

gynn(h)ev adv. *a (short) while ago* 3.2, 3.

gynt adv. *before* 2.21 (chynt), 9.14.

gyrru vn. *drive*: pret. sing. 1 gyrreis 3.3.

haedu vn. *incur* 9.28n, *deserve*: pret. sing. 3 haedawd 11.19.

hanner *half* 3.13, 13; hanner dyd *mid-day* 7.16, 10.34.

hayach adv. *almost* 13.20.

heb prep. *without* 5.5, 5, 12, etc; heb allu rif arnadunt 8.15n.

heb vb. *said* 1.10, 2.28, 31, 3.3, 7, 10, 32, 36, 4.6, 5.6, 7, 8, 10, 11, 30, etc; heb y 3.4, 4, 32, 13.15, heb yr 7.3, 9.27.

hediw adv. *today* 5.7, 6.7, 27, 7.30, 31.

heuyt adv. *also* 4.27.

heit wenyn *swarm of bees* 1.11.

hely 1.10n.

hen adj. *old* 4.4, 8.27, 10.11.

heneint *old age* 14.3.

heul *sun* 10.33, 13.26.

hi pers. pron. indep. simple sing. 3 fem. 2.19, 21, 24, 3.14, 5.11, 30, 38, 39, 8.2, 3, 10.6.

holl adj. *all* 3.6, 23, 29, 5.19, 31, 6.15, 7.18, 38, 38, 8.5, 7.8, 8.11, 31, 9.14, etc.; hollyach *in complete health* 4.1–2, 2, 10.14, 16.

hollti vn. *split*: pret. sing. 3 holltes 3.13.

hon(n) dem. pron. sing. fem. 11.21; dem. adj. fem. *this* 3.5, 9, 10, 5.1,

8.20, 32, 11.17, 12.7, 28, 32; **honn
yman** *this (here)* 10.12.
honno dem. pron. sing. fem. 9.5;
dem. adj. fem. *that* 5.36, 6.7, 20,
8.16, 9.36, 11.16.
hoyw adj. *lively, active* 5.23n.
hvn nn. *sleep* 1.9.
hwnn dem. adj. sing. masc. *this* 3.10,
4.25, 5.35, 6.9, 8.23, 24, 10.10,
13.12; **hwnn yma** *this (here)*
12.31n.
hwnnw dem. pron. sing. masc. 1.9,
2.16, 3.27, 27, 4.12, 23, 7.31, 8.32,
etc.; dem. adj. masc. *that* 2.4, 13,
15, 4.11, 26, 27, 30, 5.4, 9, 32,
6.22, 7.6, 8.17, 10.3, 36, 11.3, etc.
hwy comp. adj. *longer* 3.8n, 12.13.
hwy pers. pron. affix. simple pl. 3
5.24, 8.10, 9.21, 12.23.
hwynt pers. pron. indep. simple. pl.
3 9.27.
hyt prep. *until* 1.13, 4.11, 22, 5.2, 4,
36, 6.7, 27; *as far as, to* 4.29, 5.30,
6.13, 15, 7.11, 14, 9.31, 12.26,
13.21.
hyt ar prep. *as far as, to* 11.23.
hyt at prep. *as far as, to* 3.26, 7.7.
hyt is prep. *to below* 3.14.
hyt na conj. *(so) that . . . not* 5.15,
8.9–10.
hyt y prep. *as far as* 1.15, 4.30, 6.1,
10.20.
hyt ympenn prep. *till the end of* 2.2.
hyt yn prep. *as far as* 4.8, 13, 8.12,
9.8; **hyt yg** 4.13.
hyneif *elders* 13.6.
hynn dem. pron. sing. *this* 5.24, 34;
dem. adj. *these* 12.8.
hynny dem. pron. sing. *that* 2.16, 17,
5.1, 6.23, 7.38, 8.9, 9.1, 10.31, 32,
11.1, 12.10, 13, 20; dem. adj. pl.
those 6.29, 9.30, 12.19; **hynny o
seint** *(all) those saints* 9.28, 11.30.

i pers. pron. affix. simple sing. 1 2.7,
30, 3.3, 34, 34, 4.1, 5.39, 9.17,
31, 10.9, 12.25, 13.14.
y poss. pron. prefix. sing. 3 masc.
(before a nn. or vn.) 1.9, 16, 18,
2.15, 3.5n, 17, 18, 19, 20, 24, 28,
29, 30, 31, 4.2, 2, 7, etc., fem. 1.8,
2.24, 3.14, 29, 5.9, 29, 37, 39, 6.4,

4, 4, 7.2, 10, 12, 8.3, 33, 10.1, 5,
12; pl. 3 5.27, 9.28, 10.1, 13.6.
y *to his* (<**y y**) 2.6n, 32n, 5.16, 9.4n.
'e poss. pron. infix. sing. 3 masc.
2.26, 3.5, 5, 4.28, 5.5, 13, 14, 22,
22, etc, fem. 3.23; pl. 3 12.23.
'e pers. pron. infix. obj. sing. 3 4.10,
6.10, 8.4, 23, 29, 11.20, 12.5.
y prep. *to* 1.9, 13, 2.4, 7, 12, 15, 26,
26, 32, 32, 3.8, 10, 10, 27, 30, 34,
etc; *for* 4.6; sing. 1 **y mi** 3.8, 9, 33,
4.24, 25, 5.19, 9.30, 2 **yt** 2.7, 12.5,
masc. **idaw** 2.1, 13, 3.1, 5, 9, 23,
31, 4.7, etc., fem. **idi** 2.20, 21,
3.13, 25, 13.15, pl. 1 **y ni** 3.1, 5.35,
9.32, 34, 2 **ywch** 13.15, 16, 3 **vdunt**
4.30, 5.35, 9.21, 10.28.
y am prep. *from, around*: sing. 3
fem. **y amdanei** 7.37.
y vynyd adv. *up* 5.10n, 7.29–30, 12.6.
y gadw *to keep, to be kept* (?**y>yy**)
1.13.
y gan prep. *by, from* 2.27, 4.7, 6.21,
24, 26, 12.4, sing. 1 **y gennyf** 9.1,
pl.3 **y gantunt** 3.30.
y gilyd pron. *the other* 8.22.
yach adj. *well, healthy* 5.28.
iarll *earl*: pl. **ieirll** 8.13.
ydieithyr prep. *outside* 2.31.
yechyt *health* 6.6, 14.2.
ieuangk adj. *young* 8.28, **ieuang**
12.17; pl. **ieueing** 13.3.
ieuengtit *youth* 14.3.
ehun *alone, on his own* 2.18, 6.30; *his
own* 14.18; *only* 2.30, 3.6; pl.
ehunein *themselves* 11.5.
ell deu *both of them* 6.24.
y'm 3.32n, 6.2.
ynhev pers. pron. affix. conjunct.
sing. 1 9.1.
y'r llawr adv. *to the ground* 6.5–6,
8.3.
is prep. *beneath* 3.14.
y'th aros *waiting for thee* 9.27n.
y'th erbyn *to meet thee* 12.16.
y'th wyneb di *in thy face* 3.35.
ythagneued 12.7n.

lan 1.10n.

llad vn. *cut* 6.5, 14, *kill* 5.13, 6.11,
15; imper. sing. 2 **llad** 5.11.

llauassu vn. *dare*: subj. pres. sing. 3 **llauasso** 11.26.

llauur *labour* 13.30, 33.

llauuryaw vn. *labour* 8.21.

llauurwr *labourer*: pl. **llauurwyr** 8.11.

llall *other* 7.37.

llaw *hand* 4.1, 2, 10.15.

llawen adj. *joyful* 2.7, 3.2, 7.11, 20, 9.24, 13.12.

llawenhau vn. *to ɫe joyful, to cause joy* 12.6, 23; pret. pl. 3 **llawenhassant** 6.11.

llawer *many* 4.29, 5.8, 6.6, 10.18, *much* 2.10, 5.1.

llawuorwyn *handmaiden*: pl. **llawuorynyon** 5.29.

llawn adj. *full* 4.10, 6.20, 13.25.

llawr *ground, floor* 6.6, 15, 7.38, 8.3, 10.30, 35, 36.

lle *place* 1.12, 13, 2.4, 13, 32, 4.10, 17, 18, 22, 25, 25, 26, 27, 29, 30, 31, 5.14, 35, 7.19, 9.4 etc; *(place) where* (y) **lle** 3.16, 22, 9.8, 26, 10.7, 16, 24, 14.1, 2, 2, 5, 5, 6, 6, 7, 8, 8, 9, 9, 10, 10, 11, 11, 12, 12, 13, 14, 14, 15, 15.

llef nn. *cry, sound* 10.31, 12.10, 12.21.

lleian *nun* 2.18, 19, 20, 31, 3.3, 5, 8.14.

llen *letters, learning* 8.33.

llewa vn. *consume*: pret. sing. 3 **llewas** 2.25, 7.36, pl. 3 **llawssant** 13.21–2.

llewenyd *joy* 13.29, 33.

llewni vn. *fill* 12.11, 13.24.

lleyc *lay* 12.17.

llit *anger* 5.4.

llidiaw vn. *become angry* 1.17.

llidyawc adj. *angry* 5.7.

llith *lesson*: pl. **llithion** 3.24.

llong *ship* 2.13, 7.9.

llongwr *sailor*: pl. **llongwyr** 14.6.

llonydu vn. *quiet, appease*: pret. impers. pass. **llonydwyt** 2.12.

llosci vn. *burn* 6.15, 13.19.

llu *host* 9.26, 13.23; pl. **lluoed** 13.27.

llwyr adj. *complete, entire* 8.14.

llygat *eye* 13.9; pl. **llygeit** 3.28, 29, 30, 32, 34, 4.1, 2, 5.21.

llyma *lo here! behold!* 3.4n, 7.14, 9.10.

llyna *lo there!, behold!* 6.21.

llyncu vn. *swallow*: pres. sing. 3 **llwnck** 13.18.

llysuam *stepmother* 5.39, 6.2, 4, 4, 9.

llysuerch *stepdaughter* 5.37, 6.2.

'm pers. pron. infix. obj. sing. 1 2.7.

mab *son, youth* 1.18, 2.2, 20, 3.4, 8, 10, 18, 36, 36, 10.1, 5, 6, 7, 8, 12, 14, 16 etc; pl. **meibon** 9.17, 13.3, 6.

mal bei atuei *as if he were* 10.15n.

mal hynn *like this, thus* 11.7; also **val**.

mal y conj. *as, how* 8.7; also **val**.

mam *mother* 2.26, 10.16.

manachloc *monastery* 7.26, **manachol** 7.4.

marw adj. *dead* 2.13, 8.3, 10.5, 6; pl. **meirw** 5.20, 10.17, 12.9; **marw** vn. *die* 5.19, 10.1, 13.21.

mawr adj. *great, big, much* 7.21, 26, 32, 39, 8.5, 30 etc, adv. *greatly* 2.5, 12.9; comp. **mwy** 12.25; superl. **mwyhaf** 8.32.

mawrhau vn. *magnify, glorify*: subj. pres. impers. pass. **mawrhaer** 10.13.

mawrhydri *majesty* 13.26.

medrawd arnaw 5.5n.

medyant *power, authority* 3.5, 5.9 (-dd-).

medwl nn. *mind, care* 2.12, 22, 7.33, 10.17, 13.31.

medylyaw vn. *ponder, meditate, plan* 3.35; pret. sing. 3 **medylyawd** 1.15, 6.11, 7.25; imper. pl. 2 **medylywch** 8.25.

megys prep. *like* 12.9, 10.31, 36, 12.9.

megys y conj. *as* 11.7, 8, 13.26; *how* 7.24.

mellt *lightning* 3.12.

menegi vn. *state, declare* 7.22, 10.5; pret. sing. 3 **menegys** 8.7; plup. sing. 3 **managassei** 4.29.

merch *daughter, girl*: pl. **merchet** 13.3.

merthyr *martyr*: pl. **merthyri** 14.5.

meudwy *hermit, recluse*: pl. **meudwyot** 12.34.

mi pers. pron. indep. simple sing. 1 4.1, 6.2, 7.11, 8.29, 9.3, 29.

mis *month* 12.1.

mod *way, manner* 7.24, 11.10.

moe var. of mwy *more* 3.5, 11.24.

moes *manner, practice*: pl. moesseu 8.31.

moli vn. *praise* 3.21, 11.5; pret. pl. 3 molyassant 10.19.

molyant nn. *praise* 14.1.

mor *sea* 7.15, 9.18, 11.7, 13.19.

mor adv. *so* 7.9, 8.25.

morua *sea-marsh* 2.14.

morwyn *maiden* 5.37, 39, 6.3, 5, 8; pl. morynyonn 13.3.

mwc *smoke* 4.32, 5.1, 3, 7, 10.

myuy pers. pron. indep. reduplic. sing. 1 8.27, mivi 3.5, 7.30, 8.31, 9.7, 31.

mynach *monk*: pl. myneich 13.2.

mynet vn. *go* 2.15, 26, 3.10, 4.6, 5.39, 7.11, 15, 32, 9.4, 11.23, 24, 13.20, mynet dwylaw mynwgyl 7.20n; pres. sing. 1 af 9.11, 29, 2 ey 1.10n, 3 a 4.25, 27, 12.30; pret. sing. 3 aeth 3.26, 9.23, 12.26, 28, 13.14; imper. sing. 2 dos 2.31, 3 aet 11.24, pl. 1 awnn 5.38, 2 ewch 2.28, 5.29, 9.5, 18, ewchwi (+ affix. pron.) 9.11–12.

mynheu pers. pron. indep. conjunct. sing. 1 9.33, 13.14.

mynnu vn. *wish, desire*: pres. sing. 2 mynny 9.28; imperf. sing. 3 mynnei 10.29, mynhei 5.6; pret. sing. 3 mynnawd 2.24; plup. sing. 3 mynnassei 8.7–8; subj. pres. sing. 2 mynnych 12.5, 17.

mynnwent *graveyard* 4.27.

mynyd *mountain* 10.36; pl. mynyded 13.20.

'n pers. pron. infix gen. pl. 1 10.10; pers. pron. infix. obj. pl. 1 12.35, 36, 37.

na(t) neg. part. 3.1, 5.6, 8.24, 10.25, 26, 29, 11.26, 13.18, 19.19, 19.

na(c) neg. part. 7.3.

na ... na *neither ... nor* 2.21, 5.6, 9.25, 11.26, 27, 13.22.

nac *nor* 5.34.

nac neg. part. 3.33.

nachaf interj. *behold!* 5.18, 6.31, 7.18, 9.36, 12.3, 10, 13.23, 25, nacha 2.18.

namyn conj. *but, except* 2.24, 25, 11.17, 13.22.

naw *nine* 12.15, 13.26.

nawd *refuge, protection* 11.22, 27, 28.

nawdir *land of protection/refuge* 11.21.

neb *any one* 2.30, 4.26, 6.9, 8.22, 24, 25, y neb *the one/anyone (who)* 5.11, 11.31.

nef *heaven* 4.25, 6.15, 8.9, 10, 9.34, 12.15, 13.26.

neges *message* 9.10.

neidyaw vn. *leap*: pret. sing. 3 neidyawd 3.13.

neill *one (of two)* 3.13.

nessaf superl. adj. *nearest* 10.33, *next* 12.30.

neu conj. *or* 12.34, 34.

neur 7.4n.

newyd adj. *new* 4.4; newyd eni *newly born* 13.4.

newyn *hunger* 13.29.

ni pers. pron. indep. simple pl. 1 8.23, 9.27, 13.18; affix. simple pl. 1 5.19, 23, 34, 8.24, 9.25, 12.35, 36, 37, 13.1, 16, 20, 14.18, ny 5.19.

niuer *number, crowd* 8.17, 23, 24; yniuer 8.26n.

ninheu pers. pron. indep. conjunct. pl. 1 3.2, nynhev 9.26, 14.20.

no *than* 3.5.

nodua *refuge, protection* 11.22, 25, 31; pl. noduaeu 11.20.

noeth adj. *naked* 5.31.

nos *night* 5.36, 6.31, 9.16, 13.23; nos Pasc *Easter eve* 6.31.

ny(t) neg. part. 1.13, 17, 2.2, 2, 21, 23, 24, 3.7, etc.

nyt amgen *not otherwise, namely* 1.11, 4.28, 30, 5.19, 6.31, 7.5, 11, 9.10, 15.

nys neg. part. + 's infix. pron. sing. 3 2.28n, 29, 9.30, 11.28, 13.8, 8n.

nyth *nest* 8.1.

o interj. *oh!* 12.33.

o conj. *if* 11.23, or 11.24.

o prep. *from* 1.7, 2.8, 13, 28, 3.3, 9, 4.25, etc., *of* 1.1, 1, 1, 7, 3.18, 28, 4.10, 25, etc., + subj. of vn. 6.15; *because of* 2.10, 3.28, 5.4, 9.12, *in, as regards* 2.22, 10.17, *about* 10.31 *on* 11.2, *with, by* 4.3, *by means, through* 9.14, 11.30; sing. 3 masc. ohonaw 2.1, 10.24, 11.15, pl. 1

ohonom 8.22, ohonam 8.24, 3
ohonunt 8.18.
o achaws prep. *because of, for the
sake of* 6.16, 10.10, o achos 3.8.
o vreid adv. *hardly* 4.24.
o gwbyl adv. *in full, entirely* 7.22,
8.21.
och interj. *oh!* 13.18, 18, 19, 19.
odieithyr prep. *outside* 7.35.
odyma adv. *from here* 4.6, 5.33.
odyna adv. *then* 1.15, 3.26, 4.8, 13, 14,
15, 16, 17, 18, 22, 6.17, 10.20, 12.1.
odyno adv. *from there* 10.31.
o'e *of/from his* 1.7.
o'e 7.6n.
oet *time, interval, space* 7.9, 12.28.
oes *age, life* 2.24, 6.20, 21; pl.
oesoed; yn yr oes oesoed *for ever
and ever* 14.17.
ouer *vain* 8.21.
ouyn nn. *fear* 2.1n.
ofuynhav vn. *fear* 8.6.
offeirat *priest*: pl. offeireit 8.12,
12.34, 14.7–8.
offerenn *mass* 13.7, 10; pl. offerennev
3.24, 7.17.
ol yn ol *in succession* 3.30.
oll *all* 2.28, 3.31, 5.1, 20, 7.36,
11.17.
onnen *ash-tree* 8.1.
on(n)nyt conj. *if . . . not* 9.25, 28;
except, but 2.30, 5.16, 6.18, 10.30,
13.5.
o'r a 3.20n, 4.26, 10.19, 11.21n, 21,
22, 13.10n.
o'r blaen *in front* 10.3–4.
o'r pan *from (the time) when* 2.23.

pa adj. *what?* 6.9; pa delw *how?* 7.8.
pa beth bynnac *whatever* 12.24; pa le
bynnac *wherever* 11.25.
paham *why?* 1.18, 3.1, 5.6.
pan(n) conj. *when* 3.14, 15, 4.2, 31,
5.14, 27, 6.1, etc.
pann yw *that it is* 12.30.
paratoi vn. *prepare* 2.13; pret. sing.
3 paratoes 9.21.
parawt adj. *ready* 5.39, 7.10, 12.5.
parchu vn. *keep, reserve*: plup. sing.
3 parchassei 9.4n.
paret *wall* 2.31.
parth *part, side* 11.3, 12.32.

pawp *all, everybody* 3.9, 21, 6.15,
7.27, 8.15, 10.18 etc.
pechadur *sinner* 12.17; pl.
pechaduryeit 10.10.
pedrieirch *patriarchs* 14.7.
pellaf superl. adj. *farthest* 10.32.
penn *head* 3.12, 14, 6.2, 3, 4, 5.14
top 10.24, 29; superl. pennaf *chief*
9.15, 32, 11.19, 29.
pennadur nn. *chief, head* 8.18, 11.7,
8, 9, 15.
pennaduryaeth *chieftainship* 3.6, 9.
penydwyr *penitents* 13.2.
perued *entrails* 7.38.
peri vn. *cause* 5.35; pres. sing. 1
paraf 7.11.
person *parson*: pl. personnyeit 12.35.
perthynu vn. *relate, be appropriate*:
imperf. sing. 3 perthynei 3.20,
8.33.
peth *thing* 10.26, 12.25; pl. petheu
4.7, 13.13; y peth *that (which)*
12.4.
plwyf *people* 2.32n, 3.1.
pob adj. *every* 4.3, 11.24, 13.24, pop
10.32, 11.3, 7, 12.32.
pob kyuryw dyn *every (kind of) man*
11.21.
pob ryw *every kind of* 13.24, 33.
pob vn *every one* 2.32, 8.22.
poeni vn. *hurt, harm* 3.33.
pobyl *people* 11.16, popyl 13.7.
pony *dost thou not?* 7.2, ponyt *it is
not?* 5.35.
porthloed *harbour* 2.13.
pregeth *sermon* 2.27, 8.21, 10.24,
13.10.
pregethu vn. *preach* 2.27, 29, 33,
3.1, 7.18, 8.19, 23, 24, 26, 9.7,
10.23, 30, 36, 11.15, 16, 12.26;
imperf. sing. 3 pregethei 8.17;
pret. sing. 3 pregethawd 13.7.
prenn *tree* 8.3.
priawt adj. *married* 13.2.
prouedigaetheu *trials, tribulations*
13.31.
proui vn. *attempt* 2.29; pret. pl. 1
prouassam 8.23.
proffwyt *prophet*: pl. proffwydi
14.10.
pryt gosper *evening* 5.2n, 4–5.
prynu vn. *buy, redeem* 10.11.

putein *harlot, prostitute* 12.18.
pwy *who?* 12.35, 36, 37, 37, 37; also **bwy**.
pwy bynnac *whoever* 8.16.
pymthec *fifteen* 2.14.
pyrth *gates* 6.13.
pyscawt *fish* 11.8, **piscawt** 9.22.
pyscotta vn. *fish* 9.18.

'r def. art. *the* 2.4, 5, 6, 8, etc.
rat *grace* 3.5, 18, 8.32.
rac prep. *before*: sing. 3 **racdaw** 7.13, 26.
rac llaw adv. *later, in time to come* 14.20–21.
rac sychet 6.25n.
raco adv. *yonder* 3.8.
ragor rac *more, farther than* 11.24.
rann *part* 7.34, 39, 8.4.
rannv vn. *divide* 7.34.
redegawc adj. *running* 6.18.
rei *(the) ones, those* 1.14, 12.16, 13.2, 3, 14.6, 8.
reit *necessity* 3.9, 11.23, 24.
rif nn. *number* 8.15.
rifuaw vn. *count* 9.27.
rod *gift* 6.21.
rodi vn. *give, grant, place* 6.4, 7.35, 8.9, 10.16, 11.27, 13.11n; pres. impers. pass. **rodir** 7.6; pret. sing. 3 **rodes** 3.6, 8, 4.2, 16, 5.25, 8.8 etc., pl. 3 **rodassant** 9.21, 11.18, impers. pass. **rodet** 2.20, 9.34, 11.20; subj. pres. sing. 3 **rodho** 9.32; imper. sing. 2 **dyro** 4.1, 6.2, 10.12.
ry 5.19n, 6.15.
ryued adj. *strange, wondrous* 10.34.
ryuedawt *wonder, marvel* 11.3.
ryuedu vn. *wonder (at)* 3.35n, 8.5.
ryswr *champion, hero, soldier*: pl. **ryswyr** 14.1.
ryw *such* 6.22.

sauan *jaws* 10.11.
sant *saint* 2.31, 33, 3.3, 4.6, 20, 5.23, etc., pl. **seint** 3.6, 8.18, 19, 22, 9.8, 12,14. etc.
santes (fem.) 6.5.
sawl *so many* 13.9.
sef 1.17n, 2.19, 3.21, 35, 5.24, 6.3, 4, 12, 7.8, etc.
seuyll vn. *stand* 7.35, 10.30.

seilym *psalms* 3.23n.
sened *synod* 8.12, 15, 17, 9.26, 31, 35, 10.20, 11.15.
seraphin *the seraphim* 14.16.
sychet *thirst* 13.30; equat. adj. *so dry* 6.26n.
synnyaw arnaw 7.32n, **s. arnunt** 7.39, 12.9.
syrthaw vn. *fall* 7.37n, 10.4, **syrthyaw** 10.8, 23, 12.9; pres. sing. 3 **syrth** 13.19; pret. sing. 3 **syrthawd** 8.3, **syrthyawd** 7.36.

tat *father* 8.9, 12.37, 13.6; pl. **tadeu** 13.15.
tagneued *peace* 9.12, 12.7, 14.3.
talym 1.1n, 10.25, 12.4.
tan *fire* 4.31, 32, 5.9, 12, 6.14, 13.19.
taranau *(peals of) thunder* 3.12.
taraw vn. *strike*: pret. impers. pass. **trawyt** 7.37.
tec adj. *fair, fine* 8.28; superl. **teccaf** 12.10.
tegwch *beauty* 14.1.
teilwng adj. *worthy* 6.21, 8.25.
teir *three* (fem.) 7.34.
teyrn(n)as *kingdom* 4.25, 8.10, 9.5.
ti pers. pron. indep. simple sing. 2 1.10, 10, 2.9, 9, 10, 5.11, 10.9, 12.16, 19; affix. simple sing. 2 1.17, 2.7, 31, 3.34, 12.17, 32.
tidi pers. pron. reduplic. sing. 2 5.37, 7.1, 30.
tir *land* 1.13, 5.12, 7.16, 11.26, 13.19.
tlawt adj. *poor*: pl. **tlodyon** 13.1.
tra adv. *very* 3.29.
traet *feet* 3.14, 11.1.
torri vn. *cut, break* 7.37n; imperf. sing. 3 **torrei** 11.31.
traeth *beach* 7.11, 13.
traethu vn. *treat, discuss, recount*: pres. sing. 1 **traethaf** 13.4, impers. pass. **treithir** 1.1.
tragywydawl adj. *eternal* 3.7, 5.25, 8.10.
trallawt *tribulation* 13.31.
trannoeth *the next day, the morrow* 5.36, 37, 6.12.
tremygedic adj. *scornful* 5.17.
tremygu vn. *despise*: pret. sing. 3 **tremygawd** 1.18.
tri *three* (masc.) 1.10, 7.4.

trigyaw vn. *dwell, tarry* 3.8, 12.12.
trist adj. *sad* 5.7.
tristav *become sad* 7.8.
tristit *sorrow, sadness* 12.22, 13.22, 33.
trossi vn. *turn* 10.6.
truan nn. *wretch*: pl. **truein** 9.32; adj. *wretched, miserable* 10.4.
trugarawc adj. *merciful, compassionate*: equat. **trugarocket** 12.37.
trugared *mercy* 14.20.
trugarhav vn. *have mercy* 10.6; imper. sing. 2 **trugarhaa** 10.11.
tryded *third* (fem.) 8.3, 9.14.
tu a prep. *towards, to* 5.14; **y tu a** 7.13, 8.2.
twr *tower* 6.13.
twyllwr *deceiver* 8.8.
twymynn adj. *hot* 4.11.
ty *house* 10.7.
tyghetuen 4.7n.
tylwyth *family* 5.23, 25, 26, **tylywyth** 7.4.
tynnu vn. *draw* 6.4.
tywyssawc *chieftain, leader* 5.3, 11.6, 14, 27; pl. **tywyssogyonn** 8.13, 14.9.

vch benn prep. *above* 1.12.
vchel adj. *high* 5.4, 10.24, 36, 11.2, *loud* 3.1, 12.11.
vcheneit *sigh*: pl. **vcheneideu** 12.34.
vcheneidyaw vn. *sigh* 12.21.
vchot adv. *above* 1.14, 10.35.
vdaw vn. *howl* 5.22, 12.21, 13.2.
vfydhau vn. *obey, submit to*: pret. sing. 3 **vfydhaawd** 10.28.
vffern(n) *hell* 4.26, 27.
vn *one* 4.25, 7.35, 8.19, 12.28, 13.5, 9, *same* 9.13, *only* 10.5, 12.
vnvedwl *of one mind* 12.24.
vrdas *dignity, honour* 3.5.
vrdaw vn. *ordain, consecrate*: pres. sing. 3 **urda** 12.37; pret. impers. pass. **vrddwyt** 9.2.

wrth prep. *to* 3.36, 5.29, 33, 37, 6.2, 7.25, 8.22, 9.17, 10.8, 12.14, *on* 10.11; sing. 3 masc. **wrthaw** 1.10, 16, 2.6, 4.5, 24, 7.1, 20, 9.24, 12.3, fem. **wrthi** 10.6; pl. 3 **vrthunt** 5.31n, 9.20, 23, 10.25, 12.23.

vrth vedyd *for baptism* 3.17, 18.
vrth hynny *therefore* 7.6, 9.27, 11.14.
wy pers. pron. indep. simple pl. 3 4.31, 5.33, 9.25; also **wynt** 4.29; affix. simple pl. 3 5.15, 35.
wylaw vn. *weep* 7.8, **wylyaw** 12.20.
wylouein vn. *cry, weep, wail* 12.33, 13.18.
wyneb *face* 3.19, 35, 4.1, 12.6; **wynebclawr** 3.20n.
wynt pers. pron. indep. simple pl. 3 5.27, 9.27, 12.13; also **wy** 5.33.
wythuet *eighth* 12.28.
wythnos *week* 12.30.

y pre-verb. part. 1.1, 7, 15, 15, 18, 2.12, 12, 28, etc.
y pre-verb part. + infix. pron. obj. 3.11, 19, 8.33, 10.16, 13.26.
y bore glas 4.32, 5.1–2n.
y gyt adv. *together* 8.12.
y gyt a(c) prep. *together/along with* 2.10, 15, 4.29, 5.11, 13, 26, 7.16, etc.
y llall *the other* 7.37n.
y mywn prep. *in* 1.11, 2.32, 3.3, 5.4, 7.5, 8.1; adv. 2.32, 3.3.
y neill *the one (of two)* 3.13.
y rei *the ones, those* 12.16.
y rwg prep. *between* 2.31, 8.1; pl. 3 **y rycgtunt** 11.5.
ych poss. pron. prefix. pl. 2 *your* 12.30, 13.13.
ychen *oxen* 5.20.
ydaw vn. *leave* 2.4.
yd pre-verb. part. 2.30, 4.25, 5.14, 6.6, 13, 7.2, 39, 10.26, 12.1, 30, 13.14.
yng adj. *close* 12.10.
ym penn prep. *at the end of* 2.17.
yma adv. *here* 1.1, 2.30, *this* 14.19, **y'r hwnn yniuer yma** 8.26; **yman** 9.11.
ymadrawd *word(s), expression* 12.8, 13.12.
ymauael vn. *seize* 2.19.
ymblaen prep. *before* 11.27, **ymlaen** 11.28.
ymdangos vn. *appear*: pret. sing. 3 **ymdangosses** 3.15, 6.6.
ymdidan vn. *converse* 12.3.
ymeith adv. *away* 5.33.

ymgynnull vn. *come together, assemble*: pret. pl. 3 ymgynnullassant 8.15.

ymhoelut vn. *turn, return* 5.17, 26; pret. sing. 3 ymhoelawd 4.22.

ymoglyt vn. *avoid* 7.7.

ymparatoi vn. 2.4n; impers. sing. 2 ymparattoa 12.14.

ymrodi vn. *give oneself*: pret. pl. 3 ymrodassant 4.20–1.

ymwelet vn. *visit* 12.33; pres. pl. 1 ymwelwn 13.16n.

ymysc hynny adv. *during that time, in the meantime* 6.30.

yn predic. part. + nn. 2.21, 3.13, 7.34, etc; + adj. 3.18, 4.3, 11, 16, 21, 5.10, etc; + vn. 2.1, 18, 18, 26, 3.2, 14, 16, 18, 5.7, etc.

yn adverb. part. 2.5, 33, 33, 3.2, 6, 31, 5.25, etc.

yn prep. *in* 1.9, 12, 2.8, 9, 13, 24, 30, etc., *into* 5.15, 10.12, *on* 10.13, 11.8, 14.19, yng 3.22, yg 3.4, 4.18, 20, 11.11, y 4.15, 27, 6.17, 7.3, ym 13.24, sing. 3 yndaw 2.4n, 3.22, 6.13, 7.7.

yn poss. pron. prefix pl. 1 *our* 5.18, 19, 38, 12.22, 13.1; also an.

yn diwethaf oll *last of all* 3.31.

yn dwy *the two (fem.) of us* 5.38.

yn gyntaf adv. *first* 8.33.

yn y kyueir *about/against them* 5.17.

yn y erbyn *to meet him* 10.21–2; yn y h. *to meet them* 10.1.

yn y vlaen ef *before/ahead of him* 11.28.

yn y gylch *around him* 3.25.

ynn yach *farewell!* 13.15.

yn ouer adv. *in vain* 8.21.

yn ol prep. *after*: yn ol hynny *after that* 6.23, 12.13.

yn y byt *at all* 5.15.

yn emyl prep. *near* 10.7.

yn yr honn *in which* 11.16.

yna adv. *then* 2.12, 28, 29, 33, 3.1, 4, 17, 14, etc.

ynkylch prep. *about, around* 13.23.

ynvyt adj. *mad* 5.10.

yno adv. *there* 1.16, 2.10, 14, 3.23, 24, 4.8, etc.

ynteu pers. pron. indep. conjunct. sing. 3 masc. 2.19, 9.13, 20, 12.6, 14.19; affix. conjunct. sing. 3 masc. 2.1.

yny conj. *until* 7.13, 15, hyny 3.28; (*so*) *that* 3.13, 9.32, 33.

ynys *island* 2.9, 3.9, 10, 10, 5.1, 8.11, 32, 11.17, 25, 29, 12.28, 32, hynys 8.12.

y(r) def. art. *the* 1.12, 12, 13, 13, 18, 2.1, 4, 7, etc.

yr pre-verb. part. 1.9, 3.26, 4.8, 10, 15, 17, 18, 22, 23, 5.10, 6.17, 30, 7.8, 12, 16, 17, 8.21, 9.14, 10.6, 20, 14.2.

yr prep. *for* 9.27, 28, 29, er 11.3.

yr awr honn *this hour/time, now* 1.12, 2.8, 12.7.

yr Duw *for God's sake* 9.27.

yr honn *which* 11.16.

yr hwn(n) (a) (*the one/he*) *who* 7.28, *that (which)* 9.30n, 11.1.

yr hynn *that (which)* 7.2.

yr vn (*the*) *one* 3.31.

yr yn prep. *from, since* 1.18.

yr ys prep. *for* 2.14, 3.34n; yr ys talym *for a (long) while* 12.4.

ysgaelussaw vn. *ignore, despise*: pres. impers. pass. ysgaelussir 14.2.

ysgiwereit 5.13n, ysgwiereit 8.14.

yscolheic *scholar* 12.17: pl. yscolheig(y)on(n) 12.2, 8.

ysgriuennedic adj. *written* 4.4.

ysgrybyl 5.19n.

ysgymunaw vn. *excommunicate*: pret. sing. 3 ysgymunawd 11.30.

ysgynnv vn. *ascend, mount* 10.29.